D1806589

Current Topics in
Early Childhood Education

Volume IV

Current Topics in Early Childhood Education

Volume IV

Editor
LILIAN G. KATZ

Associate Editors
**Charlotte H. Watkins, Mima J. Spencer,
and Paula J. Wagemaker**

ERIC *Clearinghouse on Elementary and Early Childhood Education,
University of Illinois at Urbana-Champaign*

ABLEX PUBLISHING CORPORATION
Norwood, New Jersey 07648

Copyright © 1982 by Ablex Publishing Corporation.

All rights reserved. No part of this book may be reproduced
in any form, by photostat, microfilm, retrieval system, or any other means,
without the prior permission of the publisher.

Printed in the United States of America.

The material in this publication was prepared pursuant to a contract with the National Institute
of Education, U.S. Department of Health, Education, and Welfare. Contractors undertaking such
projects under government sponsorship are encouraged to express freely their judgment in professional and technical matters. Points of view or opinions do not necessarily represent the official
view or opinions of the National Institute of Education.

ISBN 0-89391-110-0(P)
ISBN 0-89391-109-7(C)   ISSN 0363-8332

ABLEX Publishing Corporation
355 Chestnut Street
Norwood, New Jersey 07648

Contents

Preface ix

1 **The Development of Bilingual and Bicultural Competence In Young Children**
Muriel Saville-Troike 1

Nature and Scope of the Process *1*
Language and Socialization *3*
Language and Cognitive Development *4*
Language Learning *7*
Language Teaching *9*
Future Directions for Research *12*
References *14*

2 **Development of Children's Racial Awareness and Intergroup Attitudes**
Phyllis A. Katz 17

When Do Racial Attitudes Begin Forming? *18*
What Are the Developmental Forerunners of Racial Attitudes? The First Three Years *19*
Racial Awareness—Its Measurement and Its Meaning *22*
Mechanisms Underlying Racial Attitude Development *26*
Attitude Acquisition: Towards a Theoretical Synthesis *41*
References *48*

3 **Motor Skill Development in Young Children: Current Views on Assessment and Programming**
Michael G. Wade and Walter E. Davis 55

Assessment of Motor Development *57*
Programming Motor Activities *64*
Summary *66*
References *67*

4 Curiosity and Self-directed Learning: The Role of Motivation in Education

Edward L. Deci and Richard M. Ryan **71**

Motivational Orientations *71*
Motivational States and the Environment *73*
Extrinsic Rewards and Feedback *75*
Information and Control *76*
Intrinsic Motivation in School Children *78*
Conclusion *83*
References *84*

5 Peer Relationship Development in Childhood

Sherri Oden **87**

Theoretical Perspectives on Children's
  Peer Relationships *88*
Social Learning *88*
Social Cognition *90*
Social Contextual *93*
The Variety of Children's Peer Relationships *96*
Support and Instruction for Children's
  Peer Relationships *108*
Conclusion *113*
References *114*

6 The Symbolic Play of Lower-Class and Middle-Class Children: Mixed Messages from the Literature

Virginia Stern **119**

Brief Description of Nine Comparative Studies *120*
Detailed Presentation of Findings of the
  Nine Comparative Studies *123*
Summary of Findings *129*
Discussion *130*
References *140*

7 Developing Cognitive Skills Through Art

Rawley A. Silver **143**

Background Literature *143*
Rationale Behind the Development of the Silver
  Test of Cognitive and Creative Skills *147*
The Test Instrument *149*
Teaching Procedures *156*
Studies Which Have Used the Silver Test *158*
Concluding Observations *170*
References *171*

8 The Kindergarten: A Retrospective
and Contemporary View
Bernard Spodek **173**

Froebelian Kindergartens *173*
The Kindergarten and Progressivism *176*
Contemporary Kindergarten Practices *179*
Conclusions *188*
References *189*

9 A Comparison of Multi-age and Homogeneous Age
Grouping in Early Childhood Centers
Paula Freedman **193**

Age Terms and Program Terms *194*
Historical Perspective *194*
The Experience of Other Countries *195*
Common Goals and Concerns in Preschool Programs *197*
Practical Considerations *202*
Conclusion *206*
References *208*

10 Caring for the Caregivers:
Staff Burnout in Child Care
*Marcy Whitebook, Carollee Howes, Rory Darrah,
and Jane Friedman* **211**

Causes of Burnout *213*
San Francisco Staff Survey *214*
Conclusions *225*
Recommendations for Improvement *226*
References *233*

How to Obtain ERIC Documents 237

The ERIC System and ERIC/EECE 239

The ERIC Clearinghouses 241

Preface

The chapters presented in the fourth Volume of *Current Topics in Early Childhood Education* fall into three broad categories, all of interest to those working directly with young children as well as to those engaged in preparing others to do so.

Three of the chapters belong in a category we might call "up-dates," for they offer recent reviews of topics presented in earlier volumes in this series. Deci and Ryan bring us recent insights into the research and issues presented in Volume II by Condry and Koslowski on intrinsic motivation and interest—a topic of central concern to teachers of children of all ages. Oden's chapter presents an up-date on the research and findings concerning peer relationships that were first brought to our attention in the chapter by Asher, Oden, and Gottman in Volume I. The rapid rate at which research is being reported in this critical area of human development suggests that regular up-dates of pertinent research may be included in the series. The chapter by Stern on the symbolic play of young children helps us to catch up on the work reported by Fein in Volume II.

A second group of chapters belongs under the heading of "perennials"—topics which come up for discussion and debate year after year by each generation of teachers and others concerned about young children. Freedman presents a review of pertinent literature on multi-age and homogeneous age grouping of young children. Saville-Troike discusses what is known to date about how children acquire a second language and considers important aspects of the relationships between bilingualism and biculturalism. Spodek presents a retrospective as well as prospective look at the role of the kindergarten, and Katz synthesizes and summarizes recent research on children's acquisition of racial awareness and on how they develop attitudes to their own and other races. Each of these chapters presents an examination of research and innovation in fields marked by much interest in recent years.

The third group of chapters deals with topics which have only recently received close attention or detailed study, although the phenomena they address are by no means new. Wade and Davis's discussion of motor skill development offers educators information on some of the modern approaches to assessing children's physical growth. Silver's chapter introduces a fresh view of the role of art in children's cognitive development and some strategies for assessing children's cognitive development through analysis of their art work. Finally, the chapter by Whitebook and her colleagues brings to our attention a topic which has been the focus of much discussion in recent months—the so-called "burn-out" syndrome affecting virtually all workers in helping professions.

Once again the variety of topics reflects the breadth and complexity of the domain of early childhood education. We are pleased to bring to readers the thoughtful and helpful insights of outstanding scholars in the field.

Lilian G. Katz, Ph.D.
Director, ERIC Clearinghouse
on Elementary and Early Childhood Education

Current Topics in
Early Childhood Education

Volume IV

1

The Development of Bilingual and Bicultural Competence in Young Children

Muriel Saville-Troike

University of Illinois at Urbana-Champaign

Millions of children in the world are acquiring one language as their "mother tongue" and subsequently learning another, either informally as they come into contact with children and adults who speak it, or formally as they receive second language instruction in the early years of schooling. Millions more are acquiring two or more languages simultaneously in early childhood as part of the natural consequence of being members of bilingual families and communities, or of having caretakers who speak different languages.

A number of questions which are related to the process of acquiring more than one language in childhood have been explored in recent years; the answers suggested thus far have important implications for all who work with children from linguistically and culturally diverse backgrounds, and for early childhood program development. Questions include the relationship of language and cognitive development, differences between simultaneous and sequential language acquisition, the effects of age on second language learning, and the relationship between bilingualism and biculturalism. Additionally, a number of factors have been identified which may either inhibit or contribute to the successful development of bilingual and bicultural competence in young children.

NATURE AND SCOPE OF THE PROCESS

The capacity to learn language is innate, and the groundwork for its development is laid with infants' earliest contacts with other human beings and with their environment. Children begin to understand and then use the language(s) spoken

1

around them because of the systematic relationship between what they hear and what is going on in the regularities and rituals of their early socialization experiences (cf. Cook-Gumperz, 1977; Halliday, 1975). Despite the great diversity of child-rearing practices and contexts, and the many differences in the structures they hear, children around the world learn whatever language is spoken by their caretakers at remarkably the same rate and in the same sequence (cf. Saville-Troike, 1982, for a survey of research on first language development).

By the time children are 7 or 8 years old, they have mastered the phonological system of whatever language has been regularly spoken around them, its basic grammatical forms (the syntactic system), and the ways in which utterances are sequenced or interact with those of others (the discourse system). They have also learned how to use language for a wide variety of purposes (pragmatics), and how to follow such sociolinguistic rules as when to speak and when to remain silent, and how to talk appropriately to persons of different statuses and roles. Developing bilingual competence entails acquiring these communicative skills in two languages, and knowing how and when to switch from one to the other.

Language acquisition is greatly affected by social circumstances. Children growing up in bilingual communities which are largely segregated (such as many of those which exist in England and the United States) may not have encountered models or social support for the use of the "standard" variety of either language (or perhaps even for a nonstandard native monolingual variety). Nevertheless, the varieties of language these children learn are as logical and systematic as any other, and are affectively more appropriate for use with family and friends than the "foreign" language of school will ever be. Claims have sometimes been made that such children are "alingual" because they do not speak a standard variety of any language, or because they code-switch between two different languages, but these ideas are based on misconceptions about the nature of language and linguistic diversity.

Code-switching in bilingual communities is commonplace and in fact constitutes the norm in many cases. The phenomenon of code-switching can probably best be understood as a sensitive process of signalling different social and contextual relations through language. The children may be exposed to the ancestral language if there are grandparents in the home, but one or both parents may use primarily the national language (if it is different), or switch from one to the other as a means of signalling closeness and informality. Such switching is likely to be most frequent between parents and their bilingual friends. The "standard" monolingual form of either language is generally used only for more formal "public" relations, and thus is less likely to be encountered by young children at home. In any event, code-switching is a highly developed linguistic skill which is normally acquired only in a "natural" learning setting, and rarely in formal school settings or by adults.

LANGUAGE AND SOCIALIZATION

The language which children learn at home is normally *part* of the native culture they acquire in the process of *enculturation, or socialization.*[1] It also serves to transmit other aspects of that culture from one generation to the next, including values, beliefs, and rules for social behavior. This intrinsic relationship of language to culture operates at an unconscious level for the most part, furthered by informal means more than by formal education, and by family and peers more than by professional educators.

Systems of formal education are themselves cultural inventions. The American, Canadian, and British educational systems, like many others, serve primarily to prepare middle-class children to participate in their own culture. Children who come into the system from other cultures or subcultures, including the lower social classes, have generally been considered "disadvantaged" or "deficient" to the degree that their own cultural experiences differ from the mainstream middle-class "norms." A number of early childhood programs have been based primarily on this rationale, and serve to provide middle-class cultural experiences to children who have been "deprived" of them. However, such programs often fail to recognize the existence and validity of the culture which the children bring with them. As a result, in the process of attempting to add a second culture, they violate the precept to accept these children "where they are," and to build on their existing strengths.

Children from non-English language and cultural backgrounds must learn the rules of the dominant culture if they are to "succeed" within its institutions and according to its values. This process of adding a second set of rules for behavior (which may coexist beside the first, replace them, or modify them) is called *acculturation.* One possible result of acculturation is *assimilation*—loss of the native culture or the merger of cultures until they are indistinguishable. Another possible result is the selective maintenance and use of both cultural systems—*biculturalism.*

The learning of culture, like the learning of language, begins with children's first experiences with the family to whom they belong, the community to which they belong, and the environment in which they live. By the time children begin their formal education, they have already internalized many of the basic values and beliefs of their native culture, learned the rules of behavior which are considered appropriate for their role in the community, and established the procedures for continued socialization; they have learned how to learn.

A major hazard in adding a second culture is that children may reject parts of their native culture without knowing or accepting comparable parts of the

---

[1] The following discussion of culture is adapted from M. Saville-Troike, *Culture in the classroom.* Rosslyn, Virginia: National Clearinghouse for Bilingual Education (1978).

second, or that they will find themselves repeatedly facing cultural interference as the rules or values of one culture conflict with those of the other in a single situation or domain. When this happens, either one culture "wins," or children must deal with emotional and cognitive stress, a situation which frequently produces feelings of inferiority or anomie.

The eventual goal for bicultural competence in minority group children can be a positive attitude toward both cultures, with a healthy balance between the two. Schools must learn more about the cultures which such children bring to school, in order to minimize potential conflict and provide a basis for adapting the curriculum to meet their learning needs. They must learn what is necessary for successful achievement in school and in the dominant society, but this need not be taught at the expense of their own culture and identity. Values, beliefs, and behaviors of the dominant culture in such domains as religion and family life may only need to be learned for passive recognition and understanding, but not necessarily adopted for active use.

LANGUAGE AND COGNITIVE DEVELOPMENT

The relationship between language acquisition and cognitive development has long been of interest, although there is still not agreement about its nature nor about how it may differ for monolingual versus bilingual children. One basic perspective, that of Piaget (1926) and his followers, is that cognitive development occurs before and quite independently of language development (cf. Bloom, 1973; Greenfield & Smith, 1976). An alternative perspective from Vygotsky (1934) and Luria (1959) is that the development of logical thought is dependent on the internalization of speech. It is the latter perspective that most clearly supports hypotheses that bilingualism in children (positively or negatively) influences their cognitive development.

Insofar as linguistic experiences may facilitate cognitive development (Cummins, 1976), or as children use language at least in part to construct their conceptual framework (Halliday, 1975), the possibility that bilingualism influences cognitive development is not necessarily incompatible with either perspective on the relationship. Further, when we consider such cognitive processes as perception, memory and recall, and categorization, the effects of both language and cultural experiences are rather generally recognized (cf. Cole & Scribner, 1974). The key question remains, however, whether learning two languages rather than one in childhood has a different effect on cognitive development, and if so, whether the effect is positive or negative.

Many early studies of the relationship between bilingualism and measured intelligence reported that bilingualism inhibited cognitive development (cf. Darcy, 1953 for a review of the literature), but these were generally conducted without control for socioeconomic status, and often with intelligence tests administered through the medium of the bilingual subjects' weaker language. They have appropriately been discounted. Many recent studies, on the other hand, report that bilingualism in childhood can accelerate the development of both verbal and nonverbal abilities (Peal & Lambert, 1962), cognitive flexibility (Ianco-Worrall, 1972), or divergent thinking skills (Landry, 1974). Some of these studies in turn may be faulted for not controlling extralinguistic variables, but it is reasonable to conclude that acquisition of two languages in early childhood in no way impedes cognitive development, and may indeed enhance it.

Evidence remains mixed concerning the effect of second language learning on cognitive development and school achievement if extensive exposure begins beyond the age of 4 or 5 years. Some (particularly middle-class) children placed in bilingual learning contexts become very successful bilinguals, but others (particularly from subordinated minority groups) do not develop full competence in either language, and do not succeed in school. Four major hypotheses have been proposed to account for this apparent discrepancy, and all four may identify factors which affect the development of bilingual and bicultural competence.

The first involves the nature of the social milieu within which learning takes place, and the relative status of first versus second language in that context. Lambert's (1975) distinction between "additive" and "subtractive" bilingualism is crucial here. *Additive bilingualism* occurs in situations where the child is a member of the dominant social class, speaks its language natively, and encounters positive attitudes and support from family and community for its continued use and development; the second language is successfully added, with no negative effects on first language competence, as in the Canadian programs which "immerse" English-speaking children in French (cf. Swain, 1978). *Subtractive bilingualism* occurs in situations where the child is a member of a minority group, does not encounter social support for continued use and development of the native language, and experiences a variety of acculturative forces; the second language is less successfully added, with a decrease in first language competence, as in United States and British programs which "submerge" minority language children in English. The negative result in terms of the development of academic and cognitive skills is not due merely to language factors, but involves such intervening variables as social status, attitudes, language functions, and self-identity.

The second hypothesis suggests that different stages of cognitive development may be involved: that is, children who are in the early concrete operational periods (6 to 8 years old) have more difficulty learning a second language than either younger or older children, yet these are precisely the years where second language teaching is concentrated for children whose first language is not the language of the school. Folk wisdom in this society has held that children have an advantage over older students in second language learning, but research does not support this conclusion (cf. Ervin-Tripp, 1974; Fathman, 1975; Snow & Hoefnagel-Höhle, 1978); older children and adolescents learn both grammatical rules and vocabulary more efficiently. [2]

The third is the *developmental interdependence* hypothesis proposed by Cummins (1979), which suggests that second language development is partially dependent on the level of first language competence which has already been reached. Related is his *threshold* hypothesis, which proposes that "there may be threshold levels of linguistic competence which a bilingual child must attain both in order to avoid cognitive deficits and to allow the potentially beneficial aspects of becoming bilingual to influence their [sic] cognitive growth" (Cummins, 1979, p. 229; see also Cummins, 1976). The basis for this hypothesis includes evidence from a study of Finnish immigrant children in Sweden which found that native language education, at least through the age of 10, is important for successful academic achievement in a second language (Skutnabb-Kangas & Toukomaa, 1976), and from similar results found for native speakers of Navajo and Spanish in the United States (Troike, 1978). These effects do not apply for children from middle-class backgrounds and with dominant or prestigious first language experiences, a fact which relates to the concept of additive versus subtractive bilingualism presented above.

Sociolinguistic factors may be further involved because of the effect they have on the types of cognitive development that school curricula foster and reward. The school, after all, is a cultural institution, and the forms of thinking that it inculcates, as well as the forms of language which are used as a medium of instruction, are culture-specific. There is greater congruity between the language used in the home background of middle-class children and that used at school than between the latter and the home language background of lower class children. Children's failure in school may thus be in part the result of their failure to acquire the culture-specific language structures and discourse forms used in the schools to mediate the teaching of cognitve skills.

This perspective is carried still further in a fourth hypothesis, which is that since procedures and content for both teaching and testing are in themselves cultural artifacts, levels of "cognitive development" and "school achievement" are primarily measures of acculturation to middle-class knowledge and language use (Troike, 1981). The fact that non-English-speaking children from middle-class backgrounds may do better in school than native English-speaking children from lower-class backgrounds suggests the importance of culture as a factor in school achievement.

Children who learn two languages simultaneously in early childhood are probably also being socialized quite naturally into a bilingual community, or

---

[2] The folk notion that young children learn a second language more easily may be due in part to the lower criteria we have for judging them "competent," and in part to young children's greater willingness to try using whatever they know.

into the two cultures these languages reflect; children from the dominant social group do not experience rejection of their native culture and pressures for acculturation, even though some children may become bicultural as well as bilingual. It is only children from subordinate groups who face the combination of (1) cultural discontinuity between contexts of first and second language development, and (2) generally negative attitudes and expectations from peers and teachers. That primary-age children tend to do even less well in such a situation than older students may be an indication of their greater vulnerability.

The answer to the question of whether learning two languages rather than one in childhood has a differential effect on cognitive development is: "probably." Assuring that this difference becomes a positive one for minority group children who are currently in a situation of subtractive bilingualism entails above all assuring that these children are not subjected to a negative valuation of their native language and culture.

LANGUAGE LEARNING

The process of simultaneous development of two or more languages in early childhood is initially the acquisition of a single system, which then becomes differentiated according to the context in which the languages are being used. If they are clearly separated in the environment—used by different people, or used in different situations—even early interference between the two is minimized (cf. McLaughlin, 1978 for a review of research on this topic). When children grow up in a bilingual environment where both languages are used by the same people and switching between languages is common, discrimination between the codes is a later development (cf. Huerta, 1977; McClure, 1977).

Children's metalinguistic awareness that they are speaking different languages also develops at a very early age in those situations where languages are kept separate by speaker or situation. One of the earliest reports, from Ronjat (1913), is about his own son's acquisition of French and German, which the boy distinguished as *comme papa* and *comme mama* at the age of only 1 year 8 months. Young Louis Ronjat may have been somewhat precocious, but other studies confirm there is conscious differentiation during the second year (e.g., Burling, 1959; Imedaze, 1967; Leopold, 1949)

When children begin learning a second language after they are 2 or 3 years old, the process is influenced by what they have already learned about their first language. The same general principles of language acquisition apply, however. Just as a child learning English natively will say *eye/eyes, hand/hands,* and then *foot/foots,* for instance, second language learners (unconsciously) induce rules and regularities from their linguistic input, and overgeneralize them as they begin using language creatively. If their native language does not include the grammatical/semantic notion "plural," they are likely to encounter negative transfer or "interference" in acquiring it in English, and the rule may develop later than if they had already learned to express the concept (even though it was by means of a very different linguistic form). The English plural is also likely to develop later (and perhaps inconsistently) if the first language did not have any *s*'s or *z*'s at the ends of words, or if it did not have any final consonant clusters as in *cats* and *dogs* (cf. Hakuta, 1974; Keller-Cohen, 1981).

In spite of some of these transfer phenomena, the order in which grammatical structures are learned in a second language is generally quite similar regardless of the age of learners or their native languages (Dulay & Burt, 1972). However, even for young children, the order in which grammatical structures in English are learned is different according to whether it is being learned as a second language or whether it is being learned as a first (native) language (Cancino, Rosansky, & Schumann, 1974; Hakuta, 1974).

Whenever people encounter a new language they usually hear the sounds through the "filter" of the first, and children learning a second language often go through a period of avoiding words which are difficult for them to pronounce. If they are interacting and making friends with young speakers of the second language, children soon begin to acquire native-like pronunciation, and outperform their parents in this aspect of developing bilingual competence. The importance of peer models in this process is highlighted by the fact that children usually learn the regional or social variety of the second language which is spoken by their new friends, rather than that spoken by the teacher or other adults. One of my Spanish-speaking kindergarten students first learned to speak English with a lisp, for instance, because his new best friend had just lost his front teeth, and Wolfram (1973) has documented that many Puerto Rican students in New York learn nonstandard black English from their black peers in the streets rather than the standard English which is modeled for them in school.

Some of children's acquisition of vocabulary in a second language is a matter of learning translation-equivalents of what they have learned in their first, but much is the process of learning new terms for new concepts and experiences. Children's vocabulary may be differentiated by domain (e.g., words for things around the house may be known in one language, things around school in another), or by which language was used when they first encountered the concept (e.g., some colors or animals may have labels in one language, some in the other). It is common for differentiation by domain to be maintained even into adulthood, unless both languages are used in the same situations.

The natural process by which their children learned English through interaction with other children in nursery school is described by Yoshida and Huang in Hatch (1978). Common phrases (such as "Get out of here!") were learned by rote and used in appropriate situations even though the meaning of the component words was not understood. Huang reports some misinterpretation, as when his son learned "I'm finished" in the context of finishing painting, and then used it only for that specific situation and not when he finished doing anything else.

Children's ability to watch other children and follow their lead nonverbally often makes it appear that they understand more of the new language than they actually do. The many nonverbal cues provided by adults talking to young children also contribute to children's ability to respond appropriately without understanding the verbal message, but often lead to an overestimation of when the children are ready to profit from verbal instruction exclusively in the second language.

Fillmore (1979) described and evaluated the results of the social strategies used by first graders learning English in a linguistically heterogeneous class, and concluded that their success depended largely on their ability to establish social contacts with the English-speaking children. This interaction both provided the necessary input for language learning and allowed these children opportunities to use the language in meaningful contexts. In a study of native English-speaking children who spent a year in a Spanish-English bilingual program without improving their command of Spanish, Edelsky and Hudelson (1979) found the main factor to be that the native Spanish-speaking children spoke only English with their English-speaking peers (thus reducing the latter's motivation and opportunity to learn Spanish).

The importance of motivation is illustrated anecdotally by the account of a Puerto Rican boy in a first grade bilingual program in New York who was English dominant and who throughout the year steadfastly resisted efforts to develop his Spanish ability. When an attractive Spanish-speaking girl entered the class in the second grade, however, he took a great interest in her, and his Spanish fluency made great strides in a remarkably short time.

In addition to the important contribution of peer interaction to second language development, peer influence can also be seen in the reluctance of some children to continue using their first language in the presence of friends who speak only the second, and even embarassment if their parents continue to do so. The development and maintenance of balanced bilingual competence is best fostered when both home and school provide a positive, supportive environment. Parents who have been upset by linguistic rejection from their preschool children have reported renewed acceptance if their children enroll in a bilingual program and learn that other children and adults also speak two languages.

LANGUAGE TEACHING

Many children can and do learn a second language without explicitly being taught, but educators cannot assume that they will "catch" one by mere exposure, like the measles or chicken pox. This sort of "osmosis" often does seem to happen when isolated children are immersed in a foreign language, as when a single family moves to another country, but sizable groups of non-English-speaking children in the United States who were required to "sink or swim" in English-only instruction have proved it is quite possible to tread water through years of exposure to a language without acquiring fluency in comprehension or use. That "method" has failed, and should not be revived. Thanks to the *Lau vs. Nichols* decision by the Supreme Court in 1974,[3] such treatment is no longer legal in the United States.

The following are basic principles which underlie the teaching of a second language to young children (adapted from Saville-Troike, 1975):

(1) All children, whether from wealthy or severely-impoverished backgrounds, can benefit from language enrichment experiences. No normal child from any cultural or social group lacks a well developed linguistic system, and no program should be based on the assumption that children from any group lack a viable language.

(2) The language and culture of the day care center, nursery school, or kindergarten should be compatible with that of the children's homes, allowing them to develop consistent self-identity and secure self-images. New elements should of course be added to children's experience, but these should be selected and presented in ways that avoid conflict.

(3) A positive self-image can be most surely fostered in a situation which emphasizes acceptance of the child's native speech and avoids depreciating it and native cultural values.

The foregoing principles are perhaps most succinctly expressed in the maxim, "Accept the child where he or she is." They may be summarized in the "First Commandment" for all education, *recognize and accept children's previous linguistic, conceptual, and cultural experience as a base on which to build, rather than as a handicap to further learning.*

Another relevant aphorism is that "Nothing succeds like success," because the converse is also true. If children who come from diverse cultural and linguistic backgrounds are penalized for their prior learnings, failure becomes a pattern of expectation for child, parents, and teachers alike. This destroys motivation and alienates children from formal learning experiences. Many of the "problems" of minority group children are not theirs, but are caused by failures of adults (even from their own social group) who evaluate them only in terms of expectations of the majority culture.

---

[3] The Supreme Court of the United States ruled in favor of Kinney Lau, a limited English-speaking student, who had brought suit against Alan H. Nichols et al. of the San Francisco school system. Mr. Justice Douglas delivered the opinion of the court, saying in part that". . . there is no equality of treatment merely by providing students with the same facilities, text books, teachers, and curriculum," and mandating "appropriate" instructional intervention (e.g., ESL and bilingual education).

Although research on second language development does not yet offer definitive answers on how best to teach young children, the following practices have been supported by both research and experience:[4]

1. Language input for second language learners should be fairly natural, but consistent and simplified. It is neither necessary nor desirable to use strictly graded instructional material, but some control of vocabulary and grammar contributes to learning. For example, blue and green should be mastered before aqua, turquoise, and chartreuse are introduced, and directions and descriptions should be given in short, simple sentences.

2. Input *must* have meaning. Words for objects and actions that can be displayed or demonstrated are much easier to teach and learn than terms for more abstract concepts. The children's native language should be used whenever it will help clarify meaning in the second. The emphasis in instruction should be on assuring *understanding*.

3. In natural language acquisition, children first use words for things that capture their attention and interest them, and this same principle applies to second language teaching.

4. Focus in language development activities should usually be on *what* is being talked about, and *not* on the language forms being used. This holds true for second language learners of all ages, but is particularly important for young children.

5. Opportunity for review and repetition should be provided, but only in meaningful contexts: that is, meaningless drill does not contribute to language development. Meaningful repetition is assured when the language being learned relates to objects and activities which will be encountered on a regular basis, and when expressions associated with "ritual" events are repeated: for example, if clean up time is introduced by, "It's time to clean up now," on one day, the same sentence should be used the next day rather than variations like, "Let's put our things away," or "I'd like to see a neat room now."

6. It is beneficial to prompt children with the right words to express what they are trying to say, but grammmatical "errors" should not be corrected when a child is trying to communicate ideas or feelings. Fluency and willingness to talk are most inhibited by correction of pronunciation, and it is most important not to treat the natural early transfer of first language phonology to the production of the second as if were a "speech impairment" or "language disability" of any kind.

---

[4] Specific instructional activities are suggested in M. Saville-Troike, *Foundations for teaching English as a second language.* Englewood-Cliffs, New Jersey: Prentice-Hall (1976).

7. Oral production on the part of children is not necessary for language learning to take place; its primary value is probably in stimulating input from others. Shy children, or children whose culture dictates against trial and error performance, should *not* be forced to speak. Natural language acquisition usually involves a period of silent assimilation.

8. Language learning activities should, if at all possible, include opportunities for children learning a second language to interact with children who are native speakers of that language (which can include cross-age peer tutoring).

9. Reading ability is the most significant instrument for assessing achievement in Western educational systems. This is greatly dependent on preliteracy experiences which transmit concepts of the functions of literacy. High priorities in early childhood education for children from families who do not have a literate tradition must be to develop concepts of these functions, and to help parents provide the kinds of home experiences which will contribute to learning to read.

10. While the importance of "reading readiness" remains controversial in early childhood education, the importance of early reading competence to overall achievement in school and reading achievement levels in later childhood is well-documented (cf. Christian, 1976; Durkin, 1966; Lado & Andersson, 1976; Lado, Hanson, & D'Emillio, 1980). Reading is learned only once, so requisite concepts and skills should be developed first in the language children understand best. In this way, children subsequently transfer their skills to their second language with little or no instruction. If bilingual education is not an available option, there is no reason to postpone reading experiences in the second language beyond the time considered "normal" for children who speak it natively.

FUTURE DIRECTIONS FOR RESEARCH

Research evidence still remains largely inadequate on a number of key points, including such matters as: (a) the relationship of bilingualism and cognitive development; (b) the relationship of larger aspects of social environment and culture to language learning; (c) the relationship of language learning to other aspects of enculturation or acculturation; (d) similarities and differences between first and second language acquisition; (e) the extent to which, and under what circumstances, success in learning through the medium of a second language is dependent on level of development in the first; (f) language learning strategies in children versus adults; and (g) the relative effectiveness of particular methods for teaching a second language. *for whom?*

With respect to the last topic (g), as for all others, it seems likely that no

Why not some ch. + some adults?

single identified method will consistently be found better than another when diverse groups of students are evaluated. Research design in this field has generally been overly simplistic, and the many known variables have not been adequately taken into account. The success of particular methods and even models for curriculum organization is likely to prove relative to particular social and cultural settings and to particular sociocultural and psychological characteristics of students. This relativistic perspective is probably necessary for assuring the validity of any research which involves such a linguistically and culturally diverse population.

An example of cultural differences in child-rearing practices influencing the appropriateness of different language-teaching methodology can be found in a California study which taught English as a second language to 5- and 6-year-old Spanish-speaking children from families of farm laborers.[5] The project—in which males learned significantly more English than females—made extensive use of games and physical activities. Most of the boys in this population had been allowed considerable freedom at home while their parents were working in the fields, and at school they were extroverted, enthusiastic about trying new games, ready chance-takers, and not inhibited about making mistakes. In accordance with traditional culture and socialization patterns, most of the girls in the population had been confined to the house and given responsibility for the care of younger siblings, even when they were only young children themselves. At school they were appropriately introverted, shy, and inhibited about trying new activities.

It can be hypothesized that the poorer second language performance of the girls was at least partially attributable to inappropriate teaching methods (which followed the best "linguistically approved" methods of the time). But if the program design had taken into account the different sociocultural and psychological characteristics of the children by differentiating methods according to sex, and perhaps by assigning boys and girls to separate treatment groups to obviate the effects of the intervening variable of cultural taboo on girls' behavior, the language learning opportunity might have been equalized, and the language learning differential might well have disappeared. Such hypotheses can and should be tested.

Obviously, not all sociocultural, psychological, and instructional variables can be controlled for research purposes, but unless they are at least accounted for, no amount of accumulation of "data" on second language development

---

[5] This study was one of the USOE cooperative reading reserch projects, and was conducted in Fresno County, California during 1964–1965 with a population of over 200 Spanish-speaking kindergarteners. It was directed by John Manning and Fred Brengelman. I was responsible for preparation of all instructional materials, demonstration of teaching methodology, and supervision of instruction for the duration of the project, and thus must take responsibility for any inappropriateness in the methods which I report.

will provide an answer to a critical question: Who learns what best under what circumstances? Small controlled studies can certainly contribute to our understanding, but their contribution is severely limited when they do not provide enough information about the subjects and the context of instruction for their results to be fitted into a cumulative picture.

It would be more convenient if we were dealing with a ''neater'' subject matter, but ignoring complexities which we know to be present must predictably yield simplistic and invalid results. Discovering which of these complexities are not significant for second language development and may thus be ignored is a matter to be decided by empirical research, not by a priori assumption or convenience.

Research design for experimental studies should either: (a) be complex enough to include a wide range of psychological and sociocultural characteristics (of children, teachers, care-taking and educational institutions, and communities) as independent variables, and a variety of carefully analyzed treatment conditions (methods, materials, and programs) as dependent variables; or (b) be of more limited scope, but have variables carefully described (and controlled for, insofar as possible) so that the results may contribute cumulatively to a larger complex grid.

All of the other research topics mentioned in relation to the development of bilingual and bicultural competence in children may also be expected to involve complex sociocultural factors. Ethnographic methods should therefore be utilized for qualitative and in-depth descriptions of the dynamics of various language development situations under different conditions as a necessary complement—and in many cases, prerequisite—to quantitative studies. Because of the paucity of data collected in the past, and the inadequacies of much previous data collection for answering the new generation of research questions which have arisen, the field to all intents and purposes remains in its infancy. Research on a variety of languages and settings is urgently needed to contribute to our still very limited state of knowledge in this complex field.

REFERENCES

Bloom, L. M. *One word at a time: the use of single word utterances before syntax.* The Hague: Mouton, 1973.

Burling, R. Language development of a Garo and English-speaking child. *Word,* 1959, *15,* 45–68.

Cancino, H., Rosansky, E. J., & Schumann, J. H. Testing hypotheses about second language acquisition: The copula and negative in three subjects. *Working papers on bilingualism* (No. 6). Toronto: Ontario Institute for Studies in Education, 1974, 80–96.

Christian, C. C. Social and psychological implications of bilingual literacy. In A. Simões, Jr. (Ed.), *The bilingual child: research and analysis of existing educational themes.* New York: Academic Press, 1976.

Cole, M., & Scribner, S. *Culture and thought.* New York: Wiley, 1974.

Cook-Gumperz, J. Situated instruction: language socialization of school age children. In S. Ervin-Tripp & C. Mitchell-Kernan (Eds.), *Child discourse*. New York: Academic Press, 1977.

Cummins, J. The influence of bilingualism on cognitive growth: A synthesis of research findings and explanatory hypotheses. *Working papers on bilingualism* (No. 9). Toronto: Ontario Institute for Studies in Education, 1976, 1–43.

Cummins, J. Linguistic interdependence and the educational development of bilingual children. *Review of Educational Research,* 1979, *49,* 222–251.

Darcey, N. T. A review of the literature on the effects of bilingualism upon the measurement of intelligence. *Journal of Genetic Psychology,* 1953, *82,* 21–57.

Dulay, H. C., & Burt, M. K. Goofing: An indicator of children's second language learning strategies. *Language Learning,* 1972, *22,* 235–252.

Durkin, D. *Children who read early.* New York: Teachers College Press, 1966.

Edelsky, C., & Hudelson, S. Resistance to the acquisition of Spanish by native English speakers in a bilingual setting. *Journal of the Linguistic Association of the Southwest,* 1979, *3*(2), 102–111.

Ervin-Tripp, S. Is second language learning like the first? *TESOL Quarterly,* 1974, *8,* 111–127.

Fathman, A. The relationship between age and second language productive ability. *Language Learning,* 1975, *25,* 245–254.

Fillmore, L. W. Individual differences in second language acquisition. In C. J. Fillmore, D. Kempler, & W. Wang (Eds.), *Individual differences in language ability and language behavior.* New York: Academic Press, 1979.

Greenfield, P. M., & Smith, J. H. *The structure of communication in early child development.* New York: Academic Press, 1976.

Hakuta, K. A report on the development of the grammatical morphemes in a Japanese girl learning English as a second language. *Working papers on bilingualism* (No. 4). Toronto: Ontario Institute for Studies in Education, 1974.

Halliday, M. A. K. *Learning how to mean: Explorations in the development of language.* London: Edward Arnold, 1975.

Hatch, E. M. (Ed.). *Second language acquisition: A book of readings.* Rowley, MA: Newbury House, 1978.

Huang, J., & Hatch, E. M. A Chinese child's acquisition of English. In E. M. Hatch (Ed.), *Second language acquisition: A book of readings.* Rowley, MA: Newbury House, 1978.

Huerta, A. The development of codeswitching in a young bilingual. *Working papers in sociolinguistics* (No. 21). Austin, TX: Southwest Educational Development Laboratory, 1977.

Ianco-Worrall, A. Bilingualism and cognitive development. *Child Development,* 1972, *43,* 1390–1400.

Imedaze, N. V. On the psychological nature of child speech formation under condition of exposure to two languages. *International Journal of Psychology,* 1967, *2* (2), 129–132.

Keller-Cohen, D. Input from the inside: The role of a child's prior linguistic experience in second language learning. In R. W. Andersen (Ed.), *New dimensions in second language acquisition research.* Rowley, MA: Newbury House, 1981.

Lado, R., & Andersson, T. (Eds.). *Early reading.* Washington, DC: Georgetown University Press, 1976.

Lado, R., Hanson, I., & D'Emillio, T. Biliteracy for bilingual children by grade 1. In J. E. Alatis (Ed.), *Current issues in bilingual education.* Washington, DC: Georgetown University Press, 1980.

Lambert, W. E. Culture and language as factors in learning and education. In A. Wolfgang (Ed.), *Education of immigrant students.* Toronto: Ontario Institute for Studies in Education, 1975.

Landry, R. G. A comparison of second language learners and monolinguals on divergent thinking tasks at the elementary school level. *Modern Language Journal,* 1974, *58,* 10–15.

Leopold, W. F. *Speech development of a bilingual child* (Vol. 3). Evanston, IL: Northwestern University Press, 1949.

Luria, A. R. The direct function of speech in development and dissolution. *Word,* 1959, *15,* 341–352.

McClure, E. Aspects of code-switching in the discourse of bilingual Mexican-American children. In M. Saville-Troike (Ed.), *Linguistics and anthropology.* Washington, DC: Georgetown University Press, 1977.

McLaughlin, B. *Second-language acquisition in childhood.* Hillsdale, NJ: Lawrence Erlbaum Associates, 1978.

Piaget, J. *The language and thought of the child.* New York: Harcourt, Brace & World, 1926.

Peal, E., & Lambert, W. The relation of bilingualism to intelligence. *Psychological Monographs,* 1962, *76,* (27, Whole No. 546).

Ronjat, J. Le développment du language observé chez un enfant bilingue. Paris: Champion, 1913.

Saville-Troike, M. *Bilingual children: a resource document.* Arlington, VA: Center for Applied Linguistics, 1975.

Saville-Troike, M. Language development. In H. E. Mitzel (Ed.), *Encyclopedia of educational research* (5th ed.). American Educational Research Association, 1982.

Skutnabb-Kangas, T., & Toukomaa, P. *Teaching migrant children's mother tongue and learning the language of the host country in the context of the sociocultural situation of the migrant family.* Helsinki: The Finnish National Commission for UNESCO, 1976.

Snow, C. E. & Hoefnagel-Höhle, M. Age differences in second language acquisition. In E. M. Hatch (Ed.), *Second language acquisition: A book of readings.* Rowley, MA: Newbury House, 1978.

Swain, M. French immersion: Early, late, or partial? *The Canadian Modern Language Review,* 1978, *34,* 577–586.

Troike, R. C. Research evidence for the effectiveness of bilingual education. *NABE Journal,* 1978, *3* (1), 13–24.

Troike, R. C. SCALP: Social and cultural aspects of language proficiency. Paper presented at Language Proficiency Assessment Symposium, Airlie House, Warrenton, VA, March 15–17, 1981.

Vygotsky, L. S. *Thought and language.* Cambridge, MA: M.I.T. Press, 1934 (reprinted in 1962).

Wolfram, W. *Sociolinguistic aspects of assimilation: Puerto Rican English in East Harlem.* Washington, DC: Center for Applied Linguistics, 1973.

Yoshida, M. The acquisition of English vocabulary by a Japanese-speaking child. In E. M. Hatch (Ed.), *Second language acquisition: a book of readings.* Rowley, MA: Newbury House, 1978.

1. Useful analysis of the current knowledge of the nature & scope of the process of language learning, of the influence of socialisation & the factors which may or may not affect cognitive development.

2. Provides the rationale for the conclusion that the dev. & maintenance of balanced bi-lingual competence is best fostered when both home & school provide a positive supportive environment.

3. Summarises the practices in 2nd language teaching which are supported by research to date.

4. Stresses the inadequacy of much research & the need for more — what is ...l Basic question. 'Who learns best under what circumstances?'

2

Development of Children's Racial Awareness and Intergroup Attitudes[1]

Phyllis A. Katz, Ph.D

Institute for Research on Social Problems, Boulder Co

People come in many varieties. They vary physically in height, weight, body type, facial features, skin color, hair color, eye color, and gender, to mention a few. At a non-physical level, they vary in temperament, disposition, language, and in political, cultural, and religious beliefs. Many of these variations are quite apparent to children. What also becomes apparent to them in the course of development is that our society places much more importance on some of these dimensions than on others. For reasons that are not entirely clear, racial and gender cues have been chosen as particularly significant ways of categorizing people.

Many beliefs about groups classified along these lines have emerged over the centuries. These beliefs are transmitted from one generation to another with such astounding efficiency that our educational institutions might have much to learn from the process. It is not too difficult to find 9-year olds who cannot read or subtract; it is virtually impossible, however, to discover children of the same age who do not know about gender or racial stereotypes.

This chapter will attempt to describe the ways in which children learn about race and form attitudes towards groups other than their own. The processes underlying this development of racial awareness and attitudes during the first ten years of life will be delineated.

How do children develop attitudes? Folk wisdom tells us that the tree grows as the twig is bent. This notion seems particularly appropriate when

[1] Preparation of this chapter was assisted by NICHD Contract No. 1-HD-92820, P. Katz, Principal Investigator. The author would like to express particular gratitude to Carol Hathaway-Clark for her research assistance and to Susie Gulbrandsen for her secretarial and editorial assistance.

considering the issue of intergroup attitude development. As Allport (1954) has suggested, early negative attitudes may be "caught, rather than taught" and once caught may be most intransigent to change. The relative imperviousness of adult prejudice to the effects of conflicting evidence and experience strongly suggests that predispositions acquired at early developmental levels may form the irrational but potent foundation for racism.

Because there is general agreement that basic attitudes are learned in child-hood, there has been a great deal of interest exhibited by social scientists in the ontogenesis of intergroup attitudes. Comprehensive reviews of some of this empirical research have been done by Proshansky (1966), Katz (1976), and Balch and Paulsen (1979); this chapter therefore will not attempt to duplicate those reviews, but rather will focus upon the basic developmental trends obtained in earlier research. It will also delineate the major theoretical viewpoints that have been offered to account for the origins of prejudice. In doing so, it will draw heavily on the present author's earlier review (Katz, 1976).

WHEN DO RACIAL ATTITUDES BEGIN FORMING?

The age at which children begin to acquire racial attitudes has been a question of continuing interest. Available evidence suggests that by 3 or 4 years of age many children make differential responses to skin color and other racial cues. The dawning of racial awareness follows what many believe to be a period of color-blindness. It should be noted that this latter belief, though widely held, appears dubious and has no empirical support, since virtually no studies have been reported with children younger than three.

There appears to be general agreement that ethnic attitudes begin to take shape and are observable during the nursery school years, although some questions exist concerning the generality of early stated preferences. According to many theorists (e.g., Goodman, 1952), the development of ethnic attitudes is integrally related to the establishment of a child's self-identity. It is typically assumed that the child must necessarily learn about which groups he/she does and does not belong to as part of the self-discovery process. At about the same time, positive and negative feelings come to be associated with various groups. In summarizing the empirical work in this area through 1965, Proshansky (1966) concludes that racial awareness (1) appears at about 3 years of age in both Black and White children, (2) increases rapidly for the next several years, and (c) is fairly well established by the time children enter first grade. Although there is some disagreement in the literature as to whether White or Black children achieve racial awareness earlier, the preponderance of evidence seems to indicate that minority children are more sensitive to racial cues and are more precocious with regard to them.

In a classic study of young children's attitudes in a Northeastern urban community, Goodman (1952) studied 103 Black and White children. One of the unique features of this frequently cited study is that the investigator made intensive observations of both the children and their families over the course of a full year. Consequently, she was able to study responses that might not have been evident to an observer who knew the children less well. According to Goodman, racial awareness was not only present at ages 3 and 4 (although there was some variability along this dimension), but 25% of the children at age 4 were already expressing strongly entrenched race-related values. White children never expressed a wish to be like a Black child, whereas Black children exhibited a great deal of denial and conflict about their evaluations of blackness. For some of the children the words were there even though the feelings were still to come, as in the case of one 4-year-old who made the haunting comment, "The people that are white, they can go up. The people that are brown, they have to go down."

One of the interesting findings reported was the discrepancy that appeared to exist between what Goodman referred to as the children's "precocious raciality" and their parents' beliefs that their children were relatively unaware of race. In another extensive and more recent sutdy of preschool children in the Northeast, conducted by Porter (1971), a sizable proportion of 3-year-old children in the sample also exhibited preferences based on racial cues, and these responses increased markedly between 3 and 5 years of age.

The presence of racial awareness in children as young as three suggests that its antecedents must have come at an earlier age—perhaps in nonverbal form. Although we do not adequately understand the parameters, some theories that have been offered will be discussed in the next section.

WHAT ARE THE DEVELOPMENTAL FORERUNNERS OF RACIAL ATTITUDES? THE FIRST THREE YEARS

There is a perceptual prerequisite involved in learning any category system. Prior to being able to define a social group, the child must be able to discriminate between groups and learn which cues are relevant for group inclusion or exclusion. Learning about people is analogous to all early concept formation. For instance, the category "cow" is defined (for young children) by the sound it makes, which is different from sounds other animals make. During early language development, young children receive considerable training of this kind, and parents reward correct classification responses. When the child correctly verbalizes "meow" to the pussy cat pictures and "bow wow" to the puppy, parents express their pleasure. Thus, it may be that both this extensive practice of classification skills and the associated reinforcement may generalize, increasing a child's predisposition for categorizing people.

Because of the perceptual prerequisite, young children's initial classifications are based upon cues which are easily discernible. This is undoubtedly why both gender and race are learned about so early. It also accounts in part for why religion and nationality cues are learned at much later stages. It is interesting to note, in this regard, that the absence of clear perceptual cues for classifying certain ethnic groups has occassionally led governments to add them. In Nazi Germany, for example, Jews were forced to wear Stars of David so that they could be more easily identified. In Truffaut's movie "The Last Metro," a story based in German-occupied Paris in 1942, a Nazi radio announcer decries the fact that is is so difficult to tell who is Jewish. "Wouldn't it be nice," he asks, "if they just all had blue skin?" The cues for learning about race are, unlike religion, more readily apparent to a young child.

The reason so little is known about the development of racial awareness during the first three years of life is that virtually no studies have been conducted with children below age 3. This state of affairs was noted in the present writer's earlier review (Katz, 1976) and remains essentially true five years later. Consequently, discussions concerning the development of racial perception during the first three years of life will be necessarily speculative. Such speculation may be important to engage in, however, for at least two reasons. First, it may serve to stimulate needed research. Second, since it has repeatedly been found that a sizable proportion of 3-year-olds and most 4-year-old children do exhibit awareness of racial cues, it is clear that the processes underlying this development must have taken place during an earlier period.

When early studies of nursery school children's racial awareness were first published (e.g., Clark & Clark, 1947; Goodman, 1952), considerable surprise was expressed at the fact that young children even noticed skin color differences. Indeed, many people still believe that children, in Rousseau-like innocence, are color-blind with respect to people. The present author has encountered several school administrators who believed that assessment of grade school children's racial attitudes would cause them to suddenly pay attention to race for the first time.

Such beliefs are clearly not supported by the evidence. Upon reflection, they are somewhat peculiar. Very young infants are obviously capable of distinguishing color cues in inanimate objects (Fagan, 1974; Gaines, 1971). Why, then, should people be exempted from this perceptual process? A study by the present author and her students, conducted with 3-day-old infants (Rose, Katz, Birke, & Rossman, 1977), found not only that facial-like configurations of varying hues were discriminated, but that infants preferred high-contrast stimuli. Thus, they followed a white face against a brown background and a brown face against a white background more actively than they followed a white face against a pink background. It may be that in very early infancy, anything that stands out visually becomes a compelling stimulus. Newborns seem to be sensitive to color cues, figure-ground contrast, border Illumination discrepancies, and configurational details as well. So much for color-blindness!

That children by age 3 should employ skin color cues as a basis for person classification, therefore, should not be surprising. Much of a child's early cognitive training employs the teaching of colors and the use of color as a classification device. What may be more surprising, however, is that nursery school children exhibit differential evaluative responses to different skin colors. White children clearly prefer the color white in both non-human and human pictures, and until relatively recently, young Black children also exhibited pro-white bias.

There are two theories that have been proposed to account for these phenomena, an early one by Allport (1954) and a more recent view postulated by Williams and his colleagues (Williams, 1972; Williams & Morland, 1976).

Allport has suggested (1954) that children evaluate other-race individuals negatively as one instance of a general fear of strange and unfamiliar things. Fear of the strange may be elicited by inanimate objects, unexpected occurrences, and, perhaps, people who look very different to the child. Allport further suggests that visible differences between people may imply other real differences to the child. This latter possibility is in accordance with cognitive-developmental theory as well (e.g., Piaget). Allport's notions were vividly brought home to the present writer when she visited a foundling home in a remote part of China several years ago. The children in the home had not had any exposure to Caucasians, and when the group walked in, several of the children between 6 and 12 months became obviously fearful, avoided us, and began to cry. Since this reaction was not elicited by unfamiliar Chinese adults, it was clear that more than simple "stranger anxiety" was involved.

Although the possibilities suggested by this view are intriguing, no systematic work with young children deriving from Allport's theory has been conducted. Thus, even assuming the validity of the "strange person" phenomenon, we do not know whether or how this earlier fear relates to subsequent attitude development. Similarly, the age when such events would have maximun developmental impact is not known. Whether such fear develops at all would seem to depend upon happenstance occurrences, and thus could not readily account for the relatively systematic effects we see later in development. Allport's reasoning suggests a modification technique which has not always been successful. It could be argued that fear of the strange might be reduced by early and frequent interracial contact. Although several studies suggest that increasing familiarity may also increase liking for previously unfamiliar stimuli (Cantor, 1972; Zajonc, Swap, Harrison, & Roberts, 1971), anecdotal evidence suggests occasions when the opposite may be true, particularly with prolonged exposure; the rearing of upper-class Southern White children by Black women did not apparently innoculate those children against negative racial attitudes.

Williams has posited an even more far-reaching theory. His position suggests that early racial preferences of Whites (and some Blacks) reflect primitive feelings about day and night. In an excellent recent review of work in the area, Williams and Morland (1976) argue that the development of the concept of race is inextricably bound with the symbolism associated with color usage. This argument is based upon several pieces of evidence. First, the color names "black" and "white" are the most frequently encountered color terms in almost all known languages (Hays, Margolis, Naroll,& Perkins, 1972). Second, considerable cross-cultural research has demonstrated that the color white is associated with positive attributes in most cultures and that the color black is linked with negative ones. Williams and Morland go on to suggest that such affective conntations generalize to skin color cues. A basic question that needs to be addressed, however, has to do with the origin of these very common linguistic patterns. The investigators speculate that pro-white bias originates from a basic human tendency to prefer light over dark. Darkness, it is argued, is intrinsically aversive because it elicits visual disorientation which leads to dark-avoidance in both humans and nonhuman primates. Because of this, darkness comes to be associated with fear , whereas lightness is associated with fear-reduction. Generalization of these trends is presumed to occur along many dimensions, including language, color, and race. Thus, it is argued that preference for lightness over darkness may be the developmental forerunner of preference for white skin. Cultural factors (i.e., language connotations, lower status associated with dark skin, etc.) merely serve to reinforce these intial tendencies.

Ontogenetically, this fascinating theory implies that there should be a relationship between a young child's fear of the dark and the negativity of his or her subsequent attitudes towards Blacks. In the only empirical effort to test this notion to date (Boswell & Williams, 1975), a modest correlation (R= .40) was found between white-black color bias in 37 5-years-olds, and their mothers' reports about their children's aversive responses to darkness. Further work in this area is clearly warranted and needed.

To summarize, by the age of 3 many children already exhibit some awareness of racial cues, although the processes underlying this development are not well investigated or understood. Children are capable of making the requisite perceptual differentiation based upon skin color (and possibly on the basis of facial features as well) quite early in life, but whether racial concepts are indeed formed seems quite dependent upon specific experiential factors, such as whether the child lives in a predominantly homogeneous or heterogeneous racial environment. Two theoretical viewpoints have been offered to account for differential evaluations of racial groups. Allport has suggested that fear of the unfamiliar underlies much of a child's response to people of other races. In contrast, Williams has argued that all children begin life with a preference for light and an aversion to dark, a tendency that continues in White children but is counteracted by other factors in minority children.

RACIAL AWARENESS — ITS MEASUREMENT AND ITS MEANING

As noted above, children are capable of making subtle and sophisticated distinctions in the world around them. Thus, what may be unusual is not that children can and do perceptually distinguish brown and white skins but that such distinctions have already taken on evaluative components by the preschool period.

In order to understand the ramifications of early racial awareness, it becomes necessary to attend to how it is actually measured in young children. By far, the most frequently employed task has been the use of doll choices. This preference task, originally employed by Clark and Clark in 1947, initially seems quite straightforward. The child is asked to choose the nice doll, the pretty one, and so on from pairs of black and white dolls. The seeming simplicity of the task may have accounted for its ready acceptance and its consequent historical significance in the *Brown* vs. *Board of Education of Topeka, Kansas* Supreme Court decision of 1954, which barred segregation in the schools partially on the basis of the Clarks' results.

Closer examination, however, reveals a number of methodological problems associated with choice instruments of this type. In most studies, the dolls differ not only in skin color cues but in eye color and hair color as well (i.e., white dolls have blonde hair and blue eyes, whereas black dolls have brown hair and brown eyes). Thus, it is not clear what cues might be accounting for the earlier-obtained preference for white dolls. Kircher and Furby (1971), for example, found that both skin color and hair type could be significant determinants of young children's preferences for pictures. Moreover, a more recent study that held hair and eye color constant (Katz & Zalk, 1974) found no preference for a doll's skin color.

Some additional problems with the use of this technique concern its psychometric properties. Reliability data have not yet been presented, despite wide usage, and it is quite conceivable that children of this age might give very different responses to the same questions a second time. Furthermore, no validity data for this task have been presented. Problems of reliability and validity are not, of course, unique to doll choice measures of racial attitudes but are applicable to a wide range of measures. Investigators employing adults are somewhat more cognizant of these issues, whereas early investigators utilizing young children have not been. Studies of children have generally assumed that in the absence of supporting evidence, a one-to-one correspondence exists between responses to the index and other behavior. Interestingly, the few studies that have attempted to assess task performance and nursery school children's actual behavior with regard to children of differing groups have not obtained positive findings. Stevenson and Stevenson (1960) have maintained, for example, that nursery school children do not exhibit same-race play preferences. The previously-referred-to study by Porter (1971) also noted that play patterns were unrelated to doll preferences, and Hraba & Grant (1970) found no relationship between doll task performance and stated friendship choices. Thus, the possibility exists that nursery school children, when confronted by a racial choice, may simply be responding in a way they feel an adult (who is often White) expects them to. Because of these varied problems, it is difficult to know how best to interpret such a measure. Despite this, the technique has been used in numerous studies.

Over the past ten years, several studies have contradicted the Clarks' earlier findings that Black children exhibit strong preferences for White dolls (Brigham & Weissbach, 1972; Butler, Cunningham, Keck & Nordquist, 1970; Datcher, Savage, & Checkosky, 1973; Fox & Jordan, 1973; Hraba & Grant, 1970; Katz & Zalk, 1974.) It is tempting to attribute such changes in children's responses to societal changes that have occurred over the past decade. The importance of the civil rights movement and Black people's developing pride in their blackness are certainly factors. Moreover, the positive exposures given to Black people by the media should not be underestimated as a potentially significant parameter for changing attitudes of children

There are several problems with the societal change interpretation, however. Results of subsequent investigation have not been completely unambiguous. Some studies (e.g., Asher & Allen, 1969; Greenwald & Oppenheim, 1968; McAdoo, 1970; Morland, 1966; Spencer & Horowitz, 1973; Williams, Best, Boswell, Mattson, & Graves, 1975) have, in fact, replicated the earlier findings regarding white doll preferences. The work of Williams and his colleagues, who used a picture preference test rather than a doll preference, has more consistently found that white figures are associated with positive adjectives and black figures associated with negative ones (Renninger & Williams, 1966: Williams & Roberson, 1967; Williams, et al. 1975). This has been true for both Black and White children at the preschool level. How, then, can one reconcile these seeming contradictions?

One possibility that follows from the methodological problems discussed above is that discrepant results may simply be reflecting the lack of reliability of the doll measure. Most investigators working with young children seem unwilling to abandon the technique however, and continue to attribute some conceptual meaning to children's preferences. It is interesting to note that older minority group children express preferences for blackness more strongly than do younger children (McAdoo, 1977). Thus, the trend may be very real, but preschool measures may be insufficiently sensitive to it.

A second possible explanation is that there may be geographic variations in children's attitudes. Interestingly, much of the work reporting more positive attitudes towards black dolls and pictures has occurred in large urban centers (e.g., Fox & Jordan, 1973; Hraba & Grant, 1970;) whereas the older attitudes appear to be more prevalent in the South and in smaller towns (e.g., Clark & Clark, 1947; Morland, 1966; Stevenson & Stewart, 1958). It might be fruitful, therefore, to conduct geographical comparisons utilizing the same instrument. Another interesting difference that emerges between those studies showing preferences and those that do not is that the latter often use Black testers. This may again tell us something about the young child's degree of sophistication; he or she may well be giving what appears to be the sociallly desirable response.

Although the whole issue of minority choices is not without controversy (cf. McQuater, & Ross 1979; Williams & Morland, 1979; Banks, 1979), the preponderance of evidence seems to this writer to suggest a growing shift towards greater minority self-esteem and positive racial identification both historically (Butler, 1976) and ontogenetically (McAdoo, 1977). Young Black preschool children in most recent studies now show either no bias or a same-race preference in choice tasks.

It should be noted that although responses of Black children have changed, the responses of young White children have not. White children never express preferences to be a member of any racial group but their own. Moreover, a multitude of studies have shown that children as young a 3 to 4 have strong positive associations to both the color and the racial group labeled "white" and negative ones to "black" in its abstract and skin color designations (Asher & Allen, 1969; Fox & Jordan, 1973; Greenwald & Oppenheim, 1968; Hardin, 1977; Hraba & Grant, 1970; Morland, 1966, 1972; Renninger & Williams, 1966; Stevenson & Stewart, 1958; Williams, Boswell, & Best, 1975). Although it is generally assumed that skin color is the most salient cue for differentiating race, two interesting recent studies looked at the role of other physiognomic cues. One, conducted by Sorce (1979), found that physiognomic features were more salient than skin color and that White children were more aware of hair features than skin color. This latter finding is particularly interesting since most doll choice tasks simultaneously vary skin, hair, and sometimes eye color. Thus, a brown-skinned, brown-eyed, and brown-haired doll is usually paired with a pink-skinned, blue-eyed, blonde-haired one. A study by Katz and Zalk (1974) which varied *only* skin color within male and/or female doll pairs (all dolls had brown hair and eyes) did not, in fact, find clear-cut preferences for white dolls. It was suggested in that study, therefore, that children may like the proverbial "gentlemen," simply prefer blondes. A study by LaCoste (1978) with 3 -to 4-year-old White children found that they were able to classify facial features for Blacks and Whites even when differential skin color cues were absent. As in the previously mentioned study, hair differences were particularly salient.

A final problem arises with regard to the theoretical relation of all preschool measures to subsequent attitude development. It is clear that all children ultimately exhibit some degree of racial awareness. It is equally clear, however, that not all children develop negative intergroup attitudes. What, then is the relationship (if any) between these earlier expressed preferences and later feelings and behaviors? Do children who exhibit early awareness develop different attitudes than those who manifest awareness later? Is intensity of awareness related to strength of later attitudes? Unfortunately, there seems to be no evidence on these issues. We know that racial awareness is a necessary condition for attitude development, but it is certainly not a sufficient one. A longitudinal study is very much needed to clarify these theoretical issues.

MECHANISMS UNDERLYING RACIAL ATTITUDE DEVELOPMENT

A number of theoretical formulations have been posited regarding the acquistion of racial attutudes. Interestingly, most of these formulations have been generated by work with adults, and extrapolations to children have been made primarily on a theoretical, rather than an empirical basis. Although all investigators in this area pay lip service to the belief that attitudes are complex and multiply determined, most theorists have, in fact, focused upon a single determinant. This section will delineate some of the major variables that have been discussed in relation to attitude acquisition.

Direct Instruction

In contrast to Allport's belief that prejudice is caught rather than taught, the song from *South Pacific* expresses the notion that "you have to be carefully taught." This latter belief may be the most commonly accepted view, both by the general public and by a number of social scientists. Why are children prejudiced? Obviously, it is is argued, because their parents are. If parents are prejudiced, they will consequently transmit such feelings to children.

Although the variable of parental instruction has considerable common-sense appeal, evidence supporting this view is scanty and inconsistent. An early study by Harris, Gough and Martin (1950), for example, suggests that there may be positive but relatively small correlations between elementary school children's racial attitudes and the attitudes of their parents. Mosher and Scodel (1960) obtained a relation between the social distance scores of 12-years-olds and the ethnic attitudes of their mothers. On the other hand, Radke-Yarrow, Trager and Miller (1952) found that kindergarten and first-grade White children often displayed negative reactions to Blacks even when their parents held more liberal attitudes. Other studies have also found no relationship to parental attitudes with either young children (Bird, Monachesi, & Burdick, 1952; Frenkel-Brunswik & Havel, 1953; Pushkin, 1967) or adolescents (Byrne, 1965). With regard to this latter study, it may be argued that the impact of parental attitudes would not be expected to be as salient during adolescence, since many additional factors—such as peer group feelings, school experiences, and type and variety of interracial encounters—have influenced earlier attitudes. If this is the case, however, than the importance of parental attitudes may have been very much overemphasized. If negative parental training can indeed be counteracted so readily, the implications for modification research are considerable.

The developmental relationship between the attitudes of children and those of their parents appears to be a complex one, which cannot readily be disentangled without longitudinal data. The expectation that direct instruction from parents is involved has not received much empirical support. Moreover, the mechanisms underlying attitude transmission have not been well delineated. Besides direct instruction, other variables to be considered in the parent-child relationship include obeservational learning and modeling (e.g., Liebert, Sobol, & Copemann, 1972). The specific timing of instruction may also be of significance. It might well be, for example, that certain early types of training leave an indelible impression, whereas later types of negative exposures are more readily changed. It is clear, however, that there is far from a one-to-one relationship between parents' and their children's attitudes.

Reinforcement Components

The mechanism of reinforcement has frequently been offered as an explanation of how children learn prejudice. According to this view, either peers or adults in the child's environment are seen as rewarding the expression of negative attitudes. The rather complex responses subsumed under the attitude construct would probably not typically be acquired under conditions of consistent reinforcement, since the communications themselves are often ambivalent (cf. Katz, Glass, & Cohen, 1973) and thus may lead to inconsistent reinforcement. Thus, for example, if first-grader Jane (White) asks her mother if she can invite her friend Lotus (Black) for lunch, the mother may say yes but she may use a slightly different tone of voice than Jane is accustomed to. When Jane asks her mother whether she may go to Lotus' house the following week, the mother may well say no, while using many circumlocutions and rationalizations. The message, then, that is often transmitted to the child is a confusing one with mixed overtones.

Despite the complexity of both the communication and the reinforcement contingencies, the possibility exists that certain basic components of racial attitudes can best be understood in reinforcement terms. The early learning involved in the affective aspects of attitudes may well fall into this category. The most active proponent of a reinforcement view has been Williams, whose theory was discussed in the previous section (since it is particularly relevant to early development). It can be recalled that Williams and his colleagues suggest that all children develop a positive bias toward light colors because of our diurnal rhythm and consequent aversion to darkness. This is reflected in the language of most cultures, which contain positive associations to the color "white" and negative ones to the color "black". This reinforces the child's initial predilections in this area, which generalize to skin color cues. The pervasive racist attitudes within our society further serve to reinforce such connections for White children. Minority group children, according to Williams, begin life with the same preferences for light colors, but positive associations to darker colors (due to contact with dark-skinned adults) soon come into play to counteract these earlier tendencies. Although Williams does not specifically discuss it, the other side of the coin should be equally true (i.e., to the extent that Black children have negative experiences with White racism, they should begin to devalue both the color "white" and the racial group).

Williams and his colleagues and students have conducted a number of studies with preschool and young grade school children which have demonstrated that (1) colors are evaluated in in accordance with the theory, particularly by majority group children; and (2) these associations do generalize to pictures of people. Two measures have been frequently used to assess these trends. The first is the Color Meaning Test (Williams & Roberson, 1967), which consists of pairs of objects or animals alike in all respects but color. The other instrument is the Preschool Racial Attitude Measure—PRAM (Williams, et al., 1975) which assesses children's associations of positive and negative adjectives to pairs of child and adult figures varying in skin color.

One of the interesting implications of this position is that if associations are formed by reinforcement, these same associations should be modifiable when the reinforcement contingencies are changed, and indeed, evidence has been offered to support this view. Interestingly, when the present author reviewed literature pertinent to attitude modification in 1974, she noted the paucity of such studies conducted with young children. This state of affairs was also noted by Proshansky (1966) in an earlier review and by Balch and Paulsen (1979), who more recently discussed some of the historical trends. Over the past decade, however, there has been a proliferation of attitude change studies. These studies have used a variety of techniques, including increasing interracial contact at the preschool level (e.g., Palmer, 1977; Goldstein, Koopman, & Goldstein, 1979), providing positive television portrayals of minorities (Goldberg & Gorn, 1979), increasing multicultural experiences (Blackwell, Silvern, & Yawkey 1976), assigning perceptual differentiation techniques (Katz & Zalk, 1978), and attempting to change pro-White/anti-Black biases by negatively reinforcing traditional responses and/or positively reinforcing pro-Black/anti-White responses (Chamberlin-Robinson, 1977; McAdoo, 1970; Shanahan, 1972; Spencer & Horowitz, 1973; Traynham, 1974; Williams & Edwards, 1969). In general, most techniques have been associated with some degree of success. Reinforcemnt procedures have worked at the preschool level, although their long-term effectiveness remains to be ascertained (Balch & Paulsen, 1979).

The relationship between children's responses to racial cues and reinforcement processes has been studied in other types of experimental paradigms, such as pitting one type of cue against another. Doke and Risley (1972), for example, attempted to assess the relative importance of race and sex as discriminative cues in the behavior of Black pre-school and grade school children. Subjects were shown pictures of a White boy and a Black girl and were taught to press a different button when each appeared. Other pictures of Black girls and White boys were then presented, and generalization on the button-pressing was obtained. Following this, a transfer task was introduced in which subjects were shown slides of Black boys and White girls. The question raised was whether the earlier discrimination was learned on the basis of skin color or gender cues. It was found that younger children generalized along the sex dimension, whereas older children (ages 9 to 12) generalized on the basis of race. The finding with young children corroborates the previously cited study by Katz and Zalk (1974) with regard to preschool children's doll preferences, in that gender cues were more salient than was skin color.

Another approach relevant to the reinforcement aspect of children's racial attitudes is concerned with the differential reward values associated with individuals of different races. The experimental paradigm employed by Katz, Henchy, & Allen (1968) demonstrates this paradigm: children participated in a rote-memory learning task and received verbal approval from either a White or Black male examiner. In this particular study, persons of the same race were found to be the most effective reinforcers (although it should be noted that some complicated interactions were obtained). With younger children, an examiner of another race may be more effective as a reinforcer (e.g., Katz. 1973). Not only are adults of different races associated with differential social reinforcement, but other evidence with young children also suggests that peers are associated with such patterns (Coates, Arnstein, & Jordan, 1973).

Investigations pertinent to children's learning behavior with same-or other-race adults (reviewed by Sattler, 1973) suggest that a wide variety of parameters are associated with how effective a person is to a child as a reinforcer. It is interesting to note that such investigations are generally categorized under the rubric of "race of examiner" effects, as if it were primarily the objective characteristics of the adult rather than the child's learned patterns that account for observed behavior differences. It is the view of the present author that this misplaced emphasis has had the effect of confusing rather than clarifying the complex patterns of results obtained. Attention has not been paid, for example, to such questions as whether a relationship exists between a child's racial attitudes and the differential reinforcing value of adults. Moreover, when adults are well-matched on other relevant variables, as was done by Yando, Zigler, and Gates (1971), some of the "racial" effects washed out. It is clear from the bewildering array of findings obtained with regard to "race of examiner" effects in children that considerably more theoretical delineation and better studies are required before unambiguous predictions can be generated.

Personality Factors and Child-Rearing Techniques

Perhaps the most widely known theoeretical treatment of prejudice is the one that attributes negative intergroup attitudes to an authoritarian personality structure (Adorno, Frenkel-Brunswik, Levinson, & Sanford, 1950). This work represents one of social science's major attempts to understand the roots of prejudice. The theory assumes that prejudice in children is generated by harsh and rigid parents. The child is viewed as having to continually submit to arbitrary and often severe parental authority. Because of the parents' uncompromising natures, the resultant hostility in the child is never permitted direct expression. Accordingly, as a defense mechanism, the child identifies with the frustrating authority figures, tends to idealize them, and displaces his or her aggressions toward out-group persons.

One of the major tenets of this theory is that prejudice serves a particular function for the individual and is integrally related to other aspects of his or her personality. The authoritarian personality type is viewed as a basically insecure person who represses impulses, views life as threatening, and perceives social relationships in terms of power. Some behavioral consequences of this syndrome are rigidity, a tendency toward stereotyped thinking, an avoidance of introspection, and excessive moralism. The authoritarian person idealizes "toughness," has contempt for "weakness," and perceives the world in sharply defined categories of black or white, right or wrong, good or bad. For the authoritarian personality, there is very little gray in the world.

The original formulations concerning the authoritarian personality were based upon an anonymous anti-Semitism scale administered to 100 college students. The eight women who scored highest and the eight who scored lowest were then given in depth interviews and projective tests. It could be argued that such a far-reaching theory was initially formulated on relatively little evidence. Nevertheless, this approach has had considerable theoretical impact and heuristic value. It has also generated a lot of controversy with regard to the adequacy of research purporting to document its suppositions (cf. Christie, 1954). The adult research with regard to this position is discussed in more detail by Ashmore and Del Boca (1976). This section, then, will only discuss evidence with children.

The most convincing study with regard to the relationship between authoritarian parents and ethnocentrism in children is the previously cited work conducted by Harris, et al. (1950). Attitude questionnaires were given to 240 fourth-, fifth-, and sixth-grade children and their parents, and positive correlations were obtained between the two sets of measures. More intensive investigation of the extreme groups demonstrated a strong relationship between maternal beliefs about child rearing and the degree of prejudice in children. The mothers of high-prejudice subjects stressed the value of obedience, preferred quiet children to noisy ones, and discouraged sex-play in their children, often by the use of physical punishment. This pattern contrasted with the more permissive practices of the mothers of low-prejudice children. Thus, the picture that emerges from this study is in accordance with the authoritarian personality theory. Several other studies have found similar results (e.g., Hart, 1957; Lyle & Levitt, 1955; Weatherley, 1963).

A continuing problem in evaluating ths research, however, has to do with the confounding of authoritarianism scores with other variables that may explain these trends equally well. As noted by several investigators (Hyman & Sheatsley, 1954; Proshansky, 1966), both intelligence and educational level are negatively related to authoritarian personality tendencies. Each of these, in turn, is related to socioeconomic level. This latter variable, in and of itself, could readily account for differences in parental beliefs about child-rearing practices. Thus, in the Harris, et al. study, the high-prejudice children may well have come from lower socioeconomic families where values might be expected to more closely approximate the ''authoritarian'' type. Without such essential controls, it is impossible to ascertain whether differences are to be attributed to parental personality or to sociocultural factors. Moreover, as other investigators (Epstein & Komorita, 1965; Proshansky, 1966) have noted, children of authoritarian parents may have acquired their attitudes via direct instruction rather than from the particular disciplinary techniques to which they were exposed.

In summary, research with regard to the authoritarian personality has provided some provocative work in this area, but is difficult to interpret. It should be pointed out that even if this research were not surrounded by methodological ambiguity, it would still be a somewhat disheartening theory from the point of view of attitude change. If the theory is correct, it follows that authoritarian parents would have to change first in order for their children to become more tolerant.

Even if one does not subscribe wholeheartedly to the theory concerning the authoritarian personality, one may still postulate that particular types of parental behavior and/or personality factors serve to instill negative racial attitudes. A study by Tabachnick (1962) attempted to test the hypothesis initially set forth by Allport (1954) that racial prejudice in children was an expression of frustration. According to this theory, individuals (both children and adults) who are unhappy with themselves or maladjusted should exhibit a tendency to take out such dissatisfaction on others who are more socially vulnerable.

Tabachnich tested 300 White fifth-grade children, employing the direct questionnaire measure of attitudes towards Blacks previously used by Gough, Harris, Martin, and Edwards (1950). Satisfaction with self was assessed by means of ''objective frustration'' caused by classifying children as underachievers, overachievers, or normal. This classification was based upon the obtained discrepancy between the child's grades and his or her IQ scores. Those children classified as underachievers by means of this rating scale were considered to be the most frustrated group. Findings revealed small (but in some instances, statistically significant) correlations between prejudice scores and self-reports of satisfaction. Thus, children who scored higher on the prejudice scale tended also to report more dissatisfaction with themselves. (The highest correlation reported, however, was −.27.) In terms of predictability, then, approximately 9% of the variability in prejudice scores could be accounted for by knowing the children's ratings of self-satisfaction. No significant relationships were obtained between degree of achievement (the investigator's objective frustration measure) and racial attitudes. Thus, it appears that personality measures may be related to attitudes, but certainly not to the degree that some theorists have contended.

The study by Tabachnick is instructive because it demonstrated some of the pitfalls frequently encountered in attempts to assess theory in this area. The correlational format of the study is typical of such investigations, and this of course, precludes saying anything about the particular nature of the relationship between personality and attitudinal variables. Even if the correlations were high (which they were not), we would not know whether the self-dissatisfaction anteceded or succeeded the development of racial attitudes, or whether some additional but unmeasured variables accounted for the concurrent development of racial prejudice and unhappiness. An additional difficulty in interpreting such findings is the reliance upon assessment of attitudes by a direct questionnaire whose validity has not been established. It would appear that social scientists sometimes try to chase butterflies with meat axes.

An example of a somewhat better controlled study with children was conducted by Epstein and Komorita (1965). These investigators attempted to assess the effects of the child's perceptions of parental discipline and particular stimulus characteristics of an out-group upon social distance scores. Social distance responses were obtained in response to pictures that were systematically varied along two dimensions: (1) social class (determined by the relative shabbiness of the clothes and surrounding environment), and (2) race (White versus Oriental). The target pictures were introduced to the sample (White middle-class children from the third to the eighth grades as a fictitious group called Piraneans. The major finding of the study was a curvilinear relationship between percieved parental permissiveness and social distance scores given to out-groups.

This finding is an interesting one, which in some ways contradicts authoritarianism theory. The children who appeared to be least prejudiced were those who perceived their parents as being either very permissive or very punitive. Those who perceived their parents as exhibiting an intermediate degree of permissiveness (one is tempted to say middle American parents) expressed the greatest social distance towards out-groups. Most theoretical positions that stress childrearing and defense mechanism components of social attitudes would generate the prediction that children whose parents are least permissive should have stronger negative attitudes towards out-groups. Such parental rigidity is, indeed, supposed to provide the motivating force behind the projection and displacement towards out-groups involved in prejudice. The study clearly does not support this expectation.

In view of the pervasive quality of most personality variables, it would be quite surprising to find that they were not related to social attitudes in some way. Nevertheless, the insistence by some theorists (e.g., Bettelheim & Janowitz, 1950) that racial attitudes in children are to be understood primarily as an outgrowth of emotional meladjustment does not seem warranted on the basis of the data available. Personality factors seem to be only tangentially related to racial attitudes or related in ways that go contrary to existing theory. Although is may be more comforting to think that highly prejudiced children must be emotionally disturbed in some way (and some undoubtedly are), the empirical evidence does not support this view unless one is willing to assume that prejudice and emotional disturbance are synonymous. Studies that measure the two constructs separately have found that they are not highly related to each other. Large numbers of children express racial prejudice but do not seem to be maladjusted in other areas.

Cognitive Aspects of Racial Attitudes

While the bulk of the evidence concerned with attitudinal antecedents has focused upon emotional determinants, some investigations of the cognitive correlates of attitudes have also been conducted and will be reviewed in this section. There are at least two ways in which cognitive components of attitudes have been conceptualized. One approach has been to view the cognitive aspects as the resultant expression of more primary & deeply-rooted personality variables. A second position has approached cognitive aspects as developmental determinants of attitudes. Until fairly recently, the first approach has been the more common one.

Concern with the thought processes underlying attitudes is not new. A number of investigators have proposed that cognitive components are central to any understanding of racial attitude acquisition. Allport, in his most comprehensive and scholarly treatment of the topic (1954), suggests that the major problem in prejudice is, in fact, a thought problem. The prejudiced individual displays what Allport calls "overcategorization" in that he or she assumes that all people placed within a class behave in the same way and exhibit the same traits. Such overcategorization is relatively impervious to new information that may logically contradict this belief. According to Allport, prejudice is not easily reversible.

The approach that regards this type of thinking as the outgrowth of personality factors (e.g., authoritarian theory) tends to conceptualize the cognitive style as disordered and the result of rigid, moralistic upbringing. According to this position, children raised in excessively strict homes acquire a tendency to "jump the gun." They categorize prematurely, overgeneralize, and resist changing categories once they are formed. Two studies are generally cited to support this position. The first one was conducted by Frenkel-Brunswik in 1948. In this investigation, high- and low-prejudice groups of children (determined by scores obtained on the California E scale) were asked to look at a series of pictures in which a cat was gradually transformed into a dog. The child's task was to label each picture. High-prejudice subjects were found to change their verbal responses more slowly from one category to another than did less prejudiced subjects, thus, supporting the theoretical expectation. The possibility exists, however, that the problem exhibited by the high-prejudice subjects was perceptual rather than cognitive (i.e., they may not have perceived the discrepant cues as readily).

A second study conducted by Kutner (1958), does not have this interpretive problem. Kutner employed sixty-7-year-old White children, dichotomized on the basis of racial attitude scores. They were given a series of conceptual tasks which included exercises in syllogistic reasoning, critical thinking, and other types of problem solving. The major finding was that the high-prejudice youngsters were defective in reasoning ability when contrasted with their agemates; furthermore, they were found to be more intolerant of ambiguity, thus providing some support for the position outlined above. Interestingly, some of the same children were observed again when they were 16 years of age, and some of the differences obtained earlier were still present (Kutner & Gordon, 1964). This latter study is one of the very few longitudinal follow-ups ever done in this area, and as such is laudable. Nevertheless, the differences between the groups might be explained more parsimoniously on the basis of obtained significant differences in intelligence test scores. It could be that high-prejudice children did not reason as well because the were less bright. There may well be differences in the cognitive styles of high- and low-prejudice children, but whether these can be attributed primarily to child-rearing practices or to other factors, such as intelligence or socioeconomic status, has yet to be determined.

As noted above with regard to the role of cognitive factors, a second view is possible which is more in accordance with cognitive-developmental theory. Within this approach, cognitive processes are considered significant in the acquisition of attitudes in their own right and and are not conceptualized as a mere outgrowth of emotional problems. The work of the major developmental theorists (e.g., Werner, Piaget) suggests some interesting parallels between the thought processes of the young child and those of the prejudiced person as described by Allport. The person who assumes that because two people are alike in one respect (e.g., blackness), they must be alike in other attributes (e.g., intelligence) is exhibiting what Piaget has labeled "transductive reasoning." According to Piaget (1928, 1951), such generalizations from the particular to the particular are characteristic of the reasoning processes of 3- and 4-year-old children. In some respects, this type of reasoning also resembles what Werner (1948) calls syncretic thought — a type of process in which a stimulus configuration is considered as changed in its entirety when only a minor component changes. Such thinking is also frequently observed in young children.

What this developmental position suggests, then, is that there is a time in a child's life when the seemingly distorted reasoning processes associated with prejudicial attitudes are quite normal. These thought processes are characteristic of early levels of maturation; in fact, racial awareness apparently begins its development in the context of both transductive reasoning and syncretic thought (i.e., in the early preschool years). Such developmental concordance may be more than coincidence. At the very least it suggests that the processes of categorization in young children be investigated much more closely than they have been.

There is no good reason to believe that children's cognitions about people differ in kind from the maturational levels exhibited in other areas of thought. Children who have difficulty, for example, in solving problems with neutral geometric stimuli that involve classification along two dimensions (e.g., Parker & Day, 1971) should have equal difficulty simultaneously categorizing a person in terms of gender and race. If children cannot understand the relationship between subordinate and superordinate classes with regard to inanimate objects (e.g., as in Piaget's experimental bead tasks), we should not assume that they will place an individual who looks somewhat different in the same category as themselves.

In an interesting recent study, Clark, Hocevar, and Dembo (1980) reported findings relevant to how children (between 2½ and 10½ years of age) understood the origins of race. These investigators found that children's reasoning about race followed a developmental hierarchy. Six levels were obtained in the types of explanations offered with regard to skin color causality. These included the following: *Level O,* lack of comprehension; *Level 1,* reference to supernatural powers; *Level 2,* arbitrary causality; *Level 3,* inaccurate physical explanations; *Level 4,* accurate physical attribution without accompanying explanation; *Level 5,* accurate physical attribution and explanation but without reference to genetics; and *Level 6,* genetic explanation. No child in the study gave a genetically relevant response. These investigators also found, in accordance with Semaj (1980) and Katz (1976), that children's level of reasoning about skin color was related to their scores on physical conservation tasks, again pointing to the importance of the cognitive context of attitude development. Some subtleties concerning the expression of children's preferences for white were also found in the Clark study as a function of race of examiner. This result substantiated earlier findings by the present author and her colleagues (Katz, Sohn, & Zalk, 1975; Katz & Zalk, 1974, 1978), pointing to the complexities involved in the measurement of racial attitudes, even with young children.

A somewhat different cognitive orientation has been proposed by Tajfel and his colleagues (Tajfel, 1969, 1973, 1979; Tajfel & Billig, 1974). In concentrating on the role played by cognitive variables in the determination of intergroup behavior, this investigator has looked at the consequences of group categorization. Tajfel argues that classifications of people into nationalities or racial groups are discontinuous and that this discontinuity gives rise to a tendency to *exaggerate* the differences *between* the classes on and given continuous dimension and to *minimize* the differences *within* each of the classes. Tajfel and Wilkes (1963) conducted a study using straight lines of varying length to demonstrate this phenomenon. Three groups of subjects were shown eight lines varying in length and were asked to estimate the length of each. When one group was asked to label the four shorter lines "A" and the four longer ones "B," they in fact exaggerated the difference in length between the "boundary" items more than did a group with either no labels or one which associated the letter with the lines in alternation sequence. Similar trends have been found for social stimuli as well (Tajfel, 1959; Tajfel, Skeikh, & Gardner, 1964). In other studies, the relationship of this phenomenon to social groups has been demostrated. When school children are divided into labeled groups, even on the basis of arbitrary and meaningless criteria, they tend to value others in their group more positively than those in the out-group (Billig & Tajfel, 1973; Tajfel & Billig, 1974).

Tajfel has clearly tapped an important underlying dimension of social categorization relevant to both gender and racial categorization. Despite the fact that much of his work has been conducted with older children and adults, his results, are very similar to those obtained in studies with younger children conducted by the present author and colleagues. (The latter studies interpret the phenomenon as perceptual rather than cognitive and thus will be discussed in the next section).

Perceptual Components of Racial Attitudes

It is commonly agreed among most investigators that perceptual differentiation of groups may be the most basic prerequisite to the development of hostile intergroup attitudes. An interesting recent study conducted with congenitally blind children in South Africa (Bhana, 1977), however, suggests that in some instances visibility may not even be a necessary precondition for prejudice to occur. In South Africa the political salience of race questions may actually overcome the need for vision, since White children who were blind were found to hold negative attitudes towards Blacks. In most cases, however, visibility is usually a necessary condition. In accordance with the previously mentioned views of Piaget, Allport suggests that visible differences between people imply real differences to the child; he goes on to suggest that this may be the perceptual foundation upon which subsequent attitudes are based.

One perceptual theory previously alluded to is Allport's (1954) postulation regarding fear of the unfamiliar. Allport's reasoning suggests that if interracial contact occurs at an early age, it should decrease strangeness and thus hinder the development of consequent negative attitudes. A study by Cantor (1972)—based upon the Zajonc, et al., 1971, "mere exposure" hypothesis—suggests that familiarity with other-race faces may be positively related to children's attitudes. There are, however, a number of problems with the "strangeness" explanation, including the rather rapid habituation that children display towards strangers.

It is possible that a systematic exploration of other factors involved in the perceptual categorization of ethnic groups may well increase our understanding of the attitude acquisition process. As was the case with cognitive parameters, perceptual factors may be viewed either as an outcome or an antecedent of the socialization process. That perceptual outcomes differ as a function of attitudes has been demostrated in adults. Highly prejudiced individuals perceive persons of another race differently than do less prejudiced individuals (e.g., Engel, 1958; Iverson & Schwab, 1967; Pettigrew, Allport, & Barnett, 1958; Reynolds & Toch, 1965), suggesting that particular perceptual styles may accompany the presence of prejudiced attitudes. This also has ramifications for eyewitness testimony (Loftus, 1979). Findings with adults, however, tell us nothing about a number of important issues that concern children, including the causal sequence of attitudinal and perceptual processes, the age at which the two processes intertwine, and the developmental course of their interaction.

The present author and her colleagues have conducted a series of interrelated studies with urban children aimed at gathering such information within a developmental context. The theoretical rationale underlying these studies assumes that the perceptual and linguistic parameters involved in group differentiation are of considerable importance in attitude acquisition. This view holds that perceptual differentiation is a function of (1) the observed stimulus charactersitics associated with individuals (i.e., their distinguishing cues), and (2) the particular labels and evaluative statements applied by peers and adults to groups. With regard to this latter factor, theories of learning (e.g., Dollard & Miller, 1950) suggest that labels and perceptions influence each other in significant ways. The association of distinctive labels to different ethnic groups would be expected to facilitate discrimination between groups (such association has been said to entail awareness of "acquired distinctiveness of cues"). In contrast, the continued use of the same name for all members within a group would be expected to reduce the capacity for differentiating among individual members. (This phenomenon is called "acquired equivalence of cues.") Each of these processes has implications for subsequent attitude development because it may either facilitate or impede the learning of other responses to groups (such as stereotyping.)

The research to be described addressed itself to a number of issues including (1) the relationship of differentiation ability to maturational level, (2) the effects of labels on person-perception, (3) the types of visual cues children use in differentiating people at various developmental levels, and (4) the relationship between attitudes and person-perception.

The first study of this sort was conducted with 192 nursery school and kindergarten children (Katz, 1973) and assessed the hypothesis that differences between members of another group are more difficult to discriminate than differences within one's own group. Black and White subjects at two preschool age levels were given a two-choice discrimination learning task that utilized drawings of faces varying in shade. Children randomly assigned to one of three groups in which they viewed either black, white, or green faces, were asked to pretend that they were space explorers and to select the "moon person" they were to bring back to earth. Choice of either the lighter or darker member of each pair was reinforced by a marble. The prediction was made that subjects would more readily learn to discriminate pairs of faces of their own race than those of another. The green-face condition was included as a control for the possible effects of unfamiliarity with other races. If the presumed difficulty of learning to discriminate other-race stimuli was due simply to unfamiliarity, green faces and other-race faces should be equally difficult to discriminate. If, on the other hand, the predicted lack of discrimination was attributable to the continued use of the same label, then other-race and green faces should elicit differential learning patterns. The latter in fact, was what was found. Children at both age levels took more trials to learn a discrimination task based on shade cues with faces of another race than with their own. More trials were not needed when green faces were used, however, suggesting that the labeling process was the important factor. Black children generally showed superior performance on all learning tasks, and younger children of both races learned more quickly when tested by an examiner of another race. These two findings suggest that color cues have differential salience, based upon the age and racial group of the children. It would appear that by the age of three, children already reveal sophisticated differential perceptual patterns associated with racial cues.

As a follow-up to this study, the same children were subsequently administered a doll preference task (Katz & Zalk, 1974). In contrast to the type of stimuli typically used in doll choice tasks, which gives subjects a choice between blonde, blue-eyed White dolls and dark-haired, brown-eyed Black dolls, the present study utilized four dolls that differed only in skin color and gender cues. Male and female dolls with brown hair and brown eyes were used. As in the Clark and Clark (1947) procedure, children were asked to tell the experimenter (either a Black or White female) which they thought was the good doll, the naughty doll, the one they liked best, etc. Results with regard to racial preferences were not in accord with those reported by earlier investigators (e.g., Asher & Allen, 1969; Clark & Clark, 1947; Morland, 1966;). The strong preferences for White dolls previously obtained were not found in this study. Preferences were based more on gender cues than on racial ones, suggesting that racial cues may not be as salient for young children as are other types of person characteristics.

In another study (Katz, Sohn, & Zalk, 1975) the developmental relationship between attitudes and perceptual factors was assessed in second-, fourth-, and sixth-grade youngsters from two racially integrated New York City public schools. Subjects were classified into high- or low-prejudice conditions on the basis of scores obtained on a multiple-choice projective instrument consisting of slides depicting ambiguous interracial situations. Subjects were asked to select, for example, which of several children was instigating an aggressive act, was winning a prize or trophy, or was being scolded by a teacher. In the perceptual task, children were asked to judge the similarity of pairs of faces that varied systematically along a number of dimensions, including skin color, shade of color, type of facial expression, type of hair, and shape of eyebrows. A factorial design was employed that varied grade level, race of child (Black or White), race of examiner (Black or White), prejudice level, and type of slide.

The clearest finding to emerge was that the high-prejudice children viewed racial cues (i.e., color and shade) as more distinctive than did low-predjudice children. This occurred with all age and racial groups. In contrast, however, other types of cues (e.g., presence of eyeglasses or facial expression) elicited more judgments that faces were "similar" from high-prejudice children viewing other-race faces. These findings are in accordance with the theoretical expectations originally advanced, but the trends were more pronounced for White than for Black children.

In the 1974 study, predictions about perceptions were made on the basis of labeling experiences that occurred many years before we saw the children. In the last study to be described in this section (Katz & Seavey, 1973), the theoretical rationale concerning language and person perception was tested directly by minipulating the labeling experiences children received. Eighty second- and sixth-grade children were randomly assigned to one of four label conditions in conjunction with two purple and two green faces, one of each color were smiling or frowning. One group was taught to associate a common name with each color pair (i.e., the two green faces had the same name and the two purple faces another). A second group was taught to associate common labels on the basis of facial expression (i.e., the two smiling faces had the same name and the two frowning ones another). A third group learned to associate a distinctive label with each of the four faces. Finally, the control group viewed the stimuli for the same number of trials but without labels. Following the labeling training, the children were asked to judge the similarity of all possible pairs of the four faces. For all the studies described in this section, the race of both the child and the examiner was varied.

As in the previously cited studies, results with regard to the White children were in accord with predictions. A significant interaction was found among race of subject, label condition, and type of stimulus-pair observed. For White children, labels that grouped stimuli on the basis of color cues augmented perceptual differentiation of color cues, whereas labels associated with facial expression enhanced the distinctiveness of expression differences. The association of four different names for each of the four faces affected the perception of color and expression cues equally. Thus, the particular types of labels used modified the subsequent perception of facial cues for White children. In contrast, however, color cues were perceived as salient by Black children even in the absence of labels, and labeling training did not significantly alter their subsequent perception.

Thus, in almost all of the studies conducted in this research program, predictions were confirmed for White children but not for Black children. The question may be raised, therefore, why this disparity exists. There are several possible explanations. First, White society does not permit Blacks to "forget" color, even if they wished to. In all studies, color cues, even "nonmeaningful" ones such as purple and green, appeared to have greater salience for Black children. Despite this increased attention to color, however, Black grade school students judged shade variations within their own race as not being an important basis for perceptual distinctiveness. This contrasts with earlier work (e.g., Freeman, Armor, Ross, & Pettigrew, 1966) suggesting that a strong positive value within the Black community was placed, upon being light-skinned. Thus, this trend toward the de-emphasis of color shade may well reflect recent strides made by Blacks in their struggle for equality and dignity. Recent Black political ideology stresses the importance of Blackness as a force for unity and pride, thus the ignoring of subtle color gradations (that may have been important to their parents in earlier years) by contemporary Black children suggests that minority group self-perceptions may indeed be changing. Although perceptual factors may well play an important role in the development of Black children's attitudes towards themselves and other groups, alternative theoretical positions may be required to delineate their development.

Since the most severe societal problems have been associated with White racism, it is interesting to note that the perceptual concomitants of White children's racial attitudes, although varied and complex, do tend to follow a somewhat predictable course which can be summarized as follows. Preschool children make distinctions on the basis of racial cues, although these may not be quite as salient as earlier work has implied when appropriate controls are included. An acquired equivalence of cues phenomenon that permits children to more readily distinguish faces of their own race from those of another race appears to be operative by 4 years of age. This relative discriminative difficulty may well reflect the fact that once individuals come to be categorized into a group, it is their defining characteristic (in this case color) that becomes the most salient feature, whereas other cues are attended to less. Perception of facial cues can be very much influenced by the labeling process, as is indicated by the way white children respond to faces categorized by either color or expression. Moreover, attitudes of white grade school children are related to their perceptions of people. Black and white faces alike in all respects but color were viewed as exceedingly different from one another by high-prejudice youngsters. Other individual differences between black faces were seen by high-prejudice children as less salient for differentiating two black faces than two white faces. Thus, contrary to the notion that children are "color-blind," these results suggest that for white children with negative racial attitudes, color, in fact, blinds.

It would appear then that perceptual mechanisms may well play an important role in the development and maintenance of prejudice. Experimental manipulations of these patterns can apparently reduce negative attitudes both on a short-term (Katz, 1973) and long-term (Katz & Zalk, 1978) basis. Thus, such patterns are not irrevocable in children. As long as adult society magnifies the differences between racial groups and ignores the individual differences between members of minority groups, however, it is laying a firm perceptual basis for the maintenance of prejudice.

Socialization and Salience of Racial Attitudes

Two additional issues merit consideration regarding the development of racial attitudes. The first has to do with who transmits information about race to the child. The second has to do with the relative salience of racial as opposed to other person cues. With regard to the first issue, commonsense notions strongly suggest that parents are the primary socializers, but research has not substantiated this supposition (Bird, Monachesi, & Burdick, 1952; Byrne, 1965; Frenkel-Brunswik & Havel, 1953; Pushkin, 1967; Radke-Yarrow, Trager, & Miller, 1952). As is the case with gender stereotypes, an increasing body of work is pointing to the importance of television (Barry & Sheikh, 1977; Greenberg, 1972; Zuckerman, Singer, & Singer, 1980) and books (Wirtengerg, 1978; Zimet, 1976) as sources of information. Even though things have changed over the past decade, a recent report of the U.S. Commission on Civil Rights (1979) suggests that race and sex stereo-typing on television continues. The President's Commission on Mental Health (1978) suggests that inadequate representation of minority groups assists in the stereotyping process. Finally, the role of peers is probably significant as well, and recent work with biracial learning teams (Devries, Edwards, & Slavin, 1978; Slavin & Madden, 1979) suggests the potency of peer behavior.

In reviewing some of the earlier work on preschool racial awareness, it sometimes appears that young children are quite bigoted. Recently, however, a number of investigators have begun to question whether race is really that salient, or whether our assessment techniques (i.e., forced-choice questions) may have exaggerated the importance of race to children. In open-ended interviews, race does not seem to be spontaneously mentioned very often by children (Learner & Buehrig, 1975; Semaj, 1981). In the only study conducted with 2½-year-olds (Boswell, cited in Williams & Morland, 1976), children chose black and white toys with equal frequency and did not associate positive adjectives with white toys unless a forced-choice was given. Generally speaking, racial cues appear to be less important to children than gender cues (Katz & Zalk, 1974; Van Parys, 1981), cleanliness (Epstein, Krupat, & Obudho, 1976), physical attractiveness (Langlois & Stephan, 1977), or age (Van Parys, 1981).

ATTITUDE ACQUISITION: TOWARDS A THEORETICAL SYNTHESIS

This chapter has attempted to review some of the more prominent theoretical positions that have been offered to account for how children aquire negative intergroup attitudes. The literature suggests a number of important trends. To summarize, relatively young children exhibit awareness of racial cues, although the salience of earlier obtained evaluations and racial preferences may have been attributable both to the particular measurement technique employed and to other methdological problems. The most obvious determinant of prejudice would seem to be parental attitudes, although the evidence regarding the importance of direct instruction is not overpowering. Reinforcement may play a role, particularly with regard to learning the cultural and linguistic connotations of color cues, which generalize in turn to skin color. Personality variables and child-rearing techniques have received considerable theoretical and empirical attention as sources of racial prejudice, but the empirical findings are inconclusive and are fraught with methodological ambiguity. Moreover, facts such as these typically lie beyond the province of social science modification, and thus such theories generate little change research. Investigations pertinent to the cognitive and perceptual components of children's prejudice are more recent but appear more promising in terms of the consistency of positive findings and their potential applicability to attitude change.

Clearly, the child is not split up neatly into the learning, personality, cognitive, and perceptual components our organization might imply; all of these areas are interrelated. Nevertheless, focus on some of these components may well have more pay-off than others. It is the contention of the present author that some of the directions taken in earlier research may well have led us into conceptual dead ends. If most preschool children show pro-white bias, for example, it makes little sense to consider such bias the outgrowth of maladaptive personality structures. If the perceptual and cognitive roots of prejudice are present in all young children, the statistically abnormal individual may well be the one whose negative attitudes are stifled. Considerably more theoretical and empirical attention to the normal developmental context in which attitude acquisition takes place appears to be needed. It is the view of the present writer that particular emphasis be give to the perceptual, cognitive, and reinforcement parameters underlying the early development of attitudes and the interrelationships that exist among these factors.

Almost all theorists in this area have used terms such as ''complex,'' ''multifaceted,'' and ''multiply determined'' to describe the ontogenesis of racial attitudes, but they have usually not applied these concepts in their own research efforts. We will, however, not develop a comprehensive understanding of how children acquire racial attitudes until more than lip service is paid to the multiplicity of concomitants. The last section of this chapter will attempt to theoretically integrate some of the diverse findings summarized above within a developmental context.

Parallels Between the Acquisition of Racial and Other Attitudes

It seems parsimonious to begin this discussion with the assumption that children's percepts and concepts about people follow the same rules as their perceptions and cognitions about other kinds of stimuli. The rules governing the effects of reinforcement should not differ whether the content of the learning concerns proper table manners or who might be welcomed as a friend. Interestingly, however, psychologists have preferred to study the processes of concept formation, perception, and learning in children by observing their reactions to relatively neutral stimuli. Those interested in racial attitudes, on the other hand, have often investigate attitudes as if they existed apart from other ongoing processes in the child. Attitudes about others neither exist nor develop in a vacuum.

The most obvious parallel to racial attitude acquisition in young children is the constellation of responses involved in sex-role learning. There are both important similarities as well as differences between the two that will now be considered. One similarity is the age at which such learning is exhibited. There is evidence that, by the age of 3, children have the rudiments of both race and gender awareness. This suggests that in both cases important events must have occurred prior to 3 years of age. Because of the relative absence of data on children younger than 3 with regard to racial awareness development, the following account is necessarily speculative, although it will draw upon evidence pertinent to acquisition of neutral concepts where relevant.

Evidence of person variability is available to the child as soon as he or she can use his or her senses. While it would not be expected that very young children would cognitively organize such variability, differential response by infants and toddlers to gender cues has been demonstrated (e.g., Jacklin & Maccoby, 1978; Lewis, 1972; Lewis & Brooks, 1975;). The process by which this occurs is not entirely clear. A number of gender cues, however, are probably used at varying points in the first two years. Voice pitch is undoubtedly a significant one. It has been found, for example, that young infants condition more quickly to high-pitched than to low-pitched voices (Blehar, 1980; Wolff, 1963). This suggests not only a perceptual skill, but perhaps also an innate adaptive mechanism that enables the infant to readily seek out those persons (typically female) who are the sources of primary reinforcement. It would be of interest to see whether infants whose primary caretaker is male (admittedly rare) may come to exhibit a preference for low-pitched voices.

Other distinctions which are probably salient relatively early in life include olfactory, tactile, and visual cues. In the olfactory area, for example, women's cosmetics are perfumed. There are also systematic differences in handling of infants by male and female adults. Although considerable within-gender variability exists in the manner that infants are picked up and held, men often exhibit more initial awkwardness and discomfort. Visual cues are apparent in a number of ways. Height differences between male and female adults may be observable to the infant at various phases of development, perhaps beginning when the child becomes locomotory. Before this time, adults bend towards infants in cribs and so systematic height differences may not be easily visible to the child. It is possible, however, that even during these early months an infant might notice different vantage points as a result of being picked up by a male or female (i.e., they are typically held higher by a male). Systematic differences in dress and/ or hair style may also be apparent. At a proximal level, skin contact with a male or female is also a differential experience. (One does not usually feel stubble on Mommy's face.) Thus gender cues are potentially discriminative in all sense modalities, although this salience may not be pronounced during the first year. Perhaps the most significant gender cue, however, has to do with differential availability: Mommy (or a female substitute) is there; Daddy is usually not.

Parents are delighted to discover that their child's first words usually include "Mommy" and/or "Daddy". The child's correct use of these nouns, together with their incorrect generalization to other adults, shows that children clearly have rudimentary gender concepts by the time they can speak. While the use of the word "Daddy" to a strange male adult might be embarrassing to a parent, the fact that it is almost never used in conjunction with a strange female adult suggests that although the child's concepts are rudimentary, they are already accurate by about 18 months of age.

A point to keep in mind at this juncture is that concepts are defined by both positive and negative instances, both by logical necessity and pedagogical practice with young children. It is difficult to imagine a parent explaining the concept "dog" to a young child without some mention of a cat. Indeed, it may be for this reason that opposites are the most frequent and most rapid responses elicited by a word association task. Juxtaposition of what is and what is not a member of a particular category is included in the definition process itself. When the concept in question refers to groups of persons, the juxtaposition of positive and negative instances may embody the seeds of future conflict at a later stage of development. This is particularly true when concepts are dichotomous rather than continuous in nature, like the exclusive concepts of male-female or black-white.

There are certain concepts about people that all young children must learn during the course of development. The distinction between self and other may well be the earliest. Many global theories of child development (e.g., those of Freud and Piaget) have stressed the importance of this distinction. Children's concepts about themselves, however, become more finely differentiated as they develop and learn about others. Concepts about others may be based upon a variety of cues, but early ones will invariably include those based upon gender, age, kinship, and race. Of these, gender may well be the earliest. As noted above, information about gender is continually given to the child from birth, both directly and indirectly. Another important person concept is age, particularly the distinction between children and adults. Although initially based upon size perceptions, this concept may later become elaborated on the basis of differential behavior prerogatives. Concepts about racial groups probably enter at a somewhat later stage, and their introduction may well be more variable, particularly for nonminority youngsters. A major similarity between racial and gender awareness development is that many of the basic perceptual and cognitive processes are completed, for both, by the time the child is ready to enter school. Children realize that both of these dimensions are significant within our society for person classification. Moreover, they can readily utilize these cues to accurately classify themselves, other children, and adults. Categorization on the basis of religion and nationality are also variable and would be expected to occur at an even later age, because they are not easily associated with highly visible types of cues.

In addition to the similarities, there are important distinctions between how concepts about racial cues and other-person characteristics are learned. One important difference has to do with the differential availability of models. Unless the child's family lives in an integrated neighborhood, a child may not have any exposure to a racially different person except on television, until he or she enters school. Thus, race concepts will inevitably enter the child's repertoire, but the timing of this will probably depend more upon chance experiential factors than upon direct and continual parental instruction.

Not only are racial concepts different with regard to timing and variability, they differ in two additional respects as well. The first has to do with the person who provides the negative instances of the concept and his or her relationship to the child. As the child learns that he is male or she is female, there is usually an opposite-sex adult present who provides a continual and complex example of the "other." As with the child-adult concept, a parent or caretaker is present to show how big people look and behave. Because of this continual interaction, it becomes difficult for the child to oversimplify the "other" too much. This is not the case with racial concepts, however. In this latter instance, unless the child grows up in an interracial family, information about race generally comes exclusively from a person who is a member of the same group, and models of the "other" may not be readily enough available to dispel misconceptions. This suggests that the age for integration may have to be much earlier than the school years to have any substantial impact.

A second important difference between the acquisition of race concepts and other person concepts is that evaluative components may be more intrinsically involved in early learning with regard to race. Although most theorists suggest that racial awareness precedes evaluation by several years, evidence pertinent to preschool children does not support this. Few children who are aware of racial cues exhibit such awareness with neutrality. It may take children quite a few years after they know they are children to ascertain that grown-up status is more valuable. Similarly, it may take a male child quite a while after he correctly labels himself a boy to have negative evaluations of girls. The fact that so few White children express the desire to be anything but white is indicative that differential status evaluations must get communicated to children quite early in life.

Attitude Acquisition: A Developmental Sequence

Based upon the investigations and theoretical considerations reviewed in this chapter, the acquisition of racial attitudes in children appears to be a complex and multifaceted process. Goodman (1964) has suggested a three-stage theory of attitude development consisting of ethnic awareness (ages 3-4), ethnic orientation (ages 4-7), and then acquisition of attitudes (ages 7 and up). The present investigator is of the belief that this is an oversimplified view. There appear to be at least eight overlapping but separable steps in the developmental sequence of racial attitude acquisition, which span approximately ten years of the child's life. These include the following: (1) early observation of racial cues, (2) formation of rudimentary concepts, (3) conceptual differentiation, (4) recognition of the irrevocability of cues, (5) consolidation of group concepts, (6) perceptual elaboration, (7) cognitive elaboration, and (8) attitude crystallization.

Early observation of racial cues. As noted earlier, a child's observation of cues associated with another race may be based upon chance environmental events. The specific effects of such observations, however, would be related to the developmental level of the child. Thus, in the first year of life, the presence of such cues may not be particularly salient, whereas later he or she is maturationally capable of processing such cues and demonstrating that difference or novelty is being observed. Whithout opportunity for such stimulus input, however, the start of this process will be delayed. Little is known about the specific developmental timetable involved here other than that it generally occurs prior to the age of 3.

Formation of rudimentary concepts. Once the child verbally expresses a differential response to an individual from another group, the chances are good that a label will be supplied by either surrounding adults or siblings. Evaluative components may also be communicated at this time. This may be accomplished either directly (e.g., ''And I don't want you to play with him'') or indirectly, through generalization from either fear of the strange (Allport, 1954), fear of the dark (Williams & Morland, 1976), or already learned connotations to colors such as black and white (Stabler, Johnson, Berke, & Baker; 1969; Williams, 1964). This stage seems to occur in many but not all children prior to 3 years of age, and it is generally complete by age 4.

Conceptual differentiation. Once a group label is provided, the child will encounter additional opportunities to observe positive and negative examples of the concept and will receive feedback for his or her responses. Both group boundaries and defining characteristics are probably taught by the utilization of verbal feedback. Is this person a member of Group X? Adult responses may be primarily informational (e.g., ''Yes, he is Black even though his skin is light, because he has broad lips and very curly hair'') or may contain evaluative components as well (e.g., ''Yes, he is Black, and I would rather that you not be too friendly with him"). In terms of concept acquisition, such evaluative responses may actually facilitate learning by providing redundancy of cues.

Recognition of the irrevocability of cues.   Kohlberg (1966) has noted that certain person-cues the child must learn about are subject to change over time, while others are not. Thus, children come to the realization that, in spite of present size differentials, they will become both older children and adults. There is growing recognition that one's status as a child is a temporary one. In contrast, applying this same reasoning to gender differences leads to an erroneous conclusion, since the child must learn that gender is (generally speaking) immutable. This concept is called "gender constancy," and it is usually developed by 5 or 6 years of age (Slaby & Frey, 1975). Clinical psychologists have repeatedly discussed the difficulties that young children prior to this age have in believing this. Little girls often believe that they will become boys, and little boys often believe that they will bear children. Early cognitions about racial characteristics may provide similar difficulties for the child. He or she must learn that racial cues, unlike size cues, do not change with age. This may well be a very complex concept for a young child, particularly because summer vacations and suntans provide continual evidence to the contrary. Since little evidence is available with regard to this factor, the age at which it typically occurs cannot be stated, although Semaj (1980) has obtained "racial constancy" in 7- and 8-year old Black children.

Consolidation of group concepts.   It is not until the child can correctly label and identify both positive and negative instances, and can recognize the immutable nature of group membership, that an accurate concept of a group can be said to exist. When consolidation occurs, the perceptual and the cognitive components of attitudes are functionally interrelated. Where evaluative content was introduced earlier, this too becomes part of the concept. On the basis of the evidence, the consolidation process typically begins during the latter part of the preschool period (i.e., by about 5 years of age) and may extend over a considerable period of time.

Perceptual elaboration.   Once the concepts of "us" and "them" are accurately established in terms of racial cues, subsequent perception of racial cues may be modified. Differences among groups may be accentuated, particularly for children exposed to heavy doses of evaluation, whereas intragroup differences, particularly of other-race people, become diminished. There is some evidence that this occurs in preschool children (Katz, 1973) and that it shows further development throughout the grade school age range (Katz, Johnson & Parker, 1970; Katz, Sohn, & Zalk, 1975). Additional evidence (Billig, 1974; Tajfel, 1969; Tajfel, Flament, Billigi & Bundy, 1971) with British grade school children suggests that affective processes inherently favor members of one's in-group, even when this group is defined quite arbitrarily and transiently. The mechanisms underlying this perceptual elaboration facilitate the learning of other differential responses to out-group individuals.

Cognitive elaboration. There has been a great deal of vacillation in the literature as to whether a child's early responses to racial cues can properly be called "attitudes." Some investigators have argued that they are, insofar as evaluative components are included. It is the view of the present author that the term "concept attitude" is a more appropriate designation of a young child's responses and that the term "attitude" be reserved for the more complex responses exhibited by older children and adults. The relationship between early concept attitudes and later attitudes is not well understood beyond the rather obvious point that the former may provide a foundation for the latter. The process by which concept attitudes or preferences become racial attitudes is what is meant by cognitive elaboration.

It is clear that a child's school experiences may be extremely important in the elaboration of racial attitudes. The particular experiences (or the lack of them) the child has with other-race children and adults, the attitudes expressed by his or her teachers and peers, will all be significant in determining future attitudes and feelings. Continuing research focus on the preschool years may well have obscured the importance of the early grade school years as focal points in attitude transition. Moreover, evidence suggests that attitudes continue to develop and differentiate during the middle childhood years.

Attitude crystallization. This phase is comparable to the last stage postulated by Proshansky (1966) and probably occurs during the later grade school years. A study of the development of racial stereotypes (Brigham, 1971) shows an increase in within-group agreement with age after the fourth grade. The effects of cultural conditioning are apparent at this level. It is as if the child has, in effect, come to terms with his attitudes. Consequently, the child probably will not "rethink" them again unless placed in a situation that requires it (i.e., if the child's social environment changes markedly). It is necessary to postulate such a stage because of the seeming intransigence of adult attitudes. Though diversity may be beautiful, the child's mind does not remain open indefinitely.

REFERENCES

Adorno, T. W., Frenkel-Brunswik, E., Levinson, D. J., & Sanford, R. N. *The authoritarian personality.* New York: Harper, 1950.

Allport, G. W. *The nature of prejudice.* Reading, MA: Addison-Wesley, 1954.

Asher, S. R., & Allen, V. L. Racial preference and social comparison processes. *Journal of Social Issues,* 1969, *25,* 157–165.

Ashmore, R. D., & Del Boca, F. K. Psychological approaches to understanding intergroup conflicts. In P. A. Katz (Ed.), *Towards the elimination of racism.* New York: Pergamon Press, 1976.

Balch, P., & Paulsen, K. *Strategies for the modification and prevention of racial prejudice in children: A rereview.* Paper presented at the 59th annual meeting of the Western Psychological Association, San Diego, April 1979.

Banks, W. C., McQuater, G. V., & Ross, J. A. On the importance of White preference and the comparative difference of Blacks and others: Reply to Williams and Morland. *Psychological Bulletin*, 1979, *86*, 33-36.

Barry, T. E., & Sheikh, A. A. Race as a dimension in children's T. V. advertising: The need for more research. *Journal of Advertising*, 1977, *6*(3), 5-10.

Bettelheim, B., & Janowitz, M. Reactions to fascist propaganda: A pilot study. *Public Opinion Quarterly*, 1950, *14*, 53-60.

Bhana, K. The relationship between perception and racial attitudes. *Behavioral Science*, 1977, *2*(4), 253-258.

Billig, M., & Tajfel, H. Social categorization and similarity in intergroup behaviour. *European Journal of Social Psychology*, 1973, *3*, 27-51.

Bird, C., Monachesi, E. D., & Burdick, H. Infiltration and the attitudes of white and Negro parents and children. *Journal of Abnormal Social Psychology*, 1952, *47*, 688-699.

Blackwell, J., Silvern, S. B., & Yawkey, T. D. *Effects of early childhood multi-cultural experiences on Black preschool children's attitudes toward themselves and Whites.* Paper presented at the annual meeting of the American Educational Research Association, San Francisco, April 1976.

Blehar, M. Development of mental health in infancy. *NIMH Science Monograph*, 1980 (No. 3).

Boswell, D. A., & Williams, J. E. Correlates of race and color bias among preschool children. *Psychological Reports*, 1975, *36*, 147-154.

Brigham, J. C. *Views of white and black school children concerning racial personality differences.* Paper presented to the Midwestern Psychological Association, 1971.

Brigham, J. C., & Weissbach, T. A. The development of racial attitudes. In J. C. Brigham & T. A. Weissbach (Eds.), *Racial attitudes in America: Analysis and findings in social psychology.* New York: Harper & Row, 1972, 35-39.

Butler, R. O. Black children's racial preference: A selected review of the literature. *Journal of Afro-American Issues*, 1976, *4* (1), 168-171.

Butler, R. O., Cunningham, J. L., Keck, S., & Nordquist, V. M. *The effects of race on the model preference of preschool children.* Unpublished manuscript, University of Tennessee, 1970.

Byrne, D. Parental antecedents of authoritarianism. *Journal of Personality and Social Psychology*, 1965, *1*, 369-373.

Cantor, G. H. N. Effects of familiarization on children's ratings of pictures of whites and blacks. *Child Development*, 1972, *43*, 1219-1229.

Chamberlin-Robinson, C. *Strategy to modify racial attitudes in black and white preschoolers.* Paper presented at the biennial meeting of the Society for Research in Child Development, New Orleans, March 1977.

Christie, R. Authoritarianism re-examined. In R. Christie & M. Johoda (Eds.), *Studies in the scope and method of "The authoritarian personality."* Glencoe, IL: Free Press, 1954.

Clark, A., Hocevar, D., & Dembo, M. H. The role of cognitive development in children's explanations and preferences for skin color. *Developmental Psychology*, 1980, *16*,(4), 332-339.

Clark, K. B., & Clark, M. P. Racial identification and preference in Negro children. In T. M. Newcomb & E. L. Hartley (Eds.), *Readings in social psychology.* New York: Holt, 1947.

Coates, B., Arnstein, E., & Jordan, J. *Racial preferences in the behavior of black and white children.* Paper presented at the society for Research in Child Development, Philadelphia, March 1973.

Datcher, E., Savage, J. E., & Checkosky, S. F. *Investigation of school type, grade, sex and race of examiner on the racial preference and awareness of black and white children.* Paper presented at the Society for Research in Child Development, Philadelphia, March 1973.

DeVries, D. L., Edwards, K. J., & Slavin, R. E. Biracial learning teams and race relations in the classroom: Four field experiments using Teams-Games-Tournament. *Journal of Educational Psychology*, 1978, *70*, 356–362.

Doke, L. A., & Risley, T. R. Some discriminative properties of race and sex for children from an all-Negro neighborhood. *Child Development*, 1972, *43*, 677–681.

Dollard, J., & Miller, N. *Personality and psychotherapy*. New York: McGraw-Hill, 1950.

Engel, E. Binocular fusion of dissimilar figures. *Journal of Psychology*, 1958, *46*, 53–57.

Epstein, R., & Komorita, S. S. Parental discipline, stimulus characteristics of outgroups and social distance in children. *Journal of Personality and Social Psychology*, 1965, *2*, 416–420.

Epstein, V. M., Krupat, E., & Obudho, C. Clean is beautiful: Identification and preference as a function of race and cleanliness. *Journal of Social Issues*, 1976, *32*(2), 109–118.

Fagan, J. F., III. Infant color perception. *Science*, 1974, *183*, 973–975.

Fox D. J., & Jordan, V. B. Racial preference and identification of black, American Chinese, and white children. *Genetic Psychology Monographs*, 1973, *88*, 229–286.

Freeman, H. F., Armor, D., Ross, M. J., & Pettigrew, T. F. Color gradation and attitudes among middle-income Negroes. *American Sociological Review*, 1966, *31*, 365–374.

Frenkel-Brunswik, E. A study of prejudice in children. *Human Relations*, 1948, *1*, 295–306.

Frenkel-Brunswik, E., & Havel, J. Prejudice in the interviews of children: Attitudes toward minority groups. *Journal of Genetic Psychology, 1953, 82*, 91–136.

Gaines, R. *Variables in color perception of young children*. Paper presented at the society for Research in Child Development, 1971.

Goldberg, M. E., & Gorn, G. J. Television's impact on preferences for non-white playmates: Canadian "Sesame Street" inserts. *Journal of Broadcasting*, 1979, *23*(1), 27–32.

Goldstein, C. G., Koopman, E. J., & Goldstein, H. H. Racial attitudes in young children as a function of interracial contact in the public schools. *American Journal of Orthopsychiatry*, 1979, *49*(1), 89–99.

Goodman, M. *Race awareness in young children*. Cambridge, MA: Addison-Wesley, 1952 (2nd ed., (New York: Crowell-Collier, 1964).

Gough, H. G., Harris, D. B., Martin, D. B., & Edwards, M. Children's ethnic attitudes I: Relationship to certain personality factors. *Child Development*, 1950, *21*, 83–91.

Greenberg, B. S. Children's reactions to T. V. Blacks. *Journalism Quarterly*, 1972, *49*(1), 5–14.

Greenwald, H. J., & Oppenheim, D. B. Reported magnitude of self-misidentification among Negro children—Artifact? *Journal of Personality and Social Psychology*, 1968, *8*, 49–52.

Hardin, M. *Examination of examiner effects on performance of the Preschool Racial Attitude Measure Test II (PRAM II): A replication*. Unpublished master's thesis, University of Arizona, 1977.

Harris, D., Gough, H., & Martin, W. E. Children's ethnic attitudes. II: Relationships to parental beliefs concerning child training. *Child Development,1950, 21*, 169–181.

Hart, I. Maternal child-rearing practices and authoritarian ideology. *Journal of Abnormal Social Psychology*, 1957, *55*, 232–237.

Hays, D. G., Margolis, E., Naroll, R., & Perkins, D. R. Color term salience. *American Anthropologist*, 1972, *74*, 1107–1121.

Hraba, J., & Grant, G. Black is beautiful: A reexamination of racial preference and identification. *Journal of Personality and Social Psychology*, 1970, *16*, 398–402.

Hyman, H., & Sheatsley, P. B. "The authoritarian personality"—A methodological critique. In R. Christie & M. Johoda (Eds.), *Studies in the scope and method of "The authoritarian personality."* Glencoe, IL: Free Press, 1954.

Iverson, M. A., & Schwab, H. G. Ethnocentric dogmatism and binocular fusion of sexually and racially discrepant stimuli. *Journal of Personality and Social Psychology*, 1967, *7*, 73–81.

Jacklin, C. N., & Maccoby, E. E. Social behavior at 33 months in same-sex and mixed-sex dyads. *Child Development*, 1978, *49* (3), 557–569.

Katz, I., Glass, D. C., & Cohen, S. Ambivalence, guilt, and the scapegoating of minority group victims. *Journal of Experimental Social Psychology*, 1973, *9*, 423–436.

Katz, I., Henchy T., & Allen, H. Effects of race of tester, approval-disapproval, and need on Negro children's learning. *Journal of Personality and Social Psychology*, 1968, *8*, 38–42.

Katz, P. A. The acquisition of racial attitudes in children. In P. A. Katz (Ed.), *Towards the elimination of racism.* New York: Pergamon Press, 1976.

Katz, P. A. Perception of racial cues in preschool children: A new look. *Developmental Psychology,* 1973, *8*, 295–299.

Katz, P. A., Johnson, J., & Parker, D. *Racial attitudes and perception in black and white urban school children.* Paper presented at the American Psychological Association, September 1970.

Katz, P. A., & Seavey, C. Labels and children's perception of faces. *Child Development,* 1973, *44*, 770–775.

Katz, P. A., Sohn, M., & Zalk, S. R. Perceptual concomitants of racial attitudes in urban grade school children. *Developmental Psychology*, 1975, *11*, 135–144

Katz, P. A., & Zalk, S. R. Doll preferences: An index of racial attitudes? *Journal of Educational Psychology,* 1974, *66*, 663–668.

Katz, P. A., & Zalk, S. R. Modification of children's racial attitudes. *Developmental Psychology,* 1978, *14*(5), 447–461.

Kircher, M., & Furby, C. Racial preferences in young children. *Child Development*, 1971, *42*, 2076–2078.

Kohlberg, L. A cognitive-developmental analysis of children's sex-role concepts and attitudes. In E. E. Maccoby (Ed.), *The development of sex differences.* Stanford, CA: Stanford University Press, 1966.

Kutner, B. Patterns of mental functioning associated with prejudice in children. *Psychological Monographs,* 1958, *72* (Whole No. 7).

Kutner, B., & Gordon, N. Cognitive functioning and prejudice: A Nine-year follow-up study. *Sociometry,* 1964, *27*, 66–74.

Lacoste, R. J. *Young children's ability to match facial features typical of race.* San Antonio, T: University of Texas at San Antonio, 1978 (ED 156 312, 19pp.)*

Langlois, J. H., & Stephan, C. The effects of physical attractiveness and ethnicity on children's behavioral attributions and peer preferences. *Child Development,* 1977, *48*, 1694–1698.

Lerner, R. M., & Buehrig, C. J. The development of racial attitudes in young black and white children. *Journal of Genetic Psychology,* 1975, *127*, 45–54.

Lewis, M. Parents and children: Sex-role development. *School Review,*1972, *80*, 229–240.

Lewis, M., & Brooks, G. Infant's social perception: A constructivist's view. In L. B. Cohen & P. Salapatek (Eds.), *Infant perception: From sensation to cognition,* (Vol. 2). New York: Academic Press, 1975.

Liebert, R. M., Sobol, M. P., & Copemann, C. D. Effects of vicarious consequences and race of model upon imitative performance by black children. *Developmental Psychology,* 1972, *6*, 453–456.

Loftus, E. F. *Eyewitness testimony.* Cambridge MA: Harvard University Press, 1979.

Lyle, W. H., Jr., & Levitti, E. E. Punitiveness, authoritarianism, and parental discipline of grade school children. *Journal of Abnormal Social Psychology,* 1955, *51*, 42–46.

McAdoo, H. P. *The development of self-concept and race attitudes in black children: A longitudinal study.* 1977. (ED 148 944 54pp.) Document not available from EDRS.

McAdoo, J. L. *An exploratory study of racial attitude change in Black preschool children using differential treatments.*Unpublished Doctoral dissertation, University of Michigan, 1970.

---

* Documents with ED numbers are available through the Educational Resources Information Center (ERIC) in microfiche and paper copy, unless otherwise noted. (For information on obtaining ERIC documents, in libraries or by mail, see page 237.) Some of these documents are also available from their original source.

Morland, J. K. A comparison of race awareness in Northern and Southern children. *American Journal of Orthopsychiatry,* 1966, *36,* 22–31.

Morland, J. K. Racial acceptance and preference of nursery school children in a southern city. In A. R. Brown (Ed.), *Prejudice in children.* Springfield: Charles C. Thomas, 1972.

Mosher, D. L., & Scodel, A. A study of the relationship between ethnocentrism in children and the ethnocentrism and authoritarian rearing practices of their mothers. *Child Development,* 1960, *31,* 369–376.

Palmer, E. L. *The public kindergarten concept as a factor in racial attitudes.* Davidson College, 1977. (ED 129 936, 9pp.).

Parker, R. K., & Day, M. C. The use of perceptual, functional and abstract attributes in multiple classification. *Developmental Psychology,* 1971, *5,* 312–319.

Pettigrew, T. F., Allport, G. W., & Barnett, E. O. Binocular resolution and perception of race in South Africa. *British Journal of Psychology,* 1958, *40,* 265–278.

Piaget, J. *Judgment and reasoning in the child.* New York: Harcourt & Brace, 1928.

Piaget, J. *The child's conception of the world.* New York: Humanities Press, 1951.

Porter, J. *Black child, white child: The development of racial attitudes.* Cambridge, MA: Harvard University Press, 1971.

President's Commission on Mental Health. *President's Commission on Mental Health: Report to the President.* (Vol. 1). Washington, DC, 1978. (ED 170 627, 101 pp.)

Proshansky, H. The development of intergroup attitudes. In I. W. Hoffman & M. L. Hoffman (Eds.), *Review of child development research* (Vol. 2). New York: Russell Sage Foundation, 1966.

Pushkin, I. *A study of ethnic choice in the play of young children in three London districts.* Unpublished doctoral thesis, University of London, 1967.

Radke-Yarrow, M., Trager, H., & Miller, J. The role of parents in the development of children's ethnic attitudes. *Child Development,* 1952, *23,* 13–53.

Renninger, C. A., & Williams, J. E. Black-white color connotations and race awareness in preschool children. *Perceptual and Motor Skills,* 1966, *22,* 771–785.

Reynolds, D., & Toch, H. Perceptual correlates of prejudice: A stereoscopic-constancy experiment. *Journal of Social Psychology,* 1965, *66* 127–133.

Rose, S., Katz, P. A., Birke, M. S., & Rossman, E. Visual following in newborns: The role of figure-ground contrast and configurational detail. *Perceptual and Motor Skills,* 1977, *45,* 515–522.

Sattler, J M. Racial experimenter effects. In K. S. Miller & R. M. Dreger (Eds.), *Comparative studies of blacks and whites in the United States.* New York: Seminar Press, 1973.

Semaj, L. The development of racial evaluation and preference: A cognitive approach. *The Journal of Black Psychology,* 1980, *6* (2), 59–79.

Semaj, L. T. The development of racial-classification abilities. *Journal of Negro Education,* 1981, *50* (1), 41–47.

Shanahan, J. K. *The effects of modifying black-white concept attitudes of black and white first grade subjects upon two measures of racial attitudes.* Unpublished doctoral dissertation, University of Washington, 1972.

Slaby, R. G., & Frey, K. S. Development of gender constancy and selective attention to same-sex models. *Child Development,* 1975, *46,* 849–856.

Slavin, R. E., & Madden, N. A. School practices that improve race relations. *American Educational Research Journal,* 1979, *16* (2), 169–180.

Sorce J. F. The role of physiognomy in the development of racial awareness. *Journal of Genetic Psychology,* 1979, *134,* 33–41.

Spencer, M. B., & Horowitz, F. D. Effects of systematic social and token reinforcement on the modification of racial and color concept attitudes in black and white preschool children. *Developmental Psychology,* 1973, *9,* 246–254.

Stabler, J. R., Johnson, E. E., Berke, M. A., & Baker, R. B. The relationship between race and perception of racially related stimuli in preschool children. *Child Development*, 1969, *40*, 1233–1239.

Stevenson, H. W., & Stevenson, N. G., Social interaction in an interracial nursery school. *Genetic Psychology Monographs*, 1960, *61*, 37–75.

Stevenson, H. W., & Steward, E., C., A developmental study of race awareness in young children. *Child Development*, 1958, *29*, 399–410.

Tabachnick, B. R. Some correlates of prejudice toward Negroes in elementary age children. *Journal of Genetic Psychology*, 1962, *100*, 193–203.

Tajfel, H. Quantitative judgment in social perception. *British Journal of Psychology*, 1959, *50*, 16–29.

Tajfel, H. Cognitive aspects of prejudice: *Journal of Social Issues*, 1969, *25*, 79–97.

Tajfel, H. The roots of prejudice: Cognitive aspects. In P. Watson (Ed.), *Psychology and race.* Chicago, IL: Aldine, 1973.

Tajfel, H. Individuals and groups in social psychology. *British Journal of Social and Clinical Psychology*, 1979, *18*, 183–190.

Tajfel, H., & Billig, M. Familiarity and categorization in intergroup behavior. *Journal of Experimental Social Psychology*, 1974, *10*, 159–170.

Tajfel, H., Flament, C., Billig, M. G., & Bundy, R. P. Social categorization and inte intergroup behavior. *European Journal of Social Psychology*, 1971, *1*, 149–177.

Tajfel, H., Sheikh, A. A., & Gardner, R. C. Content of stereotypes and the inference of similarity between members of stereotyped groups. *Acta Psychologica*, 1964, *22*, 191–201.

Tajfel, H., & Wilkes, A. L. Classification and quantitative judgment. *British Journal of Psychology*, 1963, *54*, 101–114.

Traynham, R. M. The effects of modifying color meaning concepts on racial concept attitudes in five- and eight-year old children. Unpublished Master's dissertation, University of Arkansas, 1974.

U.S. Commission on Civil Rights. *Window dressing on the set: An update.* Washington, DC: U.S. Government Printing Office, 1979.

Van Parys, M. *Preschoolers in society: Use of social roles of sex, age and race for self and others by black and white children.* Unpublished master's dissertation, University of Denver, 1981.

Weatherley, D. Maternal response to childhood aggression and subsequent anti-Semitism. *Journal of Abnormal Social Psychology*, 1963, *66*, 183–185.

Werner, H. *Comparative psychology of mental development.* Chicago, IL: Follett, 1948.

Williams, J. E. Connotations of color names among Negroes and Caucasians. *Journal of Perceptual and Motor Skills*, 1964, *18*, 721–731.

Williams, J. E. *Racial attitudes in preschool children: Modification via operant conditioning, and a revised measurement procedure.* Paper presented at the American Psychological Association, Honolulu, 1972.

Williams, J. E., Best, D. L., Boswell, D. A., Mattson, L. A., & Graves, D. J. Preschool racial attitude measure II. *Educational and Psychological Measurement*, 1975, *35*, 3–18.

Williams, J. E., Boswell, D. A., & Best, D. L Evaluative responses of preschool children to the colors white and black. *Child Development*, 1975, *46*, 501–508.

Williams, J. E., & Edwards, C. D. An exploratory study of the modification of color concepts and racial attitudes in preschool children. *Child Development*, 1969, *40*, 737–750.

Williams, J. E., & Morland, J. K. *Race, color, and the young child.* Chapel Hill, NC: University of North Carolina Press, 1976.

Williams, J. E., & Morland, J. K. Comment on Banks' "White preference in Blacks: A paradigm in search of a phenomenon." *Psychological Bulletin*, 1979, *86*, (1), 28–32.

Williams, J. E. & Roberson, J. K. A method for assessing racial attitudes in preschool children. *Educational and psychological Measurement*, 1967, *27*, 671–689.

Wirtenberg, J. *Cultural fairness in materials development. Paper presented at the skills workshop of the Women's Educational Equity Act Program, Washington, D. C., April 1978. (Abstract).*

Wolff, P. H. Observations on the early development of smiling. In B. M. Foss (Ed.), *Determinants of infant behavior, II.* New York: Wiley, 1963.

Yando, R., Zigler, E., & Gates, M. The influence of Negro and white teachers rated as effective or noneffective on the performance of Negro and white lower-class children. *Developmental Psychology,* 1971, *5* (2), 290-299.

Zajonc, R. B., Swap, W. C., Harrison, A. A., & Roberts, P. Limiting conditions of the exposure effect: Satiation and relativity. *Journal of Personality and Social Psychology,* 1971, *18,* 384-391.

Zimet, S. G. *Print and prejudice.* Kent, England: Hodder & Stoughton Educational, 1976.

Zuckerman, D. M., Singer, D. G., & Singer, J. L. Children's television viewing, racial and sex-role attitudes. *Journal of Applied Social Psychology,* 1980, *10* (4), 281-294.

Conflicting evidence.
See pages 40, 41, 42 for summaries

3

Motor Skill Development in Young Children: Current Views on Assessment and Programming*

Michael G. Wade

Southern Illinois University at Carbondale

Walter E. Davis

Kent State University

Developmental changes in a young child's motor skills are evident in the manipulatory and ambulatory activities the child exhibits. Motor skill development is an extremely important issue in the overall development of the child, for often a failure to manifest appropriate motor behavior is a signal that cognitive function may be impaired. A typical motor problem that might reflect a more general cognitive impairment is hypotonia—muscle flaccidity. (For a fuller discussion, see below). Often, general slowness in acquiring age appropriate motor skills also reflects some degree of cognitive impairment. This chapter provides a brief theoretical background to motor skill development in children, and also provides an update on the approaches to the assessment and programming of motor development.

Theoretical Background

Historically, those interested in the study of motor skill behavior have viewed motor learning and motor development as distinct entities. The former has borrowed heavily from experimental psychology for its theoretical formulations and orientations, and has concentrated on experimentally manipulating such variables as practice, feedback, age, and sex of subjects, and measuring performance change. Those theorists who have focussed on motor development have held fast to the traditional stage dependent theory of the developing child and have

---

* The support for this article came in part from NICHHD Program Project Grant #HD05951 awarded to M. G. Wade.

drawn ideas and orientations from both clinical and differential psychology. The clinical aspect is evident in the use of observational scales with children as their motor abilities develop. The differential aspects stem from the considerable research energy which has been devoted to the construction of diagnostic tests to determine the "motor age" of a young child, and to evaluate whether or not the child's motor skills are developing according to the appropriate sequence. Thus, motor development theorists have relied more heavily than motor learning theorists on correlational procedures to investigate relationships between variables such as age and sex and performance on motor skill tasks.

The traditional maturational frameworks that have been used to describe patterns of motor development in children have relied primarily on a neurologically based explanation of developing activity: that is, the appearance of motor milestones (sitting, standing, and walking) is largely determined by the maturation of the nervous system (Coghill, 1929; McGraw, 1945). These traditional views have more recently been critized by Schneirla (1966) and Connolly (1970a) for failing to give sufficient theoretical importance to the effects of motor experience on the developing organism. Results from animal studies (Bridgeman & Carmichael, 1935; Carmichael, 1934; Windle, 1940) all point to both general and localized responses occurring in the life of the organism, suggesting that progressive refinements of the developing organism's motor responses come about not only from a process of maturation but also from the effects of experience. Present day theorists in motor development (e.g., Halverson, Roberton, & Harper, 1973) who operate within stage theory recognize the role of both experience and maturation. Their major focus is on describing sequences both within and across motor skills.

With the advent of information theory (Shannon & Weaver, 1949), research on motor skill behavior developed a new language. Emphasis was placed on the individual's ability to process information. The individual was compared to a communication channel (much like a telephone switching center) with a limited capacity to process information. Research findings in the motor development literature (Connolly, 1970b; Wade, 1976) suggest that, as processors of information, children are considerably less efficient than adults. For example, when children are required to perform a motor skill (i.e., solve a motor problem), they are faced with a larger and probably very different matrix of information, and what appears simple to adults may be highly complex to children. For adults, their wider sphere of experience tends to rule out a number of hypotheses or strategies that remain conceivable to the young child faced with an identical motor problem. For example, in early game playing with a ball, children tend to "chase" the ball rather than position themselves where the ball will eventually finish. Such lack of anticipation is often a reflection of what is termed information overload for children. In informational terms, children have no redundancy (information already processed) in their systems and must therefore process more information than adults in coping with the same problem.

Although it has limitations (Connolly, 1970a; Wade, 1976), the information theory model of skilled behavior has allowed for the investigation of learning strategies which the developing child uses to develop appropriate motor skill behavior, and has provided a working model to study the process variables that contribute to the learning and development of motor activity skills.

Recently a less conventional perspective has been advanced by students of Gibson (1966). Turvey, Shaw, and Mace (1978), Fowler and Turvey (1978), Fitch and Turvey (1977) and Kugler, Kelso, and Turvey (1980) all maintain motor skill behavior can best be understood when a person is viewed within the environmental context in which he or she resides. Fundamental to this interpretation is the notion that our actions and perceptions are body-scaled.

The central idea behind body-scaled information is that objects which are perceived by the organism are defined relative to the organism's capacity for activity. Objects are distinguished not along geometrical dimensions but along activity-related dimensions. The use of the term information is owing to Gibson (1966) and does not reflect the traditional Shannon and Weaver (1949) interpretation. Conventionally, the term information reflects the idea of a limited capacity to process information as discussed above, but Gibson's use of the term defines information as the correspondence between environmental properties as they relate to the organism and the energy medium (e.g., light). Thus the metrics of activity within the environment are not related to some abstract and animal independent scale (such as feet, inches, feet per second, or pounds-weight) but are environmentally and animal functional. An object passing across the visual field is not perceived as traveling at so many feet per second, at least at the first order level; rather, questions are asked of the moving object as it relates to the organism—for example, "Can I reach it?" "Can I catch it?" "When will it hit me?" In other words, the organism acting within the environment asks "time to contact" questions of the moving object. This kind of perspective is particularly important in the wide range of motor activities which require accurate anticipatory or coincident timing behavior, such as catching and hitting balls and other moving objects.

ASSESSMENT OF MOTOR DEVELOPMENT

The importance of assessment in education is well established in both theory and practice. Assessment is conducted for such purposes as student placement, program planning and evaluation, and group comparisons. It is little wonder then, that so much time and effort has been put into the development and refinement of assessment instruments of both the motor and cognitive domains (see Ebel, 1973). Indeed, much of the assessment of early development focuses on the motor area, since (1) motor abilities are more easily and reliably observed at a very early age than are cognitive abilities; and (2) motor development is held by many to be the foundation of later cognitive development (see Piaget, 1952)

Despite the existence of a large number of instruments designed to measure motor abilities (over 300 by some counts), motor assessment is not as widespread as one might expect, and this is especially true for handicapped populations (Lewko, 1976). Also there are a number of shortcomings in both the construction and use of motor assessment instruments. In this section, four major approaches taken in motor ability assessment are reviewed, and some of the strengths and limitations associated with each approach are discussed. First is the descriptive or product oriented approach, in which a group of motor tasks is selected and each child's performance is compared with the average performance of children in his or her age group category. Scores reflect the final or end product of performance, such as the number of times the child catches a tossed ball. The second approach, termed process oriented or diagnostic, consists of evaluating tasks which are indicative of an underlying process of motor performance based on theoretical postulates. In the third approach, children are observed in activities such as running, throwing, and catching, and their performance is judged on the basis of a qualitative analysis of their movement patterns. The criterion measure in this case would be a mature or age appropriate pattern (e.g., the appropriate temporal/spatial relationships among body segments which occur during performance). In reflex testing, the fourth approach, children are evaluated on the bases of the appearance and/or inhibition of certain reflex movements according to age level.

Descriptive Approach

The descriptive or product oriented approach is traditional and based primarily on the concept that motor development follows an orderly sequence. The sequential pattern is marked by "motor milestones" (i.e., the ability to perform specific tasks such as crawling, sitting, running, jumping, and throwing). It is assumed that all children, unless severely neurologically or physically impaired, will pass through this motor sequence, although the age at which each milestone is achieved will vary. Thus, assessment scales are developed which include a number of these motor milestones and the age range in which they should appear. Children are observed to determine whether they can or cannot perform each task and are then compared with the average ability child of their age group.

The motor sequence and age ranges for these tests have been determined by the careful collection of descriptive data and the charting of progress across chronological age. The pioneer work of Shirley (1931), Bayley (1935), McGraw (1945), Gesell (1940) and others is still influential in the construction of tests of this type.

The need for quick and efficient methods to assess children at an earlier age has grown as the number of remedial education programs have grown. The

Bayley Scales (Bayley, 1969), Gesell Schedules (Gesell & Armatruda, 1949), and similar traditional instruments require considerable expertise to administer and interpret, are time consuming, and require expensive equipment. As a result, a number of tests have been constructed as screening instruments and have been primarily modifications of the Bayley and Gesell tests. Screening instruments, by definition, include a minimal number of items and are used to identify children at risk or in need of remediation. The items should well represent the assessment domain, but the test must allow for quick and easy administration so that it can be used with large numbers of children.

One of the most popular of these instruments is the Denver Developmental Screening Test (DDST—Frankenburg & Dodds, 1966). The test is administered individually and assesses gross motor, fine motor-adaptive, language, and personal-social abilities. Even though the DDST is one of the more widely used instruments, it has received considerable criticism from both researchers (e.g., Thorpe & Werner, 1974) and practitioners (see Lewko, 1976). One problem is that the DDST is often used with populations for which it not valid, and for diagnosis and program planning—purposes for which it was clearly not designed. Thus, the DDST and similiar tests lack the reliability and validity (Herkowitz, 1976; Katoff & Reuter, 1980) required to make them suitable screening instruments. The Bayley and Gesell instruments, which are technically superior, have also been criticized (e.g., Herkowitz, 1978) for failing to predict later performance. There are several factors which may contribute to the poor predictive power of these descriptive tests. One factor is that age criterion is not a valid measure of performance, since physical and neurological growth rates, which constrain the acquisition of motor skills, vary considerably among children. Another problem is the subjective judging of the acquisition of motor milestones, that is, standardizing methods of recording achievement. For example, there is little control over the various methods of prompting the child to respond such as modeling, giving verbal cues, or using manual guidance (see Ilmer & Drews, 1980).

One complaint from teachers of the handicapped is that the scoring systems of these instruments are not sensitive enough to measure changes in children whose progress is much slower than that of the average child. One attempt to alleviate this problem when testing the severly handicapped is seen in the recent work of Cohen and Gross (1979), who provide a more extensive breakdown of both fine and gross motor tasks. The disadvantage of this information is that the sequences are based on landmarks for normal child development and therefore may still be inadequate for use with multiply handicapped individuals (Mira, 1977).

Descriptive tests are of an actuarial nature in that they assess what the child can or cannot do, and therefore are most appropriately used as a screening device. Extreme caution must be exercised in using these tests for diagnostic purposes. The results of a good diagnostic test must not only indicate a motor deficiency when present but also must suggest remediation. Although aware of this need, practitioners and researchers alike often have a propensity for equating the name or label given a motor task with the process or underlying ability which predominately determines response outcome (Newell, 1976). Thus, for example, tasks labeled "balancing tasks" often are assumed to measure a child's balance ability.

Process Oriented/Diagnostic Approach

This section includes those tests whose purpose and design are diagnostic or process oriented. Some of these tests are oriented more toward gross motor tasks while others are weighted toward measuring "perceptual" attributes. The work by Oseretsky (see Doll, 1976) in Russia has had the greatest impact on motor ability testing of gross motor tasks. Oseretsky believed that motor ability is determined by neurological functioning and is primarily the responsibility of the brain. Thus, he reasoned that brain functioning could be assessed by observing a set of motor behaviors. His attempt to identify brain damage or "motor idiocy" resulted in an original test of six areas and included 85 tasks. The six areas were (1) general static balance (e.g., balancing on one foot); (2) dynamic manual (e.g., cutting a circle from paper or throwing a ball at a target); (3) general dynamic (e.g. jumping over a rope); (4) speed (e.g., making four piles with 40 match sticks as fast as possible); (5) simultaneous movement (e.g., tapping hands); and (6) dyskinesia (e.g., closing the eyes alternately). A composite score from all of the items in the test was converted into a "motor quotient" which indicated normal or abnormal motor development and in turn suggested the absence or presence of brain damage.

The Oseretsky Test was criticized because it failed to accurately identify brain damaged children (Geisler & Forster, 1960; Kiphard, 1969; both studies cited in Neuhauser, 1975). These researchers found that the six components were not actually separable and that the reliability in identifying children with brain damage was only 20%. Perhaps the strongest criticism of the original test was its extreme length, which made administration largely impractical.

The Oseretsky Test has since been adapted for use in other countries, particularly the United States (Doll, 1946) and Europe (see Nauhauser, 1975, for review). In these adaptations and subsequent revisions, researchers have attempted to correct many of the initial weaknesses described above. The most notable revisions in the United States have been the Lincoln (Sloan, 1955), Stott (Stott, Moyes, & Henderson, 1972) and the Bruininks Oseretsky (Bruininks, 1978). The latter two revisions bear little resemblance to the original Oseretsky tests.

The Stott General Test for Motor Impairment (Stott, 1966; Stott, Moyes, & Henderson, 1972) was an attempt to develop a measure of functional or presumed neurological impairment. The methodology of these researchers was to test successive experimental revisions of the Oseretsky Test on sample populations of normal and handicapped children. The result was the complete exclusion of many items and an adjustment in the pass/fail criteria and/or age level for many other items (Henderson & Stott, 1977).

The Bruininks/Oseretsky contains eight subsets and 46 items. The subtests—running speed and ability, balance, bilateral coordination, upper-limb coordination, response speed, visual-motor control, and upper-limb speed and dexterity—are based on motor components derived from factor analytic studies. Besides the complete battery, a Short Form, which consists of 14 items from the battery, is available. The scoring is based on derived scores which are compared to age equivalents or standard scores differentiated by sex. The derived scores are obtained from the raw scores by using a conversion formula (Bruininks, 1978).

An assumption of the diagnostic oriented test approach is that motor skills are general rather than specific. In other words, there are underlying motor abilities which transfer from one skill to another. Therefore, the level of performance exhibited on one skill would be predictive of the level of performance on other skills relying on the same underlying ability. By properly identifying these abilities, one could design tasks and develop an instrument to index general motor functioning. Under these assumptions, researchers, relying primarily on factor analytic studies (e.g., Bruininks, 1974; Fleishman, 1964; Rarick & Dobbins, 1975), attempted to identify these underlying abilities.

In the 1950s and early 1960s several psychologists and clinicians developed diagnostic tests weighted toward measuring perceptual-motor abilities. The most notable of these tests are the Purdue Perceptual Motor Survey (Roach & Kephart, 1966), the Southern California Sensory Integration Tests (Ayres 1964, 1974), Frostig's Development Test of Visual Perception (Frostig, Maslow, Lefever, & Whittlesey, 1963) and the Frostig Movement Skills Test Battery (Orpet, 1972). Featured on these tests are items purported to measure visual abilities (e.g., ocular control, form perception), body image and perceptual-motor match (e.g., eye-hand coordination, laterality, and directionality). These researchers hypothesized that motor performance was directly tied to perceptual abilities, which in turn were directly dependent on the central nervous system. Thus, it was held that nervous system function could be measured by assessing perceptual-motor ability.

Although these above tests are widely used (Lewko, 1977), they have come under heavy criticism. Researchers (e.g., Taylor, 1980) have found Frostig's Visual Perception Test not to measure five separate abilities as is assumed. Taylor also questioned whether the tasks (e.g., discrimination of 2-D geometric forms) tapped those perceptual abilities utilized by the child in reading and writing. The same criticism can be made with regard to motor development. It is questionable whether discrimination of 2-D geometric forms measures same perceptual ability as is required in running, jumping, and catching (see Gibson,

1979; Lee, 1978). Frostig and Ayres were also chided for failure to follow rigid standardization procedures and for making extensive and unsupported claims, particularly in the development of their earlier versions (see reviews in Buros, 1971). In addition, some practitioners have found that these tests do not relate well to their curriculum and thus are of little use in program planning (see Lewko, 1976).

Process/Descriptive Approach

Due in part to the need for assessment procedures aligned closer to program implementation, a new approach, known as the process/description approach, has emerged (Herkowitz, 1976). This approach is aimed in particular at designing tests for identifying children whose motor movements are awkward, and for testing mildly mentally handicapped children. Although this approach has not been fully developed nor thoroughly tested, it appears to hold some promise for aiding the practitioner.

In this type of test, each motor skill (e.g., throwing, catching, jumping) is selected from the program curriculum and assessed separately (e.g., Knowles, Vogel, & Wessel, 1975). The child's performance is judged on an individual basis against an established criterion of either a mature pattern (e.g., Davis, 1980; Fait, 1978, p. 78) or according to a developmental pattern (e.g., Loovis & Ersing, 1980), rather than to an age criterion as used in standardizing testing. The selection of these is based on analysis of the temporal and spatial relationships of the body parts during the performance, as described in the literature (see Wickstrom, 1977; McClenaghan & Gallahue, 1978). Thus, these testing procedures are considered to measure the process rather than the end product of performance but are descriptive rather than diagnostic.

A basic assumption in the approach is that this "mature pattern" is a biomechanically optimal performance and applies to most performers. A similar assumption is made regarding the developmental patterns which are sequential arrangements within the tasks rather than across tasks. Proponents of this type of test also adhere to the concept of motor specificity rather than generality. The notion of specificity has considerable research support, particularly that conducted by Franklin Henry during the 1950s (see Henry, 1958, 1960, for review).

Reflex Testing

Reflex behavior is a significant indication of motor development. It is fitting, therefore, that it is part of the assessment techniques used with childeren suspected of motor delay and/or mental retardation (see Newell, 1976; Molnar, 1978). Reflex testing as a major part of the neurological examination has, until recently, been conducted within the clinical setting and has followed rather standard procedures (e.g., Fiorentino, 1976; Milani-Comparetti & Gidoni, 1967).

Although the procedures are not difficult, an accurate interpretation of the results requires considerable training and experience. An appropriate use of reflex testing by trained educators is for them to do the initial identification of motor problems and to have a recommended follow-up evaluation done by a clinical specialist. Today, more and more children with motor problems are assessed in public school settings by special physical educators as well as by physical therapists; this assessment includes both reflex and motor evaluations.

In the clinical setting, reflex testing is only a part of the assessment battery used to determine the level of motor functioning and is considered to be a measure of the maturation of the neurological system. Two types of reflexes are evaluated, one of which is the "primitive" reflex. An example is the asymmetrical tonic neck reflex which is elicited in an infant by turning his or her head to one side. The normal response to this simple "stimulus" is an increase in flexor tone in the ipsilateral (same side) limbs and an increase in extensor tone in the contralateral (opposite side) limbs, thereby causing a degree of limb flexation and extension respectively. These reflexes are easily elicited at birth or shortly after and then become "integrated" into the nervous system as the child matures. Thus, while changes in muscle tone may still occur slightly from the eliciting stimulus, involuntary limb movement is inhibited by other newly established neural pathways.

Persistence of these reflexes beyond the normal age range (after 4 to 8 months for most primitive reflexes) indicates neurological impairment, even though the exact nature of this deficit is not always apparent (Patton, 1977). Absence of these reflexes at the expected time, which is usually accompanied by muscle hypotonia (floppy infant syndrome) also indicates neurological deficits but is even less suggestive of specific problems. For example, muscle hypotonia could later develop into hypertonia (as in the case of infantile spasticity), remain indefinitely, or improve with age to a normal level of motor function (Swainman & Wright, 1979).

A second type of reflex assessed is the postural adjustment reaction or the supportive reflexes, such as righting of the head in space. Another supportive reaction is derotative righting, an untwisting when a rotation is applied along the body axis. For example, if the pelvic girdle is rotated, the chest and head tend to follow reflexively. These reactions are well known to be important for the developing infant in achieving erect postures. Generally, body righting reactions begin to appear after 1 or 2 months of age in normal infants and continue to be present throughout their lives. From extensive observational studies of infants, researchers (e.g., Illingworth, 1968; Paine, Brazelton, Donovan, Droch, Hubbell, & Sears, 1964) have demonstrated a maturational sequence and timetable for the integration of the primitive reflexes and for the appearance of postural adjustment reactions, Moreover, an association between the maturation of these reflexes and the attainment of motor milestones have been shown (Hoskins & Squires, 1973; Milani-Comparetti & Gidoni, 1967).

Reflex testing has most extensively been used in evaluating infants and children suspected of having some type of cerebral palsy, particularly spasticity (the most common type), since the persistence of primitive reflexes is most evident in these cases. Recently, Molnar (1978) also demonstrated the importance of using reflex testing with mentally handicapped children. Molnar found motor delay in retarded infants (with no evidence of a physical disability) to be associated with a delay in the appearance of postural adjustment reactions. The primitive reflexes were normal for her sample, which led to the suggestion that the extended time between the dissolution of the primitive reflexes and the appearance of postural adjustment reactions contributed to the delayed motor skill development (Molnar, 1978).

As with the assessment of muscle tone and primitive reflexes, the observations of abnormal postural reactions alone do not provide sufficient information for determining precise deficits, for spinal, labyrinthine, and optical mechanisms all contribute to these automatic adjustment reactions in a cooperative and complex fashion.

PROGRAMMING MOTOR ACTIVITIES

Programming motor activities for the young child may be divided into three distinct approaches: the traditional approach, the movement education approach, and the perceptual motor approach.

The Traditional Approach

The traditional approach provides a logical series of formal motor activities that are in line with the presumed stage of the development of the child's strength and stature. The acquisition of fundamental motor tasks (see Wickstrom, 1977) is usually observable during the preschool and early school years as children develop, but as children grow older, the level of analysis required is often more complex in order to detect the subtle changes in both the character and the level of performance within each of these fundamental skills. As children progress into adolescence, the variability of their motor performance increases as they change both socially and biologically at a rate that is different from their chronological age. In other words, after puberty, chronological age per se may not provide a clear and accurate prediction regarding a child's capacity to perform a motor skill activity, because strength and growth rates vary more during this period. Thus, chronological age may sometimes be a misleading criterion for the study of changes in motor behavior.

Development in motor behavior from ages 5 years through 18 years is reflected by improvements on six fundamental groups of motor abilities. These are jumping, running, throwing, catching, balancing, and kicking. Dispersed among these fundamental motor abilities are a variety of other skills (e.g., speed, dexterity) in which children show improvement. Boys tend to improve in these skills up to the age of 18 years, while girls show improvement only up to age 14 years. As Keogh (1973) page 59 noted, it is "unusual in the senior high school if a girl runs, throws or jumps better than any but the poorer performing boy." These gains by boys are caused primarily by greater gains in strength and speed after puberty.

Movement Education

The essential idea behind movement education is in many ways embodied in the term "education through the physical" as opposed to "education of the physical." The movement education approach provides, ideally, an opportunity for the child to "discover" a variety of fundamental motor behaviors via an organized set of play and dance experiences. In the United States, motor development and elementary physical education have been influenced by movement education advocates in Europe and especially the British Isles. These advocates have sought to enhance the motor development of children via an educational system designed to help them understand the movement potential and capability of their bodies. As a result, programs of movement education are often characterized by an informal approach. Play settings are contrived by the teacher to encourage particular forms of activity, and once the child exhibits these activities the teacher seeks to improve on the quality of the movement. This approach is in sharp contrast to the traditional approach of teaching a specific activity via a formal set of teaching steps, and then, once the steps are completed, moving into another activity.

To successfully teach motor development under the movement education approach, careful planning and monitoring of both the children and the activity setting are required. If correctly carried out, a movement education approach can be extremely effective for children. If poorly planned, the approach will produce a great deal of activity but it will be misdirected and of poor quality.

Perceptual-Motor Programs

Perceptual-motor programs began to emerge in the early 1960s from the work of psychologists and clinicians, in particular Ayres (1974), Doman (see Doman, Spitz, Zucman, & Delacato, 1960), Delacato (1964, 1966), Kephart (1960), and Frostig (Frostig & Horne, 1964). These researchers were strongly influenced by earlier workers whose concern centered on children with learning difficulties (see Wiederholt, 1974, for historical review). Three basic premises underlie these various perceptual-motor programs: (1) the belief in the close tie between sensory and motor processes; (2) the contention that sensorimotor development precedes and underlies all perceptual and intellectual ability and (3) the belief that sequential motor development is mediated by and reflective of the development of the nervous system. Thus, the goal of these programs is not to treat motor disabilities but to remediate academic skills, such as reading and writing, through perceptual-motor training. Ayres' (1974) concern, for example, is not so much with improving motor skills as with improving brain function. Her program consists primarily of tactile and vestibular (balance) stimulation activities. The activities are said to improve brain-stem dysfunctions, claimed to be the source of many learning problems.

Others who adhere to the Doman-Delacato and Kephart approaches are concerned with developing specific motor patterns, believed to be prerequisites for the development of other skills, especiallly reading and writing. The Doman-Delacato program, in particular, requires strict adherence to a rigid set of activities. Doman and Delcato stress the necessity of a recapitulation of the sensorimotor sequence in order to retain the child in any motor pattern he or she might have skipped. This retraining, in turn, serves to improve nervous system function.

Balance beam walking, various locomotion patterns such as hopping and crawling, angles-in-the-snow, and ball handling are typical activities in the Kephart program. Frostig emphasizes visual training and is more eclectic in her philosophy (Frostig & Maslow, 1979). However, her program activities and many of her premises are in agreement with the other perceptual-motor theorists.

The popularity of perceptual-motor programs grew in the 1960s and 1970s but created considerable controversy. Many educators, including physical educators, special educators, and classroom reachers, were skeptical of the claim that motor learning enhances academic abilities. Several researchers (see Glass, 1967; Hammill, Goodman, & Wiederholt, 1974; Wedell, 1973, for review) attempted to substantiate the claims of the perceptual-motor theorists with intervention studies. Although the methodology of many of these studies was questionable with regard to actually being able to determine the efficacy of any program, the general findings were not supportive of perceptual motor programs' ability to enhance academic learning (see Hallahan & Cruickshank, 1973; Myers & Hammill, 1976, for a complete review). As a result, the popularity of this type of program has recently diminished (Sherrill, 1981). Today, many researchers in programming draw from all of the approaches described above.

SUMMARY

Programs and activities to develop the motor abilities of children during their formative years are integral to the process of normal development. Programs of motor activity for the young child should begin with emphasis on informality and self-discovery, to allow children to appreciate their movement capabilities. For young children, informal play settings with play equipment that encourages a variety of large muscle movements are important. Developing children must be able to appreciate the scope and potential of their motor abilities before the refinements and constraints of formal motor skills are placed upon them. As strength, dexterity, endurance, and flexibility develop, children will become receptive to the more formal motor skill activities that will become part of their experience.

REFERENCES

Ayres, A.J. *Southern California sensory integration tests.* Los Angeles, CA: Western Pschology Service, 1964.

Ayres, A.J. *Sensory integration and learning disabilities.* Los Angeles CA: Los Angeles Western Psychological Services, 1974.

Bayley, N. The development of motor abilities during the first three years. *Monograph of the Society for Research in Child Development,* 1935, *1,* 1–26.

Bayley, N. *Bayley scales of infant development.* New York: The Psychological Corp., 1969.

Bridgeman, C. S., & Carmichael, L. An experimental study of the onset of behavior in the fetal guinea pig. *Journal of General Psychology,* 1935, *47,* 247–267.

Bruininks, R. H. Physical and motor development of retarded persons. In N. R. Ellies (Ed.), *International review of research in mental retardation* (Vol. 7). New York: Academic Press, 1974.

Bruininks, R. H. *Bruininks-Oseretsky tests of motor proficiency.* Circle Pines, MN: American Guidance Service, 1978.

Buros, O. K. (Ed.) *Sixth mental measurement year book.* New Jersey: Gryphon Press, 1971.

Carmichael, L. An experimental study in the prenatal guinea pig of the origin and development of reflexes and patterns of behavior in relation to stimulation of specific receptor areas during the period of active fetal life. *Genetic physiological monographs,* 1934, *16,* 337–491.

Coghill, G. E. *Anatomy and the problem of behavior.* New York: Cambridge University Press, 1929.

Cohen, M., & Gross, P. *The developmental resource: Behavioral sequences for assessment and program planning.* New York: Grune and Stratton, 1979.

Connolly, K. J. Skill development: Problems and plans, In K. J. Connolly (Ed.) *Mechanisms of motor skill development.* New York: Academic Press, 1970a.

Connolly K. J. Response speed, temporal sequencing, and information processing in children. In K. J. Connolly (Ed.). *Mechanism of motor skill development.* New York: Academic Press, 1970b.

Davis, W. E. *Special physical education handbook.* Unpublished manuscript. University of Illinois, 1980.

Delacato, C. H. *The diagnosis and treatment of speech and reading problems.* Springfield, IL: Charles C. Thomas, 1964.

Delacato, C. H. *Neurological organization and reading.* Springfield, IL: Charles C. Thomas, 1966.

Doll, E. A. The Oseretsky scale. *American Journal of Mental Development,* 1946, *50,* 485–487.

Doman, R. J., Spitz, E.B., Zucman, E., & Delacato, C. H. Children with severe brain injuries: Neurological organization in terms of mobility. *Journal of American Medical Association,* 1960, *174,* 257–262.

Ebel, R. Li. The future of the measurement of ability II, *Education Researcher,* 1973, *2,* 5–12.

Fait, H. *Special physical education: Adaptive, corrective, developmental.* Philadlphia, PA: W. B. Saunders, 1978.

Fiorentino, M. R. *Normal and abnormal development: The influence of primitive reflexes on motor development.* Springfield, IL: C. C. Thomas, 1976.

Fitch, H. L., & Turvey, M. T. On the control of activity: Some remarks from an ecological point of view. In D. M. Landers & R. W. Christina (Eds.) *Psychology of motor behavior and sport.* Champaign, IL: Human Kinetics Press, 1977.

Fleishman, E. A. *The structure and measurement of physical fitness,* Englewood Cliffs, NJ: Prentice-Hall, 1964.

Fowler, C., & Turvey, M. T. Skill acquisition: An event approach with special reference to searching for the optimum of a function of several variables. In G. Stelmach (Ed.), *Information processing in motor control and learning.* New York: Academic Press, 1978.

Frankenburg, W., & Dodds, J. *Denver Developmental Screening Test.* Denver, CO: University of Colorado Medical Center, 1966.

Frostig, M., Lefever. W., Maslow, P., & Whittesey, J. R. B. *Developmental treatment of visual perception.* Palo Alto, CA: Consulting Psychologist Press, 1963.

Frostig, M., & Horne. D. *Teacher's guide: The Frostig program for the development of visual perception.* Chicago, IL: Follett Educational Corp., 1964.

Frostig, M., & Maslow, P. Neuropsychological contributions to education. *Journal of Learning Disabilities,* 1979, *12,* 538-552.

Gesell, A. (Ed.), *The first five years of life.* New York: Harper & Row, 1940.

Gesell, A., & Amatruda, C. B. *Developmental diagnosis: The evaluation and management of normal and abnormal neuropsychological development in infancy and early childhood* (3rd ed.). New York: Harper Row, 1978.

Gibson. J. J. *The senses considered as perceptual systems.* Boston, MA: Houghton Mifflin, 1966.

Gibson, J. J. *The exological approach to visual perception.* Boston, MA: Houghton Mifflin, 1979.

Glass, C. V. *A critique of experiments on the role of neurological organization in reading performance.* Champaign, IL: Center for the Instructional Research and Curriculum Evaluation, University of Illinois, 1967.

Hallahan, D., & Cruickshank, W. *Psychological foundations of learning disabilities.* Englewood Cliffs, NJ.: Prentice Hall, 1973.

Halverson, L. E., Roberton M. A., & Harper, C. J. Current research in motor development. *Journal of Research and Development in Education,* 1973, *6,* 59-71.

Hammill, D. D., Goodman, L. E. Wiederhott, J. L. Visual-motor processes: Can we train them? *Reading Teacher,* 1974, *27,* 469-486.

Herkowitz, J. Assessing the motor development of children: Presentation and critque of test, In M. V. Ridenour (Ed.), *Motor development: Issues and applications.* Princeton, NJ: Princeton Book Co., 1978.

Hoskins, T. A., & Squires, J. E. Developmental assessment: A test for gross motor and reflex development. *Physical Therapy,* 1973, *58,* 117-125.

Illingworth, R. S., Delayed motor development. *Pediatric Clinics of North America,* 1968, *15,* 569-580.

Ilmer, S., & Drews, J. Differential analysis of selected prompts and neurological variables in motor assessment of moderate mental retarded children. *American Journal of Mental Retardation,* 1980, *84,* 508-517.

Katoff, L., & Reuter, J. Review of developmental screening tests for infants, *Journal of Clinical Child Psychology,* 1980, *9,* 30-34.

Kephart, N. C. *The slow learner in the classroom.* Columbus, OH: Merrill, 1960.

Keogh, J. Development in fundamental motor tasks. In C. B. Corbin (Ed.). *A textbook of motor development.* Dubuque, IA: W. C. Brown & Co., 1973.

Knowles, C., Vogel, P., & Wessel, J. A. Project IACAN: Independent curriculum designed for mentallly retarded children and youths. *Education and Training of the Mentally Retarded,* 1975, *10,* 155-160.

Kugler, P. N., Kelso, J. A. S., & Turvey, M. T. on the concept of coordinative structures as dissipative structures I: Theoretical lines. In G. E. Stelman & J. Requin (Eds.), *Tutorials in motor behavior.* Amsterdam: North Holland Publishing Co., 1980.

Lee, D. N. On the function of vision. In H. L. Pick (Ed.), *Modes of perceiving.* New York: Eibbaum Press, 1978, 159–180.

Lewko, J. H. Current practices in evaluating motor behavior of disabled children. *American Journal of Teaching,* 1976, *30,* 413–419.

Loovis, E. M., & Ersing, W. F. *Assessing and programming gross motor development for children* (2nd ed.). Loudonville, OH: Mohican Textbook Publishing Co., 1980.

McClenaghan, B., & Gallahue, D. L. *Developing fundamental patterns in young and awkward children.* Philadelphia, PA: Saunders, 1978.

McGraw, M. G. *The neuromuscluar maturation of the human infant,* New York: Columbia University Press, 1945.

Milani-Compareti, A., & Gidoni E. H. *Pattern analysis of motor developmental Medicine and Child Neurology,* 1967, *9,* 631–638.

Mira, M. Tracking the motor behavior development of multiple handicapped infants, *Mental Retardation,* 1977, *15,* 32–37.

Molnar, G. E. Analysis of motor disorders in retarded infants and young children. *American Journal of Motor Development,* 1978, *83,* 213–222.

Myers, P. L., & Hammill, D. D. The perceptual-motor systems. In *Methods of learning disorders* 2nd ed.,) New York: Wiley & Sons, 1976.

Neuhauser, G. Methods of assessing and recording motor skills and movement patterns. *Developmental Medical and Child Neurology,* 1973, *17,* 369–386.

Newell, K. M. Principles of skill acquisition and their implications for assessment and prognosis, In R. E. Stadulis (Ed.), *Research and practice in physical education.* Champaign, IL: Human Kinetics Press, 1976.

Orpet, R. E. *Frostig movement skills test pattern.* Palo Alto, CA: Consulting Psychologist Press, 1972.

Paine, R. S., Braselton, R. B., Donovan, D. E., Drochbaugh, J. E., Hubbell, J. R., & Sears, E. M. Evolution of postural reflexes in normal infants and in the presence of chronic brain syndrome, *Neurology,* 1964, *14,* 1036–1048.

Patton. J. *Neurological differential diagnosis,* New York: Spunger-Verlag, 1977.

Piaget, J. *The origins of intelligence in children.* New York: International University Press, 1952.

Rarick, G. L., & Dobbing, D. A. A motor performance typology of boys and girls in the age range of 6–10 years. *Journal of Motor Behavior,* 1975, *7,* 37–43.

Roach, E. G., & Kephart, N. C. *The Perdue PMS.* Columbus, OH: Merrill, 1966.

Schneirla, T. C. Behavioral development and comparative psychology, *Quarterly Review of Biology,* 1966, *41,* 283–302.

Shannon, C. E., & Weaver, W. *The mathematical theory of communication.* Urbana, IL: University of Illinois Press, 1949.

Sherrill, C. *Adapted physical education and recreation: A multidisciplinary approach* (2nd ed.). Dubque, IA: W. C. Brown Publishing, 1981.

Shirley, M. M. *The first two years: A study of 25 babies,I Postural and locomotion development.* Minneapolis, MN: University of Minnesota Press, 1931.

Sloan, W. The Lincoln-Oseretsky motor development scale, *Genetic Psychology Monographs,* 1955, *51,* 183–221.

Stott, D. H. A general test of motor impairment of children. *Developmental Medicine and Child Neurology,* 1966, *8,* 523–530.

Stott, D. H., Moyes, F. A., & Henderson, S.E. *A test of motor impairment.* Slough: NFER Publishing Co., 1972.

Swainman, K. F., & Wright, F. S. *Pediatric neuromuscular disease,* St. Louis, MO: C. V. Mosby, 1979.

Taylor, N. E. Measuring perceptual skills that are related to the learning task. *Journal of Learning Disabilities,* 1980, *13,* 22–24.

Thorpe, H. S., & Werner, E. E. Developmental screening of preschool children: A critical review of inventories use in health and educational programs, *Pediatrics,* 1974, *53,* 362-370.

Turvey, M. T., Shaw, R. E., & Mace, W. Issues in the theory of action: Degrees of freedom, coordinative structures and coalitions. In J. Requin (Ed.).*Attention and performance VII.* Hillsdale, NJ: Lawrence Erlbaum, Associates 1978.

Wade, M. G. Developmental motor learning. In J. Keogh & R. S. Hutton (Eds.). *Exercise and sports sciences reviews* (Vol. 4). Santa Barbara, CA: Journal Publishing Affiliates, 1976.

Wedell, K. *Learning and perceptual-motor disabilities in children,* New York: John Wiley & Sons, 1973.

Wickstrom, R. L. Developmental kinesiology: Maturation of basic motor patterns, In J. H. Wilmore & J. F. Keogh (Eds,) *Exercise and sports sciences reviews* (Vol. 3). New York: Academic Press, 1977.

Weiderholt, J. L. Historical perspectives on the education of the learning disabled. In L. Mann & D. A. Sabatino (Eds.), *The second review of special education.* Philadelphia, PA; JSE Press, 1974

Windle, W. F. *Physiology of the fetus; Origin and extent of function in prenatal life.* Philadelphia, PA; Saunders, 1940.

4

Curiosity and Self-directed Learning: The Role of Motivation in Education*

Edward L. Deci and Richard M. Ryan

University of Rochester

For young children, self-directed learning is a fact of life. They are curious; they go to things that interest them, marvel at new discoveries, and drive their parents crazy with questions. For older children, however, another pattern emerges: there seems to be considerable resistance to learning, and much of the learning that they do seems to depend on directives from teachers or parents, on grades and gold stars, on various forms of external recognition.

What has happened to children's enthusiasm, their inner desire for understanding and mastering their world? Why does children's learning seem so closely tied to demands, controls and rewards? Our answers to these questions are grounded in our motivation theory (e.g., Deci, 1980; Deci & Ryan, in press-b) and in a plethora of recent research studies (Deci & Ryan, 1980). In this chapter we shall review the research and theory and then draw implications that are directly germane to early childhood education.

MOTIVATIONAL ORIENTATIONS

In essence, people can, at any given time, be in one of three different motivational states—intrinsically motivated, extrinsically motivated, or amotivated. When they are intrinsically motivated, the reward for the activity seems to be

* Preparation of this chapter was facilitated by a Research Grant (BSN 8018628) from the National Science Foundation. Any opinions, findings, and conclusions or recommendations expressed in this publication are those of the authors and do not necessarily reflect the views of the National Science Foundation.

part and parcel of the activity itself—there is no reward separate from the spontaneous feelings and thought that accompany the activity. Intrinsically motivated behavior is based in people's innate need to be competent and self-determining (White, 1959; deCharms, 1968; Deci, 1975). Curiosity, exploration, and play are examples of this type of activity. The self-directed learning of young children is paradigmatic of intrinsically motivated behavior; it is active, involving, open-minded; it includes surprise and wonder; it leads children toward mastery of their environments and provides them with the tools to be more self-determining.

When extrinsically motivated, people are working toward some external reward—it might be money, good grades, status, approval, or the avoidance of an unpleasant event. The behavior tends to be a means to some end rather than a part of the end. When extrinsically motivated, people tend to feel more pressured and less involved with the activity itself—their attention is partially focused on the desired outcome rather than on the activity. The learning of older children seems to be more extrinsic in nature—they often see it as a means to good grades, to teacher or parent approval, to compliance with deadlines and demands. The learning is no longer an expression of their curiosity and interest. As Condry and Koslowski (1979) point out, the problems with extrinsically motivated learning are that the learning tends to be less thorough and the learners tend to lose control of the learning situation.

When amotivated, people believe that they cannot have a meaningful impact on their environment, so they tend to be passive and non-responsive. They frequently feel helpless and are easily upset. Their learning is slow and seems to be painful.

Most classrooms have children that exemplify each of these motivational orientations. There are children who are curious and prefer challenges—who are interested in their work and eager for more. They seem to be intrinsically motivated and are involved in directing their own learning. Other children seem to do just what they are told to do, but they take no responsibility for themselves. They are compliant and often high achievers, but they depend on the teacher for direction and affirmation. They are extrinsically motivated; their behavior is dependent on external contingencies. Interestingly, there is a second type of behavior that is dependent on external contingencies, namely, rebellious or defiant behavior. Rebellious children are dependent on external contingencies, but they do just the opposite of what is demanded. Brehm (1966) referred to this as "reactance" and suggested that when people feel as if their freedom is threatened, they react against those threats by doing the opposite. Externally oriented people (people who are primarily oriented toward extrinsic contingencies) may be either compliant or rebellious; most often they display a mix of the two types of responding. In either case, however, they fall short of the ideal student, for they do not seem to be interested in learning for its own sake, nor do they take responsibility for their learning.

Finally, in most classrooms, there is a third type of child, the type that is passive and seems to be amotivated. Unlike the intrinsically motivated children, who are curious and spontaneous, or extrinsically motivated children, who are either compliant or reactive, amotivated children tend to act and feel helpless. They do not perform well, for they get overwhelmed by the material; it all seems too much for them.

While one could categorize most children in each classroom as falling into one of these three orientations, undoubtedly every child experiences all three of these motivational states at one time or another. It is equally true that as adults each of us is, at times, intrinsically motivated, extrinsically motivated, or amotivated. As teachers, it is particularly important to have experienced these motivational sets in ourselves, since that provides the basis for understanding the corresponding experiences of children and for grasping the conditions that produce those experiences.

With babies and preschool children, one can also observe the three motivational states. Young children are often curious and adventuresome, though at times they are also compliant, rebellious, and passive. Their patterns of behavior are less well formed than are those of older children, but the experiences that they have during the very early years lay the foundation for the pattern of being primarily intrinsically motivated, primarily extrinsically motivated, or primarily amotivated in their school-age and adult years.

MOTIVATIONAL STATES AND THE ENVIRONMENT

In the ideal classroom, one would find children who are intrinsically motivated a substantial portion of the time. Yet the ideal classroom is hard to find. Indeed, many classrooms are filled with children who are extrinsically motivated or amotivated. How does this come about? And what are the possibilities for structuring classrooms that promote intrinsically motivated learning? To answer these questions we turn to an exploration of the effects of the environment on people's motivation.

Consider first the amotivated child. Seligman (1975) and his colleagues (Garber & Seligman, 1980) have reported a great deal of research that speaks directly to this issue. They have suggested that when people operate in an environment that has response-outcome independence, they learn to be helpless. In other words, when their own behaviors do not lead to predictable outcomes, they come to believe that desired outcomes do not accrue from their own directed efforts but rather are delivered by chance or fate. In these environments, there are no clear contingencies between behaviors and outcomes, so children have no basis for learning how to achieve the outcomes they want.

There are few real-world environments that actually have response-outcome independence, in other words, environments in which there are no discernible contingencies between behaviors and outcomes. However, both home and school environments can be seen to vary in the degree to which there is inconsistency. If the cries of a hungry baby sometimes lead to its being nurtured and fed, sometimes to being ignored, and sometimes to being spanked or yelled at, the baby will have difficulty learning how to get what it wants. In these inconsistent or non-contingent environments, rewards may accrue to the child, but they do not accrue in any predictable or understandable way. In our own theorizing, we suggest that such environments undermine one's sense of personal "effectance," that is, the sense that one can competently achieve one's disired outcomes. In the absence of a contingently responsive environment, one develops a sense of failure and an expectation that continued initiations and efforts are fruitless. Frequently, this generalizes to a sense that one is worthless; in other words, it leads to low self-esteem.

Such an environment was created in a study by Hiroto (1974). He exposed college students to uncontrollable noise. Subsequently, he had them work with a finger-maze activity through which they could contingently control the noise. He found, however, that after they had learned to be helpless in relation to the noise, they failed to gain control over it, even when the control was available to them; they were passive and seemed unable to learn.

The work of Rotter (1966) and his colleagues has further highlighted the importance of environments in which there is a perceived relationship between behavior and outcomes. In environments where this relationship does not appear to exist, people develop what Rotter termed an external locus of control. Research has indicated that an external locus of control is associated with deficits in motivation and learning as well as with a variety of psychological and physical malfunctions (see Lefcourt, 1976, for a review).

In work with infants, the importance of a contingently responsive environment has also been demonstrated. This work (e.g., Ainsworth, Blehar, Waters, & Wall, 1978) has focused on mother-child interactions and has shown that when mothers do not respond consistently to their children's initiations, the children display greater anxiety—they cry more and are more upset by separations from their mothers. This evidence is quite extensive and has been collected primarily with 1-year-olds. Of course, it is difficult to say exactly what the infants' understanding of the responsiveness or non-responsiveness of their environment is like. Clearly, they have grasped whether their environment is responsively contingent (Bowlby, 1973), in other words whether they can trust the consistency and responsiveness of the environment (Erikson, 1950); however, their understanding is probably quite rudimentary and would seem more intuitive than cognitive.

These three lines of research, utilizing subjects who range from babies to adults, point unambiguously to the importance of people's need to understand contingencies. In order to be motivated, in order to function effectively and to remain healthy (Lefcourt, 1973; Deci, 1980), people must be able to perceive relationships between their behavior and the outcomes that follow; they must learn that there is the possibility for them to behave in ways that lead to predictable outcomes.

Recent research in a somewhat different vein has indicated, however, that simply having a relationship between behaviors and outcomes is not enough for intrinsically motivated, self-directed behavior. Contingencies in the environment prevent helplessness and amotivation, but they can produce an extrinsically oriented, compliant or reactive child as well as an intrinsically oriented, self-determining child. To clarify this important point, we shall turn to a brief review of relevant research.

EXTRINSIC REWARDS AND FEEDBACK

In some early studies, Deci (1971, 1972) found that when college students were paid for working on interesting activities, they displayed less intrinsic motivation in a subsequent free-choice period than subjects who had spent the same amount of time working with the activity but who had not been paid for it. In other words, the payments, which were clearly contingent, seemed to undermine students' intrinsic motivation for the activity. Their behavior seems to have become dependent on the rewards, and they were less likely to do the activity in the absence of the rewards. The undermining of intrinsic motivation by monetary rewards has been demonstrated in subjects as young as 4 and 5 years old (Anderson, Manoogian, & Reznick, 1976).

The general finding that extrinsic rewards can undermine intrinsic motivation has been replicated dozens of times with a variety of rewards, tasks, and age groups (see Deci & Ryan, 1980). For example, Lepper, Greene, and Nisbett (1973) found that rewarding preschool children with a ''good player award'' for working on an art project decreased their intrinsic motivation for working with the art materials. Ross (1975) found the same to be true when nursery school children were rewarded with desired food. Deci and Cascio (1972) found that rewarding college students with the ''avoidance of a punishment'' for doing well on an activity decreased their intrinsic motivation in much the same fashion as the more ''positive'' rewards.

It appears to be the case that the administration of rewards leads the recipients to understand their behavior as being caused by the rewards, so they subsequently perform the behavior only in the presence of a reward contingency. Rewards are not the only extrinsic factors that have been shown to undermine intrinsic motivation. Amabile, DeJong, and Lepper (1976) found that when deadlines were imposed on an activity, college students lost intrinsic motivation for the activity. Similarly, Lepper and Greene (1975) found that adults' surveillance of preschool children's behavior undermined the children's intrinsic motivation. And Deci, Betley, Kahle, Abrams, and Porac (1981) found that, when college students were explicitly directed to compete against an opponent, they lost intrinsic motivation for the activity at which they competed. Whenever people's behavior becomes controlled by some extrinsic factor, whether rewards, deadlines, surveillance, or competition, they seem to be left with less intrinsic motivation.

Earlier, we stated that intrinsic motivation is based in people's need to be competent and self-determining. Apparently, the fact of the rewards or controls undermines their sense of self-determination, for they begin to see their behavior as being determined by the extrinsic contingencies rather than by their own interest in the activity.

The competence component of intrinsic motivation can also be the means through which intrinsic motivation is undermined. Deci, Cascio, and Krusell (1973) found that when subjects failed at an interesting activity, or when they were told that they had done quite poorly, they were less intrinsically motivated than subjects who had done the same activity without the failure or without the negative feedback from the experimenter.

In sum, extrinsic rewards, externally imposed controls, and negative feedback appear to undermine intrinsic motivation and leave people's behavior dependent on external factors. This would be characteristic of the extrinsically oriented, compliant, or reactive children discussed earlier. Given this plethora of discouraging results, is there no hope?

Fortunately other studies have highlighted the factors that tend to foster intrinsic motivation. There seem to be two types of factors. One is choice. Zuckerman, Porac, Lathin, Smith, and Deci (1978) found that when college student subjects were given choice about what puzzles to work on and how long to spend working on them, they were more intrinsically motivated than subjects who were assigned the puzzles and time limits they had chosen. Swann and Pittman (1977) found similar results with young children; when the children believed they had a choice about what to play with, they were more intrinsically motivated than children who believed they had no choice.

The second factor that has been shown to enhance intrinsic motivation is positive competence feedback. When subjects get feedback indicating that they are quite competent, they seem more interested in the activity and they persist at it longer than subjects who do not get the feedback. This was found to be true for 4- and 5-year-olds (Anderson et al., 1976), for high school students (Harackiewicz, 1979), and for college students (Blanck, Jackson, & Reis, 1979). In short, just as controls and negative feedback have been shown to decrease intrinsic motivation, choice and positive feedback have been shown to increase intrinsic motivation. While many of the studies cited were done with teenagers and adults, most of the studies have been replicated with preschool and elementary school children, and all the results seem to hold across age groups.

INFORMATION AND CONTROL

The research studies presented above, along with numerous others that lend further support to the conclusions (see Deci & Ryan, 1980; Deci & Ryan, in press-b, for extensive reviews), suggest that extrinsic rewards undermine intrinsic motivation by creating a dependency between the behavior and the reward. However, one might wonder, since rewards are often used to convey competence at the activity (much like positive feedback), why they do not enhance intrinsic motivation.

Deci (1975) and Deci and Ryan (1980) have suggested that all rewards, and communications as well, have two functional aspects—a *controlling* aspect and an *informational* aspect. The function of the controlling aspect is to bring about a specific outcome. It tends to leave the recipient feeling pressure and tension. For example, if you use the reward of a candy bar to make your child clean up his or her room ("If you clean your room, I'll give you a candy bar"), you would be using the candy to control the child's behavior and the child would probably feel pressured. By contrast, the function of the informational aspect is to provide the recipient with information that is relevant for his or her performance. For example, if your child just finished practicing the piano and you thought it was particularly good, you might give him or her a candy bar as a way of saying, "That was really great." In this case, you would be using the candy bar informationally, for it simply would be providing competence feedback.

Since every reward and communication has both of these aspects, it is the relative salience of the two aspects that determines the effects of the reward or communication on intrinsic motivation. Thus, it might well be that a reward like money or praise could be administered in such a way as to facilitate intrinsic motivation by conveying positive competence information rather than attempting to control behavior. Several recent studies have found exactly that.

Enzle and Ross (1978) and Rosenfield, Folger, and Adelman (1980) both found that subjects who were paid informationally were more intrinsically motivated than subjects who were paid controllingly. Informationally rewarded subjects had been told that they would receive rewards if they performed skillfully, whereas controllingly rewarded subjects had not been told that the rewards would reflect competence. Money is generally thought to be quite controlling, so in the absence of a specific statement about its signifying competence, it was assumed that it would be perceived as controlling. The results of these two studies showed that, even though the activity and financial rewards were the same, intrinsic motivation was differentially affected by the differential salience of the informational versus controlling aspect of the rewards.

Pittman, Davey, Alafat, Wetherill, and Kramer (1980) found the same results with verbal rewards. With one group of subjects, the experimenter simply told subjects that they were doing very well at the task, whereas for a second group the experimenter told the subjects not only that they were doing well at the task, but also that that meant their data would be useful to the researchers. In both groups there was positive verbal feedback, but for the second group the fact that the experimenter seemed invested in getting good data seemed to highlight the controlling aspect of the feedback, and therefore it decreased the subjects' intrinsic motivation relative to that of subjects who were given the feedback informationally. These last three studies were all done with young adults. It is our belief, however, that the general finding is equally relevant for children.

Ryan (in press) has found that controlling feedback administered by oneself can have the same detrimental effect as controlling feedback administered by others. In his study, feedback was considered controlling when it included an evaluation of whether subjects were "doing as well as they *should* be," and it was considered informational when it simply located subjects' performance relative to the average and the maximum possible performance. Some subjects administered informational feedback to themselves, whereas others selected the evaluative (controlling) feedback that they thought was appropriate for themselves and then administered it to themselves. Ryan found that self-administered controlling feedback undermined intrinsic motivation relative to the self-administered informational feedback, just as was the case with other administered controlling versus informational feedback.

This phenomenon of the differential effect of informational versus controlling, self-administered feedback is less likely to show up in young children, for they are still in the process of internalizing the informational versus controlling structures that inform as opposed to control them. However, it is important to realize that when children grow up in informational environments, they are likely to internalize informational contingencies, whereas when they grow up in controlling environments they are likely to internalize controlling contingencies. In the latter case, they will continue to be less intrinsically motivated, for they will tend to "control" rather than "inform" themselves.

The important point from all of these studies is that the effects of rewards and communications on intrinsic motivation depend on whether they are interpreted by the recipients as being primarily informational or primarily controlling. This is very important in schools—as well as in other institutions—for rewards and communications are integral parts of educational systems. When rewards such as grades, gold stars, and verbal feedback are used controllingly, to bring about specifc outcomes, they are likely to undermine intrinsic motivation, whereas when they are used informationally, to convey competence feedback, they could maintain or enhance it.

INTRINSIC MOTIVATION IN SCHOOL CHILDREN

To test this last assertion, Deci, Nezlek, and Sheinman (1981) conducted a study in 35 fourth through sixth grade classroooms. They reasoned that teachers could be located along a continuum ranging from "highly controlling" to "highly supportive of autonomy" in terms of their general orientation toward children. Those teachers who were oriented toward control would be expected to communicate and reward controllingly, whereas those teachers who were oriented toward autonomy would be expected to communicate and reward information-ally. The former teachers tended to tell the children what they should do and rewarded the children for doing what they were told; the latter teachers en-couraged children to decide for themselves what to do and they rewarded the children for doing well.

Deci, Nezlek, and Sheinman (1981) predicted that teachers who were more control oriented would have children with lower intrinsic motivation than teach-ers who were more autonomy oriented. The results supported the prediction. In addition, children in the control-oriented classrooms had a signficantly lower perception of their cognitive competence and a lower sense of general self-worth than the children in the autonomy-oriented classrooms. A follow-up study (Deci, Schwartz, Sheinman, & Ryan, 1981) indicated that teachers' orientations can have a significant impact on the intrinsic motivation and self-esteem of children within the first two months of a school year.

In a complementary study, deCharms (1976) found that when teachers were trained to be more autonomy oriented, their pupils were more motivated than children in classrooms where the teachers had not been similarly trained. In that study, he found not only greater intrinsic motivation and satisfaction among the children in the autonomy-oriented classrooms, but also better aca-demic performance. Thus, intrinsically motivated children seem to learn better than extrinsically motivated children. The finding that intrinsically motivated people perform better at learning or other challenging activities has been con-firmed in a great many laboratory studies as well (see McGraw, 1978).

Let us now summarize the general argument and its empirical foundation. We have categorized three general types of environments: a noncontingent, non-responsive environment; a contingent, demanding, and controlling environment; and a contingent, responsive environment in which children have many choices. The non-contingent environment fosters amotivation and helplessness; the con-trolling environment fosters extrinsically motivated (compliant or reactive) be-havior; and the contingent, responsive environment fosters intrinsically moti-vated behavior.

Evidence is clear on the issue of contingency. Children must perceive a relationship between their own behavior and desired outcomes; otherwise they will tend to be amotivated and helpless. But contingency alone is not enough for intrinsically motivated children. Contingent outcomes can be quite detri-mental to children's intrinsic motivation if they are used to control rather than inform. The contingent outcomes must be responsive to children's initiations if they are to strengthen the children's intrinsic motivation and self-determination. If these outcomes make demands on or control children's behavior rather than respond to it, they can have a detrimental effect. Of course, it is more preferable to have contingent and demanding outcomes than to have non-contingent and unpredictable outcomes, for the former will at least foster extrinsic motivation. But neither represents the ideal, for neither encourages the kind of curiosity and self-directed learning that is so delightfully apparent in most 2- and 3-year-old children.

Active Learning

The abundance of research related to intrinsic motivation lends credence to the ideas that have been espoused by some educational theorists for years (e.g., Bruner, 1962; Montessori, 1967; Rogers, 1969). As Rogers put it, self-directed education will flourish in an environment that promotes active learning. A key element in such an environment is the attitude of the teacher—or as Rogers would say, the "facilitator of learning." The attitudes that seem to promote learning are ones of trust, empathy, and authenticity in the teacher. In our studies, we found that an orientation toward autonomy promoted intrinsic motivation; it is likely that autonomy-oriented teachers were more trusting and empathetic.

Active learning, according to our theory, requires the opportunity to be self-determining (to make one's own choices) and the opportunity to have an impact on the environment (to be competent and effective). In one study, Benware and Deci (1981) attempted to create an active versus a passive motivational set to explore the impact of these sets on motivation and learning. To create the active-learning orientation they asked subjects to learn some material in order to teach it to others. To create the passive set they asked students to learn the material in order to be tested on it. They reasoned that if people learned with the expectation of teaching the material to others, they would be more involved in the learning, for they would be preparing to have an impact on their environment—they would be expecting to be active and effective. Students in the two groups spent the same amount of time learning, but results indicated that the active learners were more intrinsically motivated and more satisfied than the passive learners. Even more importantly, the conceptual learning of the active group far surpassed the conceptual learning of the passive group, though interestingly, the rote learning of the two groups was the same. Passive learners memorize material well and hence will do well on memory-oriented tests, but they do not achieve the conceptual understanding that characterizes active learning. Incidentally, the active learners in this study never actually taught the material; they simply learned it with the expectation of teaching, and still they reported being highly intrinsically motivated, and their learning was more complete.

Aronson, Blaney, Stephan, Sikes, and Snapp (1978) did a number of experiments in elementary school classrooms in which they set up cooperative groups that involved each member of the group teaching things to all other members. This seemed to create a sense of interdependence and mutual goal orientation that improved attitudes, motivation, and learning. The opportunity to work together in a supportive environment was the key to effective learning.

It is important to note that an autonomy orientation in relation to learning does not mean abandoning structure; it means creating structures that allow freedom within limits (Ginott, 1972), that allow children to solve their own problems, and that provide guidance and allow children to assess their own competence. Such structures focus on outcomes rather than means, and are informational rather than controlling. With such structures, children have more opportunity to direct their learning with their own curiosity, and the result is likely to be enhanced learning and greater satisfaction.

The idea of self-directed learning within informational structures leads to some interesting paradoxes. For example, as teachers, we all want our students to succeed. Yet it can be quite detrimental to try to control them toward success. If we allow children to fail, they may be more likely to succeed. Allowing them to fail lets them choose to succeed, and once they've chosen success they will embrace it more fully. If we try to *make* our students succeed, they will either be compliant and therefore never able to take full responsibility for success, or they will be reactive and fail as a means to regain their freedom.

As teachers it is important not to become too invested in particular behavioral outcomes, for such investment is likely to lead to control and to promote feelings of failure when desired outcomes are not achieved. It is important to care about students' success, but in the final analysis the choice must be left to them. This will not guarantee success, but neither does the currently pervasive extrinsic, controlling system result in "schools without failure."

The Problems for Teachers

The main thrust of our discussion has included: first, the expressed value that a classroom full of intrinsically motivated children is the preferred classroom; and second, the assertion that autonomy-oriented, informational classroom environments are the ones that are most likely to foster intrinsic motivation in children.

For teachers this is a tall order (see Deci & Ryan, in press-a). It is easy to suggest that they implement information styles and autonomy orientations, provide contingent responsiveness to children's initiations, and be supportive of children in times of failure. However, there are many obstacles to their doing this. For one thing, most teachers find themselves in demanding systems with large classes of children who have widely varied competencies, so it is hard not to be oriented toward controlling them. Further, many children live in homes that are either non-contingent or highly controlling. Thus, the children are not accustomed to being autonomous and responsible, so the teachers may become frustrated in their attempts to support autonomy in these children. We believe it is best for teachers to attempt to support autonomy even when the children are from homes that are controlling or non-responsive, but it will take greater effort and there is less likelihood of success. Finally, teachers themselves are increasingly faced with controlling reward structures, deadlines, constraints, surveillance, and external evaluations—all factors which we previously cited as undermining intrinsic motivation. In the same way that children, in order to remain intrinsically motivated to learn, need teachers who respond to their initiations and support their mastery attempts, teachers, in order to remain intrinsically motivated to teach, need administrators who respond to their initiations and support their mastery attempts. When administrators are more autonomy oriented, when they provide teachers with opportunities to try new things, to teach in their own ways, to choose optimal challenges, the teachers seem to be more intrinsically motivated.

Unfortunately, the condition that facilitate intrinsic motivation for teachers may be more the exception than the rule. Our interviews with teachers have suggested that there are many threats to the maintenance of their intrinsic motivation. Increasingly, they report that the demands on their time and energy are growing and that the pressures toward compliance are greater. By way of illustration, consider just one example of such pressures that came up repeatedly in our discussions with teachers, namely the movement toward standardized curricula.

The Standardized Curriculum

In the modern age there is a growing trend for what many would term "accountability." This trend impacts particularly upon educational institutions, primarily because of their accessibility to the public domain. Schools are accountable to parents, taxpayers, and governments. These interest groups seek guarantees that they are getting what they paid for, and they want the results to be tangible. An outgrowth of this movement is the increasing use of large-scale, standardized curriculum projects, standardized evaluations of students, and a massive flow of paper work to document the output of teachers.

There is, presumably, some utility to the use of these procedures. We, like the teachers we interviewed, believe that there are basic skills and understandings—things like reading and writing English or having a working familiarity with arithmetic—that children should acquire. Standardized curricula have been developed to ensure that these are acquired. Nonetheless, it appears to be the case that there are some unintended, though rather serious, consequences to the imposition of standardized curricula. In the words of an experienced teacher whom we interviewed: "Even when the required material is the same that I would have taught, I resent being told how I have to teach. It just kills my motivation for teaching."

Stated in our language, the teacher was saying that the increasing standardization robs her of the opportunity to be self-determining and that seems to be undermining her intrinsic motivation. It is difficult for her to maintain an informational, autonomy orientation when she herself feels over-controlled.

Along with the packaged curricula come increased paper work, surveillance, and evaluation. On this score the evidence is clear; if standardized curricula tend to kill interest and motivation, the increased emphasis on evaluation drives another nail in the coffin. These added demands deplete the energy of teachers who, under other conditions, might invest their efforts in the classroom, where they are needed. Increased demands in an educational environment where there are diminishing resources and fewer teacher's aides also feed into a sense of helplessness that prevents teachers from accomplishing the goals that the majority of them value most.

Insofar as standardized curricula are a given, if they are here to stay, the best that can be hoped for is that they be administered more informationally. If administrators had a less evaluative and more supportive orientation toward the teachers who have to use them, perhaps the teachers could maintain greater enthusiasm and supportiveness in teaching the material to the children. In turn, the children might be more intrinsically motivated to learn the material.

CONCLUSION

Most educators agree that an important goal of the educational process is helping students to be self-directed and interested in learning. They want children to learn the fundamentals and to use them in creative problem-solving. In motivational terms, they want children to be intrinsically motivated.

The goal of having intrinsically motivated children may be best achieved when teachers themselves are intrinsically motivated, when they are excited, involved, self-directed, and trying new things. When teachers are intrinsically motivated, they will, it seems, be more supportive of children's attempts at independence and mastery, and they will be more informational in the use of rewards and communications. The children need supportive teachers, teachers who are oriented toward autonomy, but, in order for teachers to remain autonomy oriented and to encourage intrinsic learning, they themselves will need to feel supported, they themselves will need to have opportunities to be competent and self-determining. If the climate of the educational system were to become more informational and autonomy oriented, then the various people who learn and work in the system would undoubtedly experience more intrinsic motivation for their learning and working.

REFERENCES

Ainsworth, M. D. S., Blehar, M. C., Waters, E., & Wall, S. *Patterns of attachment.* Hillsdale, NJ: Lawrence Erlbaum Associates, 1978.

Amabile, T. M., DeJong, W., & Lepper, M. R. Effects of externally imposed deadlines on subsequent intrinsic motivation. *Journal of Personality and Social Psychology,* 1976, *34,* 92–98.

Anderson, R., Manoogian, S. T., & Reznick, J. S. The undermining and enhancing of intrinsic motivation in pre-school children. *Journal of Personality and Social Psychology,* 1976, *34,* 915–922.

Aronson, E., Blaney N., Stephan, C., Sikes, J., & Snapp, M. *The jigsaw classroom.* Beverly Hills, CA: Sage, 1978.

Benware, C., & Deci, E. L. *The quality of learning with an active versus passive motivational set.* Unpublished manuscript, University of Rochester, 1981.

Blanck, P., Jackson, L., & Reis, H. T. *Effects of verbal praise on intrinsic motivation for sextyped tasks.* Paper presented at the American Psychological Association Convention, New York, September 1979.

Bowlby, J. *Attachment and loss, II. Separation: Anxiety and anger.* New York: Basic Books, 1973.

Brehm, J. W. *A theory of psychological reactance.* New York: Academic Press, 1966.

Bruner, J. S. *On knowing: Essays for the left hand.* Cambridge, MA: Harvard University Press, 1962.

Condry, J., & Koslowski, B. Can education be made intrinsically interesting to children? In L. Katz (Ed.), *Current topics in early childhood education* (Vol. 2). Norwood, NJ: Ablex Publishing Co., 1979.

deCharms, R. *Personal causation: The internal affective determinants of behavior.* New York: Academic Press, 1968.

deCharms, R. *Enhancing motivation: Change in the classroom.* New York: Irvington, 1976.

Deci, E. L. Effects of externally mediated rewards on intrinsic motivation. *Journal of Personality and Social Psychology,* 1971, *18,* 105–115.

Deci, E. L. Intrinsic motivation, extrinsic reinforcement, and inequity. *Journal of Personality and Social Psychology,* 1972, *22,* 113–120.

Deci, E. L. *Intrinsic motivation.* New York: Plenum, 1975.

Deci, E. L. *The psychology of self-determination.* Lexington, MA: D.C. Heath, 1980.

Deci, E. L., Betley, G., Kahle, J., Abrams, L., & Porac, J. When trying to win: Competition and intrinsic motivation. *Personality and Social Psychology Bulletin,* 1981, *7,* 79–83.

Deci, E. L., & Cascio, W. F. *Changes in intrinsic motivation as a function of negative feedback and threats.* Paper presented at Eastern Psychological Association Convention, Boston, 1972.

Deci, E. L., Cascio, W. F., & Krusell, J. *Sex differences, positive feedback and intrinsic motivation.* Paper presented at the Eastern Psychological Association Convention, Washington, D.C., May 1973.

Deci, E. L., Nezlek, J., & Sheinman, L. Characteristics of the rewarder and intrinsic motivation of the rewardee. *Journal of Personality and Social Psychology,* 1981, *40,* 1–10.

Deci, E. L., & Ryan, R. M. The empirical exploration of intrinsic motivational processes. In L. Berkowitz (Ed.), *Advances in experimental social psychology* (Vol. 13). New York: Academic Press, 1980.

Deci, E. L., & Ryan, R. M. Intrinsic motivation to teach: Possibilities and obstacles in our colleges and universities. In J. Bess (Ed.), *New directions for teaching and learning.* San Francisco, CA: Jossey-Bass, in press. (a).

Deci, E. L., & Ryan, R. M. *Intrinsic motivation and human behavior.* New York: Plenum, in press. (b).

Deci, E. L., Schwartz, A. J., Sheinman, L., & Ryan, R. M. An instrument to assess adults' orientations toward control versus autonomy with children: Reflections on intrinsic motivation and perceived competence. *Journal of Educational Psychology,* 1981, *73,* 642–650.

Enzle, M. E., & Ross, J. M. Increasing and decreasing intrinsic interest with contingent rewards: A test of cognitive evaluation theory. *Journal of Experimental Social Psychology,* 1978, *14,* 588–597.

Erikson, E. *Childhood and society.* New York: Norton, 1950.

Garber, J., & Seligman, M. E. P. (Eds), *Human helplessness.* New York: Academic Press, 1980.

Ginott, H. G. *Teacher and child.* New York: Avon, 1972.

Harackiewicz, J. The effects of reward contingency and performance feedback on intrinsic motivation. *Journal of Personality and Social Psychology,* 1979, *37,* 1352–1363.

Hiroto, D. S. Locus of control and learned helplessness. *Journal of Experimental Psychology,* 1974, *102,* 187–193.

Lefcourt, H. M. *Locus of control.* Hillsdale, NJ: Lawrence Erlbaum Associates, 1976.

Lepper, M. R., & Greene, D. Turning play into work: Effects of adult surveillance and extrinsic rewards on children's intrinsic motivation. *Journal of Personality and Social Psychology,* 1975, *31,* 479–486.

Lepper, M. R., Greene, D., & Nisbett, R. E. Undermining children's intrinsic interest with extrinsic rewards: A test of the "overjustification" hypothesis. *Journal of Personality and Social Psychology,* 1973, *28,* 129–137.

McGraw, K. The detrimental effects of reward on performance. In M. R. Lepper & D. Greene (Eds.), *The hidden costs of reward.* Hillsdale, NJ: Lawrence Erlbaum, Associates, 1978.

Montessori, M. *The discovery of the child.* New York: Ballentine, 1967.

Pittman, T. S., Davey, M. E., Alafat, K. A., Wetherill, K. V., & Kramer, N. A. Informational versus controlling rewards, levels of surveillance, and intrinsic motivation. *Personality and Social Psychology Bulletin,* 1980, *6,* 228–233.

Rogers, C. *Freedom to learn.* Columbus, OH: Merrill, 1969.

Rosenfield, D., Folger, R., & Adelman, H. When rewards reflect competence: A qualification of the overjustification effect. *Journal of Personality and Social Psychology,* 1980, *39,* 368–376.

Ross, M. Salience of reward and intrinsic motivation. *Journal of Personality and Social Psychology,* 1975, *32,* 245–254.

Rotter, J. B. Generalized expectancies for internal versus external control of reinforcement. *Psychological Monographs,* 1966, *80,* (1, Whole No. 609).

Ryan, R. M. Control and information in the intrapersonal sphere: An extension of cognitive evaluation theory. *Journal of Personality and Social Psychology,* in press.

Seligman, M. E. P. *Helplessness.* San Francisco, CA: Freeman, 1975.

Swann, W. B., & Pittman, T. S. Initiating play activity of children: The moderating influence of verbal cues on intrinsic motivation. *Child Development,* 1977, *48,* 1128–1132.

White, R. W. Motivation reconsidered: The concept of competence. *Psychological Review,* 1959, *66,* 297–333.

Zuckerman, M., Porac, J., Lathin, D., Smith, R., & Deci, E. L. On the importance of self-determination for intrinsically motivated behavior. *Personality and Social Psychology Bulletin,* 1978, *4,* 443–446.

5

Peer Relationship Development in Childhood*

Sherri Oden

Wheelock College

The preschool playground. Several children are playing in the sandbox. There are some giggles of fun. There are some cries. From the sidelines, the adults watch. Children's relationships with peers—whether with acquaintances, friends, classmates, or adversaries—are important influences in children's development. The influence of parents and educators in children's peer relationships is more limited than in any other developmental context; the adult can only observe, inquire, and wait to be consulted. The peer relationship is thus the most independent sphere in the child's development. Perhaps this is one of the reasons why it is so fascinating to consider, so critical to understand its significance in children's development.

Researchers of child development have often acknowledged that peer interaction is an important part of childhood, but only recently have these researchers made strides in outlining the major processes by which children become acquainted, share common experiences, coordinate activity, and get along with each other amid a variety of circumstances and over time. Accordingly, the main perspective taken in this paper is that peer relationships in childhood provide more than incidental social experiences, and constitute social contexts beyond those in the family. In the context of peer relationships, children's development continues to progress as children expand their experiences and increase their knowledge. Three major directions in this research are examined in this discussion. The first section of this chapter provides a review of the major theoretical perspectives and empirical research on children's peer relationships

---

* Paper prepared while on leave at Harvard Graduate School of Education.

in child development. In the second section, the findings of this research are related to questions that educators and parents may ask as they observe peer interaction in the classroom, home, or neighborhood. Throughout these two sections, the implications for children's social experience in the school and at home are discussed and future research directions are proposed. In the last section, the role of adults in the development of children's peer relationships is reviewed according to available evidence, and methods for supporting and instructing children in peer relationship development are discussed. Various types of curriculum activity are then examined for their potential influence on peer relationships, especially those relationships between children of different ages, races, sexes, and abilities.

THEORETICAL PERSPECTIVES ON CHILDREN'S PEER RELATIONSHIPS

There is no single theoretical model that provides a description of the critical elements and processes in children's peer relationship development. Although all the models to be discussed here are based on major child development theories (social learning, cognitive developmental, and social contextual) they differ in their fundamental assumptions about the origin, nature, and course of human development. Each model, however, offers a viewpoint on children's peer relationships that may constitute either a challenge or confirmation of our ideas as educators, parents, or researchers. This section of the paper examines a selection of these models in terms of the following question: What are the social conditions (the activities and experiences encountered by the child in the family, neighborhood, and schools) which appear to influence social, cognitive, and language development in children's peer relationships?

SOCIAL LEARNING

The major theoretical position of the social learning perspective is that children learn to seek, engage in, and benefit from peer relations in the family, neighborhood, and school through reinforcement and imitation. In addition, some theorists (e.g., Bandura, 1977; Parke, 1970) have pointed to the importance of conceptual modeling through direct or indirect instructions. According to social learning theorists, children are thought to initiate peer interaction because they are reinforced for doing so by adults, have viewed other children interacting, have received prompts or instructions, or all of these. A parent or preschool teacher may often say to a young child, "Go on, say 'Hi' to Billy" or "Go over and show your friend Alice your new toy" or "Good! You're such a friendly boy (or girl)," or when a social attempt is ignored or rebuked by a child's peer, "Maybe he'll play with you later" or "You should let Alice play with the toy, too." To parents and teachers such commentary, feedback, direction, encouragement and empathy is most often a spontaneous part of conversations with children.

Children are thus socialized to enter into and maintain peer interactions and to form friendships, and adults have some influence on that process. As children's peer contacts first begin, parents and other caregivers are in close proximity—most often on the periphery such as the same room, the kitchen, or the porch—and are available for giving attention, reinforcement, suggestions, discussion, and, if needed, direction and intervention (Ainsworth, 1973). Infants with more secure attachments to parents, compared to those with less secure attachments, have been found at age 18 months (Easterbrooks & Lamb, 1979) and at 3½ years (Waters, Wippman, & Sroufe, 1979) to be more responsive to peers.

In preschool, kindergarten, and primary school, children interact in larger peer contexts with increasingly less adult presence. As yet, little research is available on how peers in these contexts socialize each other compared to how adults socialize children. For example, Shatz and Gelman (1973) found that in mixed age peer interaction, the 4-year-old children modified the structure of their speech in order to communicate more effectively with younger children (2-year-olds). Mangione (1981) found a similar pattern among dyads of 5- and 7-year-old children. Over the course of the elementary school years, children also increasingly base their self-evaluations on comparisons with characteristics of their peers (Ruble, Baggiano, Feldman, & Loebl, 1980). Evidence from several research programs indicates that peers also socialize each other in sex role behavior (e.g., Dweck & Bush, 1976; Lamb & Roopnarine, 1979).

Further research is needed on the content of children's interactions in order to clarify to what extent children's interactions provide unique contributions to their developmental changes, or simply reinforce their already acquired behavior. To what extent, for example, does a child's new social learning extend beyond the family—the primary instrument of socialization? Peers appear to provide each other with additional sources of information and example, partly because they are not, strictly speaking, at that same level in every respect. For example, two children may differ in age, sex, ability, or interest and thus represent resources not likely to be available in a given child's own family. The peer group is thus thought by Hartup (1978) and others to expand the child's socialization.

Since peers interact over time and with increasing independence from adults, and share common territories (the sidewalk, schoolyard, classroom), they are also likely to develop their own unique standards and expectations for social behavior. Ladd and Oden (1979) interviewed third- and fifth-graders on how they would help a classmate who was being made fun of by peers, being yelled at by a peer, or having schoolwork problems. The children were also asked how they would help the classmate when he or she was alone and still unhappy after such events. Many of the helpful strategies most often suggested by children appeared to differ from the kinds of strategies adults might recommend. For example, for situations in which other peers were present, adults might recommend moralizing strategies, "I'd tell those kids that it's not nice to do that," or negotiate-mediate strategies, "I'd talk to that other kid to get him to stop." However, children in this study infrequently mentioned such strategies. Rather, order-command strategies were frequently suggested, "I'd say to those kids, 'Stop it!' " Instruct strategies were highly frequent for both the peer group and "alone with the classmate" situations. These strategies included direct instruction on how to tell teasing peers to "cut it out" or the yelling peer to "bug-off"; an explanation of what to do next time; and a demonstration of how to solve a schoolwork problem. In this study, children who lacked knowledge of which strategies were appropriate, according to peer standards, tended to be less liked by their peers as indicated by sociometric assessment. Isolation or rejection by peers may, in part, result from a lack of socialization from the peer group or from a child's reluctance to participate or cooperate with specific peer norms.

Overall, social interaction and relationship skills, from the social learning view, are developmental in that they become more extensive and complex over time as experience and learning diversifies and increases. As children have increasing opportunities to interact with particular peers, they prefer the company of particular peers. Two children may thus seek ways to increase the frequency or extend the length of time with each other, or in the course of interacting, they may simply experience stronger positive feelings and/or more ease in revealing thoughts and feelings. In this way each shares his or her individuality and a friendship relationship is thought to develop. According to the social learning perspective, these friendships should provide the opportunity for reciprocal positive reinforcement, modeling, and instruction. Hartup (1978) has pointed out that these relationships appear to be characterized by their reciprocal nature; that is, each child provides a similar degree and/or type of positive reinforcement, such as affection, encouragement, sympathy, and help. These peer dyad contexts should provide more intense socialization opportunities and, at the same time, due to the element of mutual affection, should allow more room for the expression of individuality, thus constituting an unique opportunity for peers to learn from one another. If a child had only one friend, while of great value, in the absence of other positive peer interaction, this could be too limited an experience in peer relationship development. On the other hand, it might be that such a relationship serves to launch each child into additional peer relationships.

SOCIAL COGNITION

Inspired largely by the cognitive theory of Piaget (1932), some researchers have focused on how children structure the social world and how they understand or construe what they observe, learn about, and experience. In this view, it is the growth in social thought that marks social developmental achievements. This progression is viewed as representing qualitatively different stages or levels in one or more social-cognitive domains, such as the growth of the ability to know other persons (e.g., Peevers & Secord, 1973), the ability to distinguish one's own perspective from that of another (e.g., Selman, 1981), the ability to distinguish moral from conventional problems (Turiel, 1978), and knowledge of the interpersonal world (Youniss, 1978).

According to an interpretation of Piaget's writing (1932) by Youniss (1978), "Interpersonal relations are the topic of social thought" (p. 214). According to this view, social knowledge is interactive and consists of different kinds of relations that become known through interpersonal exchanges. Thus a child learns of authority relations in interaction with parents, teachers, and other adults, and later, through interaction with peers, of equal status relations in which rules are established by cooperative agreement among equals. Youniss more specifically proposed that social interactions are functional relations and may be understood by studying how interactions operate. "Interactions serve to: (a) establish a relation; (b) keep a relation going; (c) correct a relation when it goes awry; (d) intensify a relation; (e) terminate a relation; and (f) change a relation from one mode to another" (p. 221). Particular behavioral actions may vary across these types of relations or within a given type, yet it is the growth in understanding of social processes that is the important focus here.

Children increasingly appear to gain knowledge of how to construct social interactions with peers; they learn how social interaction progresses and how to coordinate activity with others. Youniss and Volpe (1978) gathered data by interviewing children 6 to 14 years old on the subject of how friendship relations are formed, maintained, threatened, repaired, and terminated. These data indicate that with time, experience, and development, children's understanding of a friend relationship changes from one based on the sharing of physical activities, through the sharing of resources, being kind or nice to each other, especially when in need, to one based on a unique match of two different personalities. It may be helpful for teachers and parents to consider that the child's definition of friendship may differ from the adult view and yet to realize that the child's understanding is constantly undergoing exploration and revision.

For example, children's conceptions and acts of distributive justice among peers, commonly referred to as the process of dividing materials, space, and time were investigated by Damon (1979). Findings indicated an increasing ability among children to establish a fair method for the distribution of goods (for example, candy) even when a simple, equal division was not possible. Children of elementary school ages are less likely than preschoolers to keep material goods just for themselves, while older children are more likely to divide resources by some reasonably fair criterion, for example, which child tries harder. This developmental trend was found in experimental situations as well as in interviews. Studies also indicate that children who have persistent difficulty in fair distribution are likely to experience more peer conflict.

Children appear quite early to distinguish social and conventional behavior and moral issues. Turiel (in press) argues that social developmental progress does not necessarily follow in a uniform pace or direction; some domains may develop rather early and remain little changed in any fundamental sense, whereas other domains may undergo continual change. In support of this, Bigelow (1977) contends that some aspects of the friendship-making process, such as ego reinforcement and sharing with others, may continue to be important expectations of friends as children develop; other behaviors may not. Similarly, data from several studies indicate that as children develop they become increasingly aware of psychological dispositions and personality characteristics (e.g., Livesley & Bromley, 1973), and of the difference between intentions and actions (Baldwin & Baldwin, 1970); even at quite young ages, they appear to have these capabilities to some degree. Turiel (in press) argues that there is not one central social cognitive system, but different rule systems for different cognitive domains which are not directly dependent or structurally interrelated. Thus, while progress in a child's understanding of moral issues may affect his social conventional understanding, the one would not determine the other. Conventional issues include manners, styles of dress, and so forth, whereas moral issues pertain to respect for another person's rights and physical welfare.

As children's social development progresses, they become less egocentric; that is, they become increasingly able to see or comprehend a perspective other than their own. The growing capacity for social perspective-taking, originally discussed by Piaget, may undergo stage-like changes as Selman (1981) argues, or may be a social interaction method as Turiel suggests. In either case, role-taking is an important ability evidenced early in children's development that has been found to undergo considerable change with time and experience (Selman, 1981). To understand, predict, or anticipate another person's likely feelings, attitudes, and actions is dependent on the ability to see both shared characteristics or similarity between oneself and another, and to know there are differences. The social perspective-taking process seems to require the ability to find ways to learn about the differences between oneself and another, communicate about these differences, and deal with them.

Some researchers have recently viewed social-cognitive processes as social inference or reasoning processes centering mainly on the ability to comprehend psychological motives behind actions, to accurately attribute causes, and to predict likely consequences of social actions and likely actions of another person in a given circumstance (see Shantz, 1975, for a review). Among the more compelling proposals, Stein and her colleagues (e.g., Stein & Goldman, 1981) propose that much of the way social events are understood and organized at a cognitive level may be in a narrative structure. In this model, children learn to solve social problems in much the same way they comprehend and process the elements of a story, which include consideration of the setting, the initiating event of the story, the internal responses and reactions of the main character, attempts by the main character to overtly deal with a problem or to seek a goal, and the consequences of these actions for the main character.

In sum, the social cognition perspective emphasizes the role of growth in the social-cognitive processes involved in the child's social development. In this view, the nature and course of a child's peer relationships are determined not simply by the child's previous learning, but also by his or her cognitive approach to the social world that influences peer interactions and relationships. At the same time, however, experience with peers presents continued challenges to the child's assumptions about the workings of the social world.

SOCIAL CONTEXT

The major focus of the social contextual perspective theorists (even more so than social learning and cognitive perspective theorists) is on the social context. Social contextual perspective theorists comprise an interdisciplinary group which includes anthropologists, ethnologists, psychologists, sociologists, and linguists within psychology and sociology. Although these researchers differ in their interpretation of the particular kind of role the social context has in children's relationship development, the importance of studying the various systems in the child's peer contexts is stressed.

According to the social contextual view, a given social context is thought to differ in its structure and specific mechanisms from other contexts and may thus define, limit, or structure the nature and purpose of particular peer relationships. Denzin (1977) argues that to fully achieve a theory of the relationship between self and society, a theory must clarify the childhood socialization process. To Argyle (1969), the study of small group process is particularly important to the understanding of social interaction. Children and adults experience several different groups—the family, school (or work) groups, and friendship groups, each of which differs in its purpose, membership, structure of authority, procedure, and status hierarchy. Children thus learn to operate in a number of different school, neighborhood, and friend groups.

The social experience and conduct of children also reflects a given culture. According to Much and Sweder (1978), the cultural process involves "situations of accountability" in which cultural control and negotiation take place. When some "breach of social expectation" occurs, an accusation may be made, an explanation or account requested, and an evaluation provided which includes a cultural rule or message. Much and Sweder propose that there are at least five rule types: "(1) regulations (or laws); (2) conventions (or customs); (3) morals (or ethics); (4) truths (or beliefs); and (5) instructions (techniques, recipes, or 'know-how')" (p. 19). For example, a child is likely to learn or be reminded that there is a rule against stepping ahead of a peer in line when he or she actually breaks that rule, or that hurting someone physically is wrong when the moral rule is violated. Similarly, regarding social conventions, a child may learn that to his peers he talks too loudly, wears funny clothes, or eats sloppily. Much and Sweder point out, however, that there is continual negotiation within groups as to which kind of behaviors are different, but acceptable, or not acceptable, tolerable or intolerable, morally right or wrong, allowable or not allowable, correct or incorrect.

A particular feature of peer interaction is participation in negotiation processes. Corsaro (1981) proposes that children have far more opportunity to negotiate in the peer context than in the family context. The children may select which peers they prefer to interact with and negotiate with by weighing their personal needs with the social context. Corsaro conducted an observational study of peer interaction in a nursery school over a year's time. He found that children's peer activities in the nursery school context were continually susceptible to disruption, either from other peers wanting to join an activity or use the materials, or from a change in the overall activity of the curriculum schedule. In this context, which Corsaro compared to an adult cocktail party, friendship making seemed more a function of the mutual ease with which two children could initiate or join an activity, and perhaps negotiate how to resume it at a later time or protect the activity, their "interactive space," from continual invasions. Personal characteristics of playmates may have little importance to friends in this type of context unless the friendship is additionally pursued after school.

Negotiation is also integral to games and activities. Fine (1981) studied preadolescent boys who participated in little league baseball in several communities. His observations confirmed the importance of 'chums,'' as Sullivan (1953) originally referred to preadolescent male friends. At this point in development and in these contexts boys learn to negotiate their roles in games and other activities. They master such techniques for "getting along" as threatening, trading favors, using reason, "backing off," or "leaving the field." Through such activities, preadolescents develop considerable self-presentation skills in which they come to discover what Cooley (1902) originally called the social self-concept (knowledge of how one is perceived by others), and at the same time learn how to communicate personal views of themselves to peers.

Activities which enhance participation of children in peer interaction are thus important to children's peer relationship development. The research of Hallinan (1981) and Hallinan and Tuma (1978), for example, indicate that small group activities foster the development of friendships. What, then, are the elements of contexts such as activities, games, and discussions which contribute to relationship development? Sociolinguistic and pragmatic perspectives on the communication process have recently presented additional approaches toward gaining a greater understanding of the social meaning of these interactions. For example, Garvey and Hogan (1973) propose that children's early orientation to activities may promote the acquisition and use of verbal forms of interpersonal contact, and that, as children develop language and learn methods to converse and sustain verbal interaction, activities become less important.

A critical skill in discussion context is turn-taking. The research of Ervin-Tripp (1979) and others on how children learn to take turns in conversations illustrates some of the specific pragmatics of language actually used in children's social interaction. (Bates, 1976, refers to pragmatics as having to do with the rules that direct the use of language in context.) These researchers demonstrate that learning to take turns in conversations involves learning the rules for how to begin, sustain, and terminate conversations. Conversational skills, however, also include the application of shared meaning; for example, by clarifying or repairing miscommunications and by asking questions in both direct and indirect forms.

The child also learns that conversational techniques such as interrupting the speaker, changing the subject, or proposing a topic may indicate which person has the greater authority in a conversation, as in parent-child or teacher-child discussions. Other conversations are characterized by a "balance" between peers, or by peer competition. Mishler (1979), who analyzed the conversations of 6-year-old children as they were bargaining to trade popcorn and cookies, proposed that it was important to consider the social context of the conversation, that of bargaining for a trade, in order to understand and predict the structure of the conversation and the meaning of the interaction. He concluded that the children's conversations in the context of trading are structured around not giving the upper hand to other children, which is signalled by being the first one to offer the trade. Researchers in future studies could similarly assess conversational structures in friendship-making contexts. For example, it would be interesting to determine how much peers like each other, or in a conflict of interest situation to assess whether the friendship relationship has an effect. Conversational structure may also provide insight into the status of the relationship, that is, to what extent the children are friends, strangers, and so forth. Studies of mixed-age interaction (e.g., Garvey & Hogan, 1973; Mangione, 1981; Shatz & Gelman, 1973) have found that language patterns of mixed- and same-age peers differ in that older children will modify the complexity of their speech to approximate that of younger children.

The social contextual view of children's peer relationship development thus focuses on peer relationships as contexts in which the child learns to operate. The three perspectives reviewed, however, have common threads—the reciprocal nature of human relations, the increasing role of peers in children's behavioral and cognitive development, the role of the larger social environment in children's peer experiences, and, most important, the further contributions of peer relationships to the child's development beyond the family as additional sources of modeling, information, feedback, challenge, and support.

THE VARIETY OF CHILDREN'S PEER RELATIONSHIPS

The discussion of recent research on children's peer relationships will now proceed with an emphasis on the research findings rather than the theoretical conceptions. The findings are organized according to the information and implications they provide for educators and parents on the variety of children's peer relationships.

Strangers and Newcomers

How do Children Get to Know Each Other? Studies with very young children have recorded that even at 1 year of age children show a definite interest in other children (Lee, 1975; Lewis, Young, Brooks, & Michalson, 1975). Lewis et al. (1975) conducted one of the few studies on peer interaction among infants. In the basic study, 16 groups of four infants were observed with their mothers in a room. One half of the group of children were 12 months and the other half were 18 months of age. Although the infants stayed near their mothers, both age groups looked more at the peers than at the mothers. In a second study, children of approximately 12 months of age were paired with either a "friend" or a stranger peer for two sessions. The "friends" were infants who had had a minimum contact of two occasions during the previous two weeks. The infants were more likely to touch, seek proximity, look at, and imitate the familiar peer than the unfamiliar peer. In a study by Mueller and Lucas (1975), young children's reciprocal interaction was found to be facilitated by mutual interest in toys and other physical objects. Mueller and Brenner (1977) found a similar pattern in a 7-month longitudinal study of children from 12 to approximately 18 months of age. In this study, they also found that the familiar peers engaged in more sustained peer interactions, which in turn facilitated the development of their social skills, thereby enabling them to further sustain their interactions.

At first, a child who is a newcomer to a group of other children may be physically and verbally quite reticent (McGrew, 1972). Considerable time may be spent with the newcomer and his or her peers looking at each other. In McGrew's study of nursery school children, the newcomer children tended to make consistent strides across the first five days toward participation in the classroom activity, and, although their general physical mobility increased, their verbal interaction was not markedly different. A follow-up observation, several months later, indicated that the children who had been newcomers were behaving and participating in the same ways and with the same frequencies as the other children. Foote, Chapman, and Smith (1977) studied 7- and 8-year-old children who were either friend or stranger pairs as they watched a comedy film. The children who were strangers were much more constrained in their behavior in general and toward each other than were the friend pairs. Newcomb, Brady, and Hartup (1979) found that in both competitive and cooperative task situations, first- and third-grade children paired with either a friend or nonfriend classmate were far more animated in the friend pairs. Gottman and Parkhurst (1979) found similar trends among 13 young children (from 2 to 6 years) who were paired with either their best friend or with a stranger. In this study, friends were more likely to participate in conversation rather than a collective monologue and to engage in fantasy play.

In a recent study designed to determine the social processes occurring during children's initial acquaintanceship, Oden, Herzberger, Mangione, and Wheeler (1981) observed 5-, 6-, and 7-year-old, same-age, same-sex dyads who were strangers to each other prior to the beginning of the study. The children were paired to play with art materials on five successive days for brief periods of time, and their interactions were video-taped from behind a two-way mirror. The children's interactions, especially in the initial sessions, reflected a wariness between the peers (a finding consistent with previous such investigations with younger children). The transcriptions of their conversations showed that the children tended to become more comfortable and less constrained, more interested in each other's activity, and more interested in getting to know one another as the sessions progressed.

Overall, the findings from several studies show that infants, preschool, and primary school age children tend to "hang back" at first when confronted with an unfamiliar peer. It may be that the children test out the potential for a friendly versus an unfriendly response, or are simply uncertain of how to proceed. Parents and teachers are often observed encouraging children to get to know each other by telling them to say hello, say their names, or invite each other to participate in an activity. Such encouragement appears to be a source of children's learning how to initiate interaction in the early phases of peer acquaintance, but it seems important not to criticize children for their wariness or hesitation when faced with an unknown peer in the interest of encouraging children to become friends.

Friends and Best Friends

How do Children Become Friends? As discussed earlier, several researchers (e.g. Damon, 1979; Selman, 1981; Youniss, 1978) have investigated children's conceptions of friendship. These researchers found that younger children (before the age of 9) say their friends are those with whom they play and share things, whereas in middle childhood (9 to 10 years) friends are those who like each other and help each other. Among preadolescents, friends are those who understand each other and share personal thoughts, feelings, and secrets. Selman proposes that the social role-taking or perspective-taking process is the central mechanism by which this progression in friendship occurs. Youniss focuses more on children's increasing ability to collaborate and reciprocate—in short, to interact mutually. However, each investigator stresses children's ability to like one another and to form affectional bonds as essential features of friendship development, a contention supported in the study by Oden et al. (1981). These researchers found that, when asked, elementary school age children suggested that liking to play together and having fun were important bases of friendships.

Although young children may have difficulty articulating and/or recalling to adults what they think about in the friendship-making process, the 5-, 6- and 7-year-old children in the Oden et al. (1981) study appeared to be quite aware of the specific actions of each other throughout the five play sessions. This study revealed that children begin to know each other by sharing information, including information about self, family, and friends, their activities, interests, values, and personal characteristics. At the same time, they develop ways to allow for individual activity by sharing materials and space, and taking turns. Children also explore the possibility of joint activity by attempting to plan what, where, when, and how they might do something of mutual interest. During an activity, children also share general knowledge and information, and provide assistance or support. Throughout, children attempt to discover or even test out the personal and emotional characteristics of each other by teasing, direct inquiry, or openly showing or stating feelings and attitudes. Children are also likely to discover the limitations of a developing relationship and may need to find ways to prevent or alleviate disagreements or conflicts. The following conversations from the transcripts of the Oden et al. (1981) study illustrate the acquaintance process observed. The more common questions children asked each other and which set the "getting acquainted" process in motion were about age or grade. For example:

Child A	Child B
How old are you?	
	Six and a half.
So am I. I'll be seven.	
My birthday is . . . on . . .	
	Ooh. This is sticky clay.
Six more years and I'll be sixteen.	
Yeah. Seven more years I'll be seven-	
teen. Three more years I'll be . . . thir-	
teen. One more year, I'll be seven.	
	Me too.

* * * * * *

Child A	Child B
	What grade are you in?
Second.	
	I'm in—I'm in first.

Child A	**Child B**
Did you—did you flunk kindergarten?	
	How did you know?
Your mother—my mother told—your mother told my mother and my mother told me. My friend, she's eight years old and she's in second grade. Shouldn't she be in third grade?	
	Yes. She flunked.

* * * * * *

As the children were becoming acquainted, considerable portions of their conversations revolved around planning individual and joint activities and ways to use the materials. Some had few problems agreeing on matters, while others had to negotiate.

Child A	**Child B**
Oh, these are the pens that go with it.	
	I wanna do it. I wanna do it, too! Hold it, we can share these.
I want this—I want the other one.	
	You can use anything you want. Oh, look, why don't you use this?
That's chalk and I don't wanna play with chalk.	
	Me neither. (Sings) I'm gonna draw something. Hold it.
We gotta share the markers. The mark— the markers go with this (pointing to own materials) anyways.	
	Why don't you use these? They're better than these . . . (points to other markers).
I want to use those. (Points to B's markers)	
	I'm using these.
We'll share those . . . Yeah.	
	We got two packs.
So?	
	Hold it. These two packs are more than one pack.
I know I want the—(starting to escalate voice) We share.	
	Shh. We . . . share.

* * * * * *

The children in this study found ways to interact constructively, and in most cases their mutual liking increased. Several dyads also increasingly exchanged information about each other, shared their activity, and planned to maintain the relationship after completion of the study.

In one of the sessions, a more structured art activity was provided via a battery-operated toy which spun a small sheet of paper around as each child used magic marker pens to make circular designs. The toy was highly attractive to the children and use of it appeared to present considerable challenges to all the children to distribute turns equitably. An in-depth analysis was then conducted in a second study to examine the conflict resolution processes among children who are just getting to know each other (see Oden et al., 1981). This situation appeared to provide a socialization experience for some children.

Child A	**Child B**
	I'm gonna do it.
You're not gonna do it!	
	Yeah, I am.
Billy! It's mine!	
	This is mine!
Would you (mumbles) . . . all right! I quit! I'm not doin' nothin'.	
	But you got it. You had a turn.
You always . . . I didn't even do anything!	
	Yeah, you did.
What?	
	A design.
Nothin'—I didn't, I didn't do nothin'.	
	Yeah you did, keep it on!
No, I didn't. Bill—all right!	
	All that, all that I was tryin' to do. . . .
Well, let me have a turn!	
	All that I was tryin'—I . . . you got a turn.
I did not! (screams and throws down a pillow)	
	Yeah, you did.
No, I didn't, I . . .	
	Stop arguing. Don't yell—see that tape recorder? Just . . . you can do it now. We have to share, ya know.
Yeah (mumbles) but you gotta give me a turn.	
	I did give you a turn.
What'd ya call that thing? Nothin'. I don't	

like it. If I don't like it let me have another turn.

        Ya can't always have your . . . your way.

I know that, but . . .

*(Child B sets up paper
for Child A to use)*

        The first time is neat. Don't try to chop
off the tops.

Chop off the tops?

        Yeah. Like these parts. Like this part
right here. Why don't you try short-stop?

Kay . . . Where's red?

        Red! I think this is red.

Gimme a purple.

        Hey, these might work. These work.

Aw, look what I did in the middle!

        Oh great. Wanna try green? Here's a
green.

I—I'm trying grey.

        Tiny green now.

Wait—I'm gonna see what it looks like.
But I'm gonna turn it back on, okay?

        Yeah, but then it's my turn.

All right . . .

*   *   *   *   *   *

Interestingly, by the end of the 10-minute session, children in most dyads had shared the toy to a nearly equal extent of time, even though they switched the toy back and forth for varying lengths of time. Also, nearly every dyad worked out a system allowing for the child awaiting his or her turn to participate in some way, for example, handing the pens or selecting colors. The potential for a lack of equity was a critical issue here and may be a critical issue in enhancing or detracting from friendship building (see Wheeler, 1981). Among those children who seemed to be forming friendships in the current study, situations involving conflicts of interest did seem to present a catalyst of sorts:

Child A	**Child B**
	It's my turn.
I'm gonna show this to my Dad. You want me to turn it on? Cause we're best friends, right?	
	No, I'm not ready. Okay, now . . .

We're best friends, right? So we could
turn it on. It's fun. It's fun. Isn't it a lot
of fun? Ooo, I need more paper. No, too
much paper. Huh,
Waa! Yours is gonna be much better.

I can still fit a lot of colors in.

Yeah. Oooh. That's pretty.
I'm gonna put some on the outside.

Nice. Okay.

Oh, I'm sorry for being in the way.

I hope this turns out.

Please use black. It's pretty. See.

I don't want to use black.

It's real pretty. Please it's really pretty.

Okay.

See? It's pretty.

It makes the picture pretty. I know.

Oh, that's pretty.

But it's gonna turn out awful. It is awful.

No, just . . . no it's not gonna turn awful. See? See that.

You have . . . three, right? I have two.
Can I do another one? Right now.

Right now? You could do somethin' else.
Why don't you do somethin' else. Cause
friend do . . . don't play really all that
together . . . like . . . you know.

Well you're my . . . you know, best
friend that I can play with. Cause I don't
have any other friends in the neighborhood. Hey, want to get each other's address.
I'll give you my address . . .

I don't know my, um, address, but . . .
(gives phone number).

Give me your phone number then. I'll rip
this piece of paper in half. You write it
down and I'll write it down. . . .

All right . . .

*(Children quickly write
down phone numbers.)*

You better get goin' on your picture.

All right, now, here's mine.

* * * * * *

Gottman and Parkhurst (1979) stress the importance of studying the interactions of actual friends. From their data on preschoolers, they have formulated a model which they suggest may predict whether young children will become friends. In this hierarchical model, Gottman and Parkhurst propose that the application of specific social skills is important if children are to begin to develop a friendship. The first skill in the model is the ''connectedness'' of the dyad's conversation and the clarity of their communication. The second skill is conversation that leads to establishing similarity in interests, feelings, and so forth. Third, when a ''common ground'' and agreements are solidly established, ''contrasts'' or individual differences between the children become interesting to them. The ability to resolve conflicts and have squabbles ''burn out'' appears to be important throughout the friendship-making process. The final level is the ability of the children to interact in fantasy play, including role-playing, playing monsters, television characters, and so forth. In these interactions, the children can express feelings, explore differences, test each other's patience and limits, and resolve conflicts in less threatening ways.

Gottman and Parkhurst also suggest that older children participate more in ''activity talk,'' which may indicate that they are less interested in making new friends and/or in mastering the friendship making process. This proposal remains to be explored, however. It may be that older children are more activity oriented as a function of the nature of the school context. Activities in school environments may receive increasing focus and the friendship-making process may thus become more integrated into the structure of the classroom, the schoolyard, and planned games.

If Gottman and Parkhurst's model is valid, a large degree of similarity between individuals seems important in childhood friendships as it is in adult interpersonal attraction (Berscheid & Walster, 1969). Reviews by Asher, Oden, and Gottman (1977) and Hartup (1978) reported on a number of correlational studies which found that children like or prefer to play with or be friends with children who are similar to them in personal status characteristics such as age, sex, race, and cultural background. However, Hartup pointed to the fact that children do have friends of different ages and might have more of these friendships if environments such as classrooms were differently structured. Singleton and Asher (1979) found that cross race interactions became more positive with greater opportunity to interact, although friendships were not really increased. Serbin, Tonick, and Stenglanz (1977) found that when opposite sex interactions were encouraged by teachers, they increased. Perhaps it is only when interaction between children of a different age, sex, or race is actually encouraged that children may discover similarity and attraction, and develop friendships with each other. It seems unfortunate that characteristics other than behavior or personality should constrain children from getting to know another who may potentially become a friend.

In summary, the process from acquaintance to friend may be a gradual one and the particular issues that emerge as important may vary according to the children's developmental level, previous experiences, or individual personalities, values, and interests. It appears that children may become friends and best friends when they have sufficient opportunities to get to know each other. Even where such opportunities exist, children may need to be encouraged to look beyond obvious differences and find a common ground to which they can relate. Providing children with activities that are likely to be interesting to both or many children may be helpful. Encouraging children to learn more about each other may also help children focus on more substantive issues. Educators and parents are likely to find that children will seek their help for clarification and information about how to unravel a misunderstanding or resolve a conflict. On such occasions, adults can help a child express his or her ideas and feelings, discover ways to learn the other child's perspective, and examine solutions that take into account both children's perspectives. (Further discussion of the adult role in peer relationships is provided in the last section of this chapter.)

Acquaintances, Playmates and Classmates

Do Children Have Many Friends? Several investigators, using sociometric questionnaires, have investigated the number of children's friends, especially in school (Asher & Hymel, in press; Gronlund, 1959; Hallinan, 1981; Singleton & Asher, 1979). According to research conducted by Asher and his colleagues, approximately 5 to 10% of elementary school children are not named by any of their classmates as a best friend on sociometric questionnaires. For example, 23 out of 205 third- through fifth-graders in one sample received no nominations as an "especially liked" friend. Of the 23 children, 11 children received no negative nominations from same sex peers. A child could therefore be well liked or accepted by peers, but have no close or best friends in a given classroom. Further, a child could have one or more best friends and be quite disliked by some other classmates, and so forth. According to Peery (1979), children can be popular, amiable, isolated, or rejected.

Although most children in school do have one or more close or best friends either in their classroom, in another classroom, or elsewhere (in the neighborhood, in a club), there has been insufficient attention to the other types of peer relationships that a child experiences. A child's constellation of peer relationships may be differentiated according to familiarity, attraction, and liking, and according to whether the attraction or liking is reciprocal or unidirectional. First, peers with whom a child interacts include the peers he or she finds attractive, peers he or she does not find attractive, and peers he or she has overlooked. Finally, among playmates, a child may have one or more best or close friends and may even have an adversary or two. Considering the complexity of the possible types and levels of children's peer relationships, part of a child's peer social development is likely to include his or her investigating and understanding the range of possibilities. More research is needed on the social-cognitive and behavioral processes inherent in the range of children's peer relationships.

Cooper, Ayers-Lopez, and Marquis (in press) have stressed the importance of studying peers in teaching and collaborating roles. In peer socialization, children, including those not considered as friends, appear to be resources for each other for instruction, information, and evaluation. The one-fourth to one-half of peer interaction in which there is a more modest degree of liking or attraction is also a part of children's peer relations, as indicated in studies employing sociometric analyses. Hallinan and Tuma (1978), for example, employed a sociometric questionnaire in 18 upper elementary school classrooms in which children were asked to indicate their best friends, friends, and nonfriends. The data revealed that 49% of the children's choices were in the friend category, with the other half split between the best friend and nonfriend categories. Fine's study (1981) of preadolescent boys in little league baseball found that 18% of the possible relationships were rated as close friends, 31% as friends, and 2% disliked, leaving 47% who were neither friends nor disliked.

Peer relationships are thus varied in their degree of liking and purpose of the interactions. It may be that learning to interact cooperatively in an activity with another child who is not a friend and may not be especially likeable or attractive is an important early experience for constructive participation in work or recreational activities in adulthood. Furthermore, when children are encouraged to learn to interact with many children, more equal opportunity for all children to participate in the full range of academic experiences in school is enhanced, and some children may also increase their pool of potential peer relationships.

Cliques and Cohesive Groups

What Types of Peer Groups do Children Form and What is The Influence of Membership in Such Groups? Research has indicated that cliques (mutual friend groups) do exist among elementary school children, often as a function of mutual preference for friends of the same age, sex, and race, as discussed in the previous sections and further by Asher et al. (1977) and Schofield (1981). Hallinan (1979) studied classroom cliques (mutual friend groups) from over 60 fourth- through sixth-grades and found that 29% of the classrooms had no cliques at all. More cliques were found in the sixth-grade; larger sized classrooms had more and larger cliques. However, the majority of the cliques were not stable in peer membership across the school year. (Interestingly, the type of classroom organization—for example, open, traditional—did not appear to be related to the existence or stability of cliques.)

According to the cognitive-developmental perspective (e.g., Turiel, in press), children might not begin to explore the concept of a group, including its purpose and membership requirements, until middle childhood, when cognitive operations are more advanced. It is during this period of childhood that clubs, for example, have been observed to become more interesting to children. Hallinan's research (1981) indicates that, in this culture, boys are much more likely to form groups of three or more friends, whereas girls appear to elect dyadic friends, although they do participate in group activities. Research on actual peer groups and their development in the social context is important, and to date quite overlooked. Studies should focus not only on friend groups, but also on "work" groups. The implications of such research would be informative to educators, in particular, but might also clarify some relationships between social and cognitive processes.

When children are given more opportunities to mix in group activities and helped to participate, especially in discussions, they may gain greater knowledge and understanding of each other. Friendships may then develop and thereby enhance the cohesiveness of more diverse peer groups. Hallinan and Tuma's (1978) study of 18 elementary classrooms found that those children who had the same reading teacher, and who also spent greater time in reading groups over the course of the school year, tended to develop more friendships in their group. Friendships were enhanced from nonfriend to friend status and from friend to best friend status without a decline in other best friendships. An evaluation of two first grade classrooms found similar results (Moss & Oden, 1980). In each classroom, two groups listened to stories read to them by the teacher twice a week over a six week period. They then participated in a discussion of each story's structure, including a discussion of the language, setting, characters, plot, problem or conflict events, attempts toward solution, motivation of the characters, and the overall purpose of the story. One of the groups in each classroom listened to stories about making friends and getting along with others, while the other group listened to stories about the difficulties of bears living in the natural habitat. A third group in each classroom listened to both sets of stories, but were asked only for their initial reaction to the stories. Children in the groups which had discussion, regardless of the content of the stories listened to, increased their mutual liking ratings of group members on posttest sociometric assessments. The group which did not participate in discussions slightly decreased their mutual liking ratings of group members. Cherry-Wilkinson and Dollaghan (1979), who examined the language used by children in first grade reading group discussions, offer some explanation as to why discussions increase liking of group members. They found that discussion contexts provide opportunities for children to experiment with strategies for more effective communication with their peers.

Although little is known about group experience in children's peer relationship development, it seems that children tend to form groups, as they do friendships, largely on the basis of similarity in salient personal characteristics, such as race, cultural background, and physical capability. This tendency may be especially isolating for children who differ from classmates or neighbors on one or more characteristics that place them in the minority. Even where there are several children of some particular characteristic or similar characteristics in a classroom, peer groups may become polarized as each group has difficulty interacting with "those other kids." Groups based on same sex or race are the most common examples of this tendency. Again, as noted above, when children are encouraged to interact with each other, such barriers may give way to the formation of more diverse, yet cohesive peer groups.

Adversaries and Isolates

Why Are Some Children Disliked or Alone? Some children do seem more likely than others to become engaged in an adversary relationship with their peers. Numerous studies have used observational methods and sociometric questionnaires to identify children who often seem to be at the center of fights, arguments, and other such social activity (e.g., Johnston, Deluca, Murtaugh, & Diener, 1977), and children who appear to be disengaged from their peers, on the periphery of peer interaction and relationships or, as Gottman (1977) described, "hovering."

The nature of the isolation experience of some children may also be variable. A child sometimes, for example, might interact negatively with peers and at other times remain quite uninvolved or withdrawn from peer interactions. These children may lack knowledge of how to effectively interact with their peers. Children may also interact negatively with peers mainly in specific types of circumstances—for example, group discussion—or with a specific peer group in the classroom. Putallaz and Gottman (1981) recently conducted research which illustrated that many children who were not well accepted by peers behaved as though they were newcomers to a setting, that is, unaware of peer norms and conventions for interaction. Even when they were interacting with children of similar low peer status, their behavior proceeded in a fashion that seemed likely to bring on rejection or negative interaction. Perhaps some children are self-defeating as a function of past experiences in their family and/or with peers who were rejecting toward them; they expect to be rejected. In some cases, children may simply lack socialization of basic norms and moral actions either from their family or from infrequent peer relationships that have the continuity of friendships. As indicated earlier, Ladd and Oden (1979) found that in middle childhood the children who were less liked by peers also tended to be less aware of peer norms for being helpful to their peers.

It is important to conduct research on the origins of peer social isolation to determine the duration of the isolation, and the original and current causes, including the critical situations and behavioral characteristics that lead to such isolation. Although children who are not well liked or accepted by peers may not share an equivalent profile, they do share an equivalent problem—isolation from positive peer interactions, relationships, and socialization.

Recent research on social skills instructional methods with low-accepted and isolated children has indicated that interventions are helpful. Several intervention studies have instructed low-accepted children in positive social behaviors (e.g., joining activities, sharing materials, taking turns, asking questions, offering useful suggestions), and have provided structured opportunities for peer interaction resulting in improvement in the children's peer acceptance (Gottman, Gonso, & Schuler, 1976; Gresham & Nagle, 1980; Ladd, 1981; Oden & Asher, 1977). A variety of research and educational interventions have been found helpful to children's overall social development, and these methods may be employed by teachers, parents, and counselors with children who have difficulty in peer relationships (Cartledge & Milburn, 1980; Furnam, Rahe, & Hartup, 1979; Roedell, Slaby, & Robinson, 1977; Shure & Spivack, 1978; Stocking, Arezzo, & Leavitt, 1980). Some of the intervention methods may be incorporated into educational and parenting methods to enhance children's peer relationships or to prevent or attenuate persistent problematic peer relationships.

Some children may not lack social skills but because they differ, as noted earlier, on some salient characteristic (race, cultural background, sex) they may encounter social rebuffs or neglect from peers—a situation that can lead to isolation, segregation, or mutual antagonism (see Scholfield, 1981). Similarly, several studies (e.g., LaGreca & Mesibov, 1979) have found that children who have some physical or learning disability, and who are then "mainstreamed" into a classroom with peers of more typical development, may not be accepted by these children.

When isolation from peer relationships is a stable condition, as some data indicates it can be (e.g., Oden & Asher, 1977), children are limited in their overall developmental experience. Some evidence indicates that social isolation or problematic peer relationships in childhood may be related to social and emotional difficulty in young adulthood (e.g., Cowen, Pederson, Babigian, Izzo, & Trost, 1973). There is no available evidence, however, that *positive* peer relationships in childhood constitute a foundation for or have some influence on future positive relationships in adulthood. This would be an interesting direction for future research.

SUPPORT AND INSTRUCTION FOR CHILDREN'S PEER RELATIONSHIPS

The role of educators and and parents in children's peer relationship development depends upon many factors, including cultural values, current social issues, the individual child, the peer group, and the curriculum. Although some parents may feel that the teacher should have a limited role in their children's social development, peer social experience does take place within the teacher's sphere in day care centers, preschools, in the classroom, on the playground, and at camp, scouts, and little league. Yet the parent's role also continues to be a factor in children's social development. Children's peer relationship development in school is also likely to be affected by major social events in the society—for example, the integration of children with diverse racial and cultural membership, mainstreaming of children with physical or learning difficulties, changing sex role expectations, and the increasing use of media and computers in the classroom. The major focus of this section, however, is the role of adults in children's peer relationship development. The adult's participation in children's peer relationships includes two major roles: (1) an adult person, experienced and knowledgeable about social interaction and relationships with peers; and (2) the architect and director of the curriculum and activity context in which children interact with peers.

Support and Instruction from Educators and Parents

What do you say to a child who tells you, "No one likes me at school," or "Jennifer and I had a fight," or "Mike's not my friend anymore," or "Alan's always bossing me around!" A supportive style of communication in discussions about a child's peer relationships is probably a necessary beginning element (see Stocking et al., 1980, for a review). Reinforcing or praising children's positive social interaction with peers is likely to enhance communication and discussion, while the use of sarcasm or interruption are likely to block effective communication (see Robin, Kent, O'Leary, Foster, & Prinz, 1977). Parents and teachers should also ensure that their discussions of peer relationships with children are relevant to the children's levels of development and understanding. At the same time, however, adults should avoid platitudes like, "Oh, everybody likes you," "He'll forget about it," or "You'll feel better tomorrow." Usually, after some questioning and some listening, an adult will readily find a response that satisfies the child's search for a caring, interested, listening, and reassuring adult. Essentially, in these discussions, according to research in child development, the adult is both a model and a coach who helps the child toward an understanding of social interaction and relationship formation processes.

Methods for enhancing discussions with children may be discovered by comparing ideas with other adults. A number of such methods, however, have been examined by researchers. Some methods have been applied in schools, and their effectiveness has been evaluated. Other methods have been applied as a part of research studies, but constitute models which may be adapted for various situations according to the individual child and adult, the particular peer group, or the particular situation. Several methods are highly similar in that they engage the child in learning to describe, propose, and evaluate aspects of social interaction and relationship formation. More specifically, key features of these methods include:

(1) Describing a problem or event (e.g., a fight, trying to join a group, being teased);

(2) Describing one's own feelings, behaviors, and perspectives;

(3) Considering the likely perspective of the other peer or peer group;

(4) Suggesting a number of strategies that are potential solutions to a "problem" (e.g., a quarrel) or potential means of attaining a goal (e.g., making friends);

(5) Considering the likely impact of a strategy for oneself and the other peer or peer group.

A number of researchers have examined the critical features of such discussion methods in order to determine why they are effective. Meichenbaum and Goodman (1971) and Bash and Camp (1980) consider a critical feature to be the "talking-out-loud" aspects which children increasingly learn to do on their own before taking a course of action. In this way, children are likely to behave less impulsively and with more judiciousness prior to such action. Spivack and Shure (1974) and Shure and Spivack (1978) characterize these types of discussions between adult and child as "dialoguing," in which the child learns to think about how to rectify his or her problematic social behavior before selecting a course of action. The problem-solving process includes thinking of alternative solutions, thinking of the consequences of such actions, and means-ends thinking, that is, ways to put plans into action. Several social problem-solving scripts and programs, along with opportunities to try out actions, have been found effective in enhancing positive social behavior of children (see Urbain & Kendall, 1980).

Methods which are highly similar to social problem-solving methods, but have been applied more specifically to enhancing peer interaction, are referred to as "coaching" or social skill instruction. As previously discussed, these methods have been effective interventions with children found to be low in peer acceptance or to have a few friendships in school. In this research (Covill-Servo, 1982; Gresham & Nagle, 1980; Ladd, 1981; Oden, 1980; Oden & Asher, 1977), children participate in a number of "coaching" sessions in which they are first instructed by an adult in social skill concepts that are correlated with peer acceptance measures and represent general norms for social behaviors with peers. For example, Oden and Asher (1977) instructed children in the following social skills for playing a game with another child: participation (getting started in a game or activity, paying attention), cooperation (taking turns, sharing materials), communication (talking with the other child, listening), and validation-support, referred to as friendly, fun, and nice (being friendly, offering help or encouragement). Each child was then given an opportunity to play a game with a classmate. Following this, the adult and child reviewed the social skills previously instructed in light of the peer play experience (see Oden, 1980, for further details). Elements of the Oden and Asher study were replicated by Gresham and Nagel (1980) and Covill-Servo (1982). In the Gresham and Nagle study, children viewed a film with a narrative soundtrack providing instruction in the skills used in Oden and Asher's study. Results were comparable to those of Oden and Asher. The Covill-Servo study replicated Oden and Asher's social skill instruction, with both classmates and nonclassmates as peer partners for the play sessions. Play experience with children from the child's major peer group (e.g., the classroom) appeared to have a greater impact on the children's social participation and acceptance by peers. The children in Ladd's (1981) study made gains in specific social skills (e.g., asking positive questions, giving useful suggestions) as well as peer acceptance. This social skill instruction procedure included a guided rehearsal by the adult as each dyad played games. These findings also indicate that simply learning new skills and interacting with other children may not alter acceptance by classmates if opportunities to interact with peers are not increased in the classroom.

In summary, adult conversations with children about their peer relationships appear to be an important resource in helping children develop friendship skills. Numerous styles or methods of talking with children appear to be helpful to them. An adult who is open to talking with his or her child about peer relationships is also likely to further enhance the adult-child relationship.

Influence of Curricula and Activities

A curriculum for children's social development is ongoing in the classroom or family even though it may be implicit or "hidden" (Cartledge & Milburn, 1980; Johnson, 1981). Katz and Zalk (1978) and Lockheed and Harris (1978), among others, found that when children interact in curriculum activities which include mixed-sex and race groups, stereotypes tend to be lessened and a greater general openness to intergroup activities results. In general, the research evidence indicates that in order to promote children's social development, the preschool and elementary school curriculum should provide children with opportunities to (1) interact with their peers so that they can learn to know and get along with each other and begin and sustain friendships; (2) interact in pairs and in small groups; (3) interact with many different children in the classroom; (4) interact with many different children in various situations (e.g., in classroom instructional activities, in language arts and media experiences, on the playground); and (5) discuss issues in human relations (e.g., rights of individuals, cooperation in the group, resolving conflicts).

Children are also likely to benefit from opportunities to interact with peers outside the school context, such as at each other's homes, in clubs, scouts, art activities and/or family outings (the circus, zoo, or picnics). The inclusion of a sibling should also be considered in activities where they may enjoy or profit from being included. (The role of siblings would seem important in children's peer relationship, but this is an area which needs investigation.)

In curriculum planning, educators and parents need to include various types of activities that foster children's general education as well as positive peer relationships. Language arts activities, as well as music, drama, art, and children's literature, for example, are important in helping children express individual feelings, ideas, and creativity, and in enhancing their understanding of reciprocity and fairness in human relations. Accordingly, language activities represent a potential for greater knowledge and understanding between children and for helping children interact with children of a different race or cultural background, age, sex, and physical or learning ability. Several studies have found that reading and discussing stories about children who differ on some characteristic, such as a physical disability (e.g. Mauer, 1979), help children to have more receptive attitudes toward each other in future interactions. Discussing stories from children's literature (e.g., Serow & Solomon, 1979) or from television (e.g, Slaby & Quarforth, 1980) can help children to be more aware of sex and race sterotypes and what may be incorrect or inaccurate about these stereotypes.

Academic projects may also be constructed so that children learn the role of cooperation in group effort. Those elements of the curricula designed to maximize children's knowledge of cooperative problem-solving are likely to be most beneficial to children when employed as an integral feature of classroom activity. It is important to balance the goal structures of activities so that children experience activities that are structured for cooperation as well as for assertiveness. Research evidence indicates that subjects such as math, spelling, vocabulary, geography, and so forth can be structured for group cooperation, and that such cooperation tends to enhance children's peer relationships while at the same time improving their cognitive abilities and academic achievement (Johnson, 1981). In general, engaging small groups of children in these activities allows every child to make some contribution to the group interaction. Large group activities also have their place. Physical education and sports activities, for example, are known to enhance group effectiveness and still foster friendships in larger groups (e.g., Fine, 1981).

Group discussion on issues of interest may include controversy and this can result in an enhancement of the peer group (Johnson & Johnson, 1979). Topics of controversy might be handled by discussion and activities that extend from the discussions, such as a classroom newspaper or a debate. Various discussion formats and topics should be considered (e.g., Mehan, 1979; Johnson, 1981); however, there are some issues that should be highlighted or receive specific attention in discussions or debates. These issues include specific events in the classroom and/or issues in human relations in society. Discussions could take place in relation to a television program, current event, slides, a story from children's literature, or by role playing. The discussion of issues in human relations should help children to examine stereotypes and get to know each other at the same time. Examples of general themes that are especially relevant as children progress through the preschool and elementary school years include:

(1) Learning how to include a child who tries to join a classroom activity;
(2) Learning to appreciate many of the diverse characteristics of classmates, playmates, and friends;
(3) Learning how to understand the perspective of another child whose values or situation may differ from one's own;
(4) Learning how to help another who may be in distress or having some problem, such as learning a skill, finding the way around the school, making friends, or getting along with classmates; and
(5) Learning how to determine fair ways to utilize space and resources within a group.

These kinds of issues may also be pursued in special discussions to help solve problems over everyday issues, including participation of both sexes in games in the playground or in a specific section of the room (e.g., block building area, playhouse); refusal of a child to sit next to another child at the art table; teasing or bullying another child who may appear to be lost, upset, unaware of how to do something, or who is usually very quiet; pushing ahead of others in line; stealing someone's supplies or abusing someone's property; and settling arguments by physical fights. The use of role-playing and puppets for acting out potential solutions to such situations has been found effective for clarifying perspectives and consequences of social actions (see Cartledge & Milburn, 1980).

It is also interesting to consider the potential challenge that television and computers in the classroom will present for curriculum planning. Rather than increasing competition and isolation from peer relationship development, this technology could result in greater mastery of the basic academic skills and provide greater time for children to learn to apply or practice their skills in projects and joint endeavors. In any curriculum planning, activities should be examined for their potential for enhancing chilren's peer relationship development as well as their academic learning.

CONCLUSION

Peer relationships among children appear to provide contributions to children's social development. Children do not simply interact with peers; they develop relationships with peers which provide unique social contexts in the children's development. In a peer relationship, a child experiences interaction with another child who is of a similar level of experience and competence and yet who is different enough to provide a resource for enrichment of his or her own experience. Children also learn to develop cohesive peer groups—they learn how to resolve conflicts through negotiation and cooperation, and they learn how to compete with one another and yet maintain their own individuality. They learn how to form and sustain friendships. Although the influence of adults in children's peer relationships is limited, their role is important in ensuring that classroom curricula, and activities in schools and the community, provide sufficient opportunities for children to develop relationships with their peers.

REFERENCES

Ainsworth, M. D. S. The development of infant-mother attachment. In B. M. Caldwell & H. N. Ricciuti (Eds.), *Review of child development research* (Vol. 3). Chicago, IL: University of Chicago Press, 1973.

Argyle, M. *Social interaction.* London: Methuen, 1969.

Asher, S. R., & Hymel, S. Children's social competence in peer relations: Sociometric and behavioral assessment. In J. D. Wine & M. D. Smye (Eds.), *Social competence,* New York: Guilford Press, in press.

Asher, S. R, Oden, S. L., & Gottman, J. M. Children's friendships in school settings. In L. G. Katz (Ed.), *Current topics in early childhood education* (Vol. 1). Norwood, NJ: Ablex, 1977.

Baldwin, C. P., & Baldwin, A. L. Children's judgments of kindness. *Child Development,* 1970, *41,* 29–47.

Bandura, A. *Social learning theory.* Englewood Cliffs, NJ: Prentice-Hall, 1977.

Bash, M. S., & Camp, B. W. Teacher training in the 'think-aloud' classroom program. In G. Cartledge & J. F. Milburn (Eds.), *Teaching social skills to children.* New York: Pergamon Press, 1980.

Bates, E. Pragmatics and sociolinguistics in child language. In D. M. Morehead & A. E. Morehead (Eds.), *Normal and deficit child language.* Baltimore, MD: University Park Press, 1976.

Berscheid, E., & Walster, E. H. *Interpersonal attraction.* Reading, MA: Addison-Wesley Publishing Co., 1969.

Bigelow, B. J. Children's friendship expectations: A cognitive-developmental study. *Child Development,* 1977, *48,* 246–253.

Cartledge, G., & Milburn, J. F. (Eds.), *Teaching social skills to children,* New York: Pergamon Press, 1980.

Cherry-Wilkinson, L., & Dollaghan, C. Peer communication in first grade reading groups. *Theory Into Practice,* 1979, *28,* 267–274.

Cooley, C. H. *Human nature and the social order.* New York: Scribner's, 1902.

Cooper, C. R., Ayers-Lopez, S., & Marquis, A. Children's discourse during peer learning in experimental and naturalistic situations. *Discourse processes,* in press.

Corsaro, W. A. Friendship in the nursery school: Social organization in a peer environment. In S. R. Asher & J. M. Gottman (Eds.), *The development of children's friendships.* New York: Cambridge University Press, 1981.

Covill-Servo, J. L. The modification of children's low-peer status from a socio-psychological perspective. Unpublished doctoral dissertation, University of Rochester, Rochester, NY, 1982.

Cowen, E. L., Pederson, A., Babigian, H., Izzo, L. D., & Trost, M. A. Long-term follow-up of early detected vulnerable children. *Journal of Consulting and Clinical Psychology,* 1973, *41,* 438–446.

Damon, W. *The social world of the child.* San Francisco, CA: Jossey-Bass, 1979.

Denzin, N. K. *Childhood socialization,* San Francisco, CA: Jossey-Bass, 1977.

Dweck, C. S., & Bush, E. S. Sex differences in learned helplessness (1): Differential debilitation with peer and adult evaluators. *Developmental Psychology,* 1976, *12,* 147–156.

Easterbrooks, M. A., & Lamb, M. E. The relationship between quality of infant-mother attachment and infant competence in initial encounters with peers. *Child Development*, 1979, *50*, 380–387.

Ervin-Tripp, S. Children's verbal turn-taking. *Developmental pragmatics*, New York: Academic Press, 1979.

Fine, G. A. Friends, impression management, and preadolescent behavior. In S. Asher & J. M. Gottman (Eds.), *The development of children's friendships*. New York: Cambridge University Press, 1981.

Foote, H. C., Chapman, A. J., & Smith, J. R. Friendship and social responsiveness in boys and girls. *Journal of Personality and Social Psychology*, 1977, *35*, 401–411.

Furman, W., Rahe, D. F., & Hartup, W. W. Rehabilitation of socially withdrawn preschool children through mixed-aged and same-age socialization. *Child Development*, 1979, *50*, 915–922.

Garvey, C., & Hogan, R. Social speech and social interaction: Egocentrism revisited. *Child Development*, 1973, *44*, 562–568.

Gottman, J. M. Toward a definition of social isolation in children. *Child Development*, 1977, *48*, 513–517.

Gottman, J., Gonso, J., & Schuler, P. Teaching social skills to isolated children. *Journal of Abnormal Child Psychology*, 1976, *4*, 179–197.

Gottman, J. M., & Parkhurst, J. T. A developmental theory of friendship and acquaintanceship processes. In W. A. Collins (Ed.), *Minnesota symposium on child psychology* (Vol. 13). Hillsdale, NJ: Lawrence Erlbaum, Associates, 1979.

Gresham, F. M., & Nagle, R. J. Social skills training with children: Responsiveness to modeling and coaching as a function of peer orientation. *Journal of Consulting and Clinical Psychology*, 1980, *18*, 718–729.

Gronlund, N. E. *Sociometry in the classroom*. New York: Harper, 1959.

Hallinan, M. T. Structural effects on children's friendships and cliques. *Social Psychology*, 1979, *42*, 43–54.

Hallinan, M. T. Recent advances in sociometry. In S. R. Asher & J. M. Gottman (Eds.), *The Development of children's friendships*. New York: Cambridge University Press, 1981.

Hallinan, M. T., & Tuma, N. B. Classroom effects on change in children's friendships. *Sociology of Education*, 1978, *51*, 270–282.

Hartup, W. W. Children and their friends. In H. McGurk (Ed.), *Issues in childhood social development*. London: Methuen, 1978.

Johnson, D. W. Student-student interaction: The neglected variable in education. *Educational Researcher*, 1981, *10*, 5–10.

Johnson, D. W., & Johnson, R. Conflict in the classroom: Controversy and learning. *Review of Educational Research*, 1979, *49*, 51–70.

Johnston, A., Deluca, D., Murtaugh, K., & Diener, E. Validation of a laboratory play measure of child aggression. *Child Development*, 1977, *48*, 324–327.

Katz, P. A., & Zalk, S. R. Modification of children's racial attitudes. *Developmental Psychology*, 1978, *14*, 447–461.

Ladd, G. W. Effectiveness of a social learning method for enhancing children's social interaction and peer acceptance. *Child Development*, 1981, *52*, 171–178.

Ladd, G. W., & Oden, S. The relationship between peer acceptance and children's ideas about helpfulness. *Child Development*, 1979, *50*, 402–408.

LaGreca, A. M., & Mesibov, G. B. Social skills intervention with learning disabled children: Selecting skills and implementing training. *Journal of clinical child psychology*, 1979, *8*, 234–241.

Lamb, M. E., & Roopnarine, J. L. Peer influences on sex-role development in preschoolers. *Child Development*, 1979, *50*, 1219–1222.

Lee, L. C. Toward a cognitive theory of interpersonal development: Importance of peers. In M. Lewis & L. A. Rosenblum (Eds.), *Friendship and peer relations*. New York: John Wiley & Sons, 1975.

Lewis, M., Young, G., Brooks, J., & Michalson, L. The beginning of friendship. In M. Lewis & L. A. Rosenblum (Eds.), *Friendship and peer relations.* New York: John Wiley & Sons, 1975.

Livesley, W. J., & Bromley, D. B. *Person perception in childhood and adolescence.* London: Wiley, 1973.

Lockheed, M. E., & Harris, A. M. *The effects of equal status cross-sex contact on students' sex stereotyped attitudes and behavior.* Paper presented at the Annual Meeting of the American Educational Research Association, Toronto, Canada, 1978.

Mangione, P. L. *Children's mixed- and same-age dyadic interaction.* Paper presented at the biennial meeting of the Society for Research in Child Development, Boston, April 1981.

Mauer, R. A. Young children's responses to a physically disabled story-book hero. *Exceptional Children,* 1979, *45,* 326–330.

McGrew, W. C. Aspects of social development in nursery school children with emphasis on introduction to the group. In N. Burton-Jones (Ed.), *Ethological studies of child behavior.* New York: Cambridge University Press, 1972.

Mehan, H. "What time is it, Denise?" Asking known information questions in classroom discourse. *Theory Into Practice,* 1979, *28,* 285–294.

Meichenbaum, D. H., & Goodman, J. Training impulsive children to talk to themselves: A means of developing self-control. *Journal of Abnormal Psychology,* 1971, *77,* 115–126.

Mishler, E. G. "Would you trade cookies with the popcorn?" The talk of trades among six year olds. In O. K. Garnica & M. L. King (Eds.), *Language, children and society.* New York: Pergamon Press, 1979.

Moss, J., & Oden, S. *Developing narrative competence and peer relationships in a language arts curriculum.* Unpublished manuscript, University of Rochester, Rochester, NY, 1980.

Much, N. C., & Sweder, R. A. Speaking of rules: The analysis of culture in breach. In W. Damon (Ed.), *New directions for child development: Moral development.* San Francisco, CA: Jossey-Bass, 1978.

Mueller, E., & Brenner, J. The origins of social skills and interaction among playgroup toddlers. *Child Development,* 1977, *48,* 854–861.

Mueller, E., & Lucas, T. A developmental analysis of peer interaction among toddlers. In M. Lewis & L. A. Rosenblum (Eds.), *Friendship and peer relations.* New York: John Wiley & Sons, 1975.

Newcomb, A. F., Brady, J. E., & Hartup, W. W. Friendship and incentive condition as determinants of children's task-oriented social-behavior. *Child Development,* 1979, *50,* 878–881.

Oden, S. The child's socal isolation: Origins, prevention, intervention. In G. Cartledge & J. Milburn (Eds.), *Teaching social skills to children: Innovative approaches.* Elmford, NY: Pergamon Press, 1980.

Oden, S., & Asher, S. R. Coaching children in social skills for friendship making. *Child Development,* 1977, *48,* 495–506.

Oden, S., Herzberger, S. D., Mangione, P. L., & Wheeler, V. A. Children's peer relationship development: An examination of social processes. In *Conference on boundary areas in psychology: developmental and social.* Nashville, TN: Vanderbilt University, June 1981.

Parke, R. D. The role of punishment in the socialization process. In R. A. Hoppe, G. A. Milton, & E. C. Simmel (Eds.), *Early experiences and the processes of socialization.* New York: Academic Press, 1970.

Peery, J. C. Popular, amiable, isolated, rejected: A reconceptualization of sociometric status in preschool children. *Child Development,* 1979, *50,* 1231–1234.

Peevers, B. H., & Secord, P. F. Developmental change in attribution of descriptive concepts to persons. *Journal of Personality and Social Psychology,* 1973, *27,* 120–128.

Piaget, J. *The moral judgment of the child.* London: Routledge and Kegan Paul, 1932.

Putallaz, M., & Gottman, J. Social skills and group acceptance. In S. R. Asher & J. M. Gottman (Eds.), *The development of children's friendships.* New York: Cambridge University Press, 1981.

Robin, A. L., Kent, R., O'Leary, D., Foster, S., & Prinz, R. An approach to teaching parents and adolescents problem-solving communication skills: A preliminary report. *Behavior Therapy,* 1977, *8,* 639–643.

Roedell, W. C., Slaby, R. G., & Robinson, H. B. *Social development in young children.* Monterey, CA: Brooks/Cole, 1977.

Ruble, D. N., Boggiano, A. K., Feldman, N. S., & Loebl, J. H. *Developmental Psychology,* 1980, *16,* 105–115.

Schofield, J. W. Complementary and conflicting identities: Images and interaction in an interracial school. In S. R. Asher & J. M. Gottman (Eds.), *The development of children's friendships.* New York: Cambridge University Press, 1981.

Selman, R. L. The child as a friendship philosopher. In S. R. Asher & J. M. Gottman (Eds.), *The development of children's friendships.* New York: Cambridge University Press, 1981.

Serbin, L. A., Tonick, I. J., & Sternglanz, S. Shaping cooperative cross-sex play. *Child Development,* 1977, *48,* 924–929.

Serow, R. C., & Solomon, D. Classroom climates and students' intergroup behavior. *Journal of Educational Psychology,* 1979, *71,* 669–676.

Shantz, C. V. The development of social cognition. In E. M. Hetherington (Ed.), *Review of child development research* (Vol. 5). Chicago, IL: University of Chicago Press, 1975.

Shatz, M., & Gelman, R. The development of communication skills: Modifications in the speech of young children as a function of listener. *Monograph of the Society for Research in Child Development,* 1973, *38* (5, Serial No. 152).

Shure, M. B., & Spivack, G. *Problem-solving techniques in childrearing.* San Francisco, CA: Jossey-Bass, 1978.

Singleton, L. C., & Asher, S. R. Social integration and children's peer preferences: An investigation of developmental and cohort differences. *Child Development,* 1979, *50,* 936–941.

Slaby, R. G., & Quarfoth, G. R. Effects of television on the developing child. In B. W. Camp (Ed.), *Advances in Behavioral Pediatrics,* 1980, *1,* 225–266.

Spivack, G., & Shure, M. B. *Social adjustment of young children.* San Francisco, CA: Jossey-Bass, 1974.

Stein, N. L., & Goldman, S. R. Children's knowledge about social situations: From causes to consequences. In S. R. Asher & J. M. Gottman (Eds.), *The development of children's friendships.* New York: Cambridge University Press, 1981.

Stocking, S. H., Arezzo, D., & Leavitt, S. *Helping kids make friends.* Allen, TX: Argue Communications, 1980.

Sullivan, H. S. *The interpersonal theory of psychiatry.* New York: Norton, 1953.

Turiel, E. Social regulations and domains of social concepts. In W. Damon (Ed.), *Social cognition.* San Francisco, CA: Jossey-Bass, Inc., 1978.

Turiel, E. Domains and categories in social cognitive development. In W. Overton (Ed.), *The relationship between social and cognitive development.* Hillsdale, NJ: Lawrence Erlbaum Associates, in press.

Urbain, E. S., & Kendall, P. C. Review of social-cognitive problem-solving interventions with children. *Psychological Bulletin,* 1980, *88,* 109–143.

Waters, E., Wippman, J., & Sroufe, L. A. Attachment, positive affect, and competence in the peer group: Two studies in construct validation. *Child Development,* 1979, *50,* 821–829.

Wheeler, V. A. *Reciprocity within first-grade friend and nonfriend dyads in a conflict of interest situation.* Unpublished doctoral dissertation, University of Rochester, Rochester, NY, 1981.

Youniss, J. The nature of social development: A conceptual discussion of cognition. In H. McGurk (Ed.), *Issues in childhood social development.* London: Methuen, 1978.

Youniss, J., & Volpe, J. A relational analysis of children's friendship. In W. Damon (Ed.), *New directions for child development. Social cognition* (No. 1). San Francisco, CA: Jossey-Bass, 1978.

6

The Symbolic Play of Lower-Class and Middle-Class Children: Mixed Messages from the Literature

Virginia Stern

Bank Street College

Which of the following statements is true?

1. The symbolic play (dramatic play) of middle-class preschool children differs in almost every way from that of lower-class children of the same age.
2. There are very few systematic differences in the symbolic play of middle-class and lower-class children of preschool age.

If a poll were taken of teachers, psychologists, and other observers of young children, it is likely that a high proportion would subscribe to the first statement. Moreover, if questioned further, they would also interpret the difference to mean that symbolic play not only occurs more frequently among middle-class children, but also that it is of a higher quality than that of lower-class children.

This belief in the superiority of the play of middle-class children, triggered by observations in Head Start centers where large numbers of children from "poverty-level" families attended preschool educational programs for the first time, was reinforced by the publication in 1968 of Smilansky's book, *The Effects of Sociodramatic Play on Disadvantaged Preschool Children*. In this book two studies were described—a preliminary comparative study, and a study of the effects of training on the symbolic play of lower-class children. In the preliminary study, Smilansky compared the symbolic play of two groups of children attending preschool classes in Israel. One group (which she characterized as "disadvantaged") consisted of lower-class children of immigrants from Middle Eastern and North African countries; the other (called "privileged") consisted of middle-class children of European descent. She described the play of these two groups as being at opposite poles with respect to the incidence, elaboration, and complexity of symbolic play. The impact of her findings is due not only to the fact that her study was the first of its kind, but also to the inferences she drew from the findings that the play of the privileged children was more advanced cognitively than that of the disadvantaged children, and that the latter needed specific training to learn to play symbolically.

That the Head Start children did not seem to engage in symbolic play as much as and/or in the same ways as did the middle-class children who attended independent nursery schools and who had, until then, been the usual subjects of investigations of symbolic play, was a source of concern to those who believed that young children learn primarily through play and that symbolic play is important for children's cognitive and affective development.

This, in addition to a more general concern about the difficulties experienced in school by children from economically impoverished homes (which was one of the reasons for the establishment of the Head Start program), led to a rash of studies aimed at documenting the specific differences in cognitive functioning between lower- and middle-class children as well as the sources of these differences (Bloom, Davis & Hess, 1964). On the basis of their findings, many of the investigators prescribed, and often translated into reality, intervention programs designed to overcome the "cognitive deficits" which they found in disadvantaged preschool children (Feldmann, 1964). Smilansky's work stimulated the introduction of programs aimed at teaching lower-class children to play symbolically and encouraged studies of the effects of training on young children's play.

Despite the renewed interest of researchers in play in general, and in symbolic play in particular, there have been very few comparative studies of the symbolic play of lower- and middle-class children. Of those studies that have been done, some support Smilansky's findings, others contradict them.[1] Moreover, if looked at in close detail, the picture that emerges from these studies is more confusing than enlightening, and offers more questions than answers about both findings and methodology. The sources of these differences in results are important to consider in relation to further research in the field. In this paper, I shall summarize briefly the nine most relevant comparative studies in an effort to clarify their disparate findings, discuss some of the problems involved in this kind of research, and finally, outline possible next steps.

BRIEF DESCRIPTION OF NINE COMPARATIVE STUDIES

Smilansky (1968) compared the symbolic play of middle-class and lower-class 3- to 6-year-old children. For evaluation of the children's play, she chose six elements which she considered essential to symbolic play. Four of these apply

---

[1] This review does not cover studies of the effects of training.

to symbolic play in general (that is, when the child is playing alone or with others), and two to sociodramatic play (in which two or more children interact). Because her findings are almost entirely descriptive and she does not report on these six elements systematically, it is difficult to disentangle them from additional, more qualitative aspects of symbolic play which she also discusses. One can, however, find scattered (though often unclear) references to all of them.

In this comparative study, Smilansky found differences between the two groups on all dimensions studied except for the content of play themes and of the roles the children enact. She states that while all six elements were observed in the symbolic play of middle-class children at age 3, most of the elements were lacking in the play of lower-class children from ages 3 to 6. From this she concluded that the differences between the two groups are not due to differences in *rate of development* but involve a difference in basic style.

Questioning Smilansky's finding that the children of Middle Eastern and North African immigrants do not develop the ability to engage in symbolic play, Eifermann (1971) studied the symbolic play of 6- to 14-year-old lower- and middle-class Israeli children in two elementary schools.[2] She found that more lower-class 6- and 7-year-olds (of the same cultural background as Smilansky's sample) engaged in symbolic play than middle-class 6- and 7-year-olds. Eifermann suggests that lower-class children reach the peak of symbolic play at a later age than do middle-class children; that is, there is a developmental lag in the symbolic play of lower-class children. She considers that her findings refute Smilansky's conclusion.

Two American psychologists also based their studies on Smilansky's work. Griffing (1980) used Smilansky's six play components[3] and found statistically significant differences (in the same direction as Smilansky) between 5- and 6-year-old black middle-class and lower-class children with regard to all six components. In contrast to Smilansky, Griffing defined her categories clearly, and used a more refined system for coding play (4-point rating scales) and statistical methods for determining differences between the two groups. In general, her study was more carefully executed and, unlike several of the other studies, she did not confound ethnicity and social class.

Rosen (1974) compared the play of black lower-class and white middle-class kindergarten children as a prelude to an intervention study with a sample of lower-class children. She found that the white middle-class kindergarten children engaged in more sociodramatic play, and often at a more sophisticated level, than the black lower-class children (p. 926). However, she does not define sophistication.

Rubin, Maioni, and Hornung (1976) compared the symbolic play of middle-class and lower-class 3- and 4-year-old Canadian children, with respect

---

[2] This was part of a large scale, systematic study, conducted in 14 schools, grades 1 through 8, aimed mainly at challenging Piaget's theory that all games with rules are competitive.

[3] Several of which she defined somewhat differently.

to Parten's (1932) social play hierarchy and Smilansky's translation of Piaget's three play stages into the following four categories: functional play, constructive play, dramatic play, and games with rules. Rubin et al. found a marginally significant difference between the two groups with respect to "cooperative" symbolic play. The lower-class children engaged in less cooperative symbolic play than the middle-class chilren.

Smith and Dodsworth (1978) compared the "fantasy" (symbolic) play of 3- and 4-year-old children from middle- and working-class backgrounds in England. The study was designed to examine quantitatively Eifermann's developmental lag hypothesis at the preschool age range. They used three criteria (which the investigators have shown to be developmental indices that determine whether a developmental lag exists): (1) "elaborated" use of objects relative to "replica" use; (2) the number of participants in play; and (3) the length of play episodes. They also investigated the amount of group play and the level of verbalization and compared their findings with Smilansky's. Since statistically significant differences were found between middle-class and lower-class children with respect to two of their criteria as well as verbalization, they concluded that "the data give some support to Eifermann's developmental lag hypothesis" (p. 189).

Golomb (1975) compared the symbolic as well as other kinds of play[4] of 3- to 6-year-old middle- and upper-middle-class American children with that of lower-class children of the same age. She constructed a complex symbolic play scale combining a number of play behaviors, some of which are coded as separate categories by other investigators. She also coded several of the play-scale components individually. In addition, several of her categories, which in other studies apply to symbolic play alone, include other play activities. She found no systematic differences between the two groups on any of the symbolic play variables investigated, nor in the developmental changes which occurred in each social-class group.

In studying the play of English children, Tizard, Philps, and Plewis (1976b) investigated the influences of social class and educational orientation of the preschool centers attended. In addition to symbolic play, their social-class comparisons included a wide range of other kinds of play activities (sand play, rough and tumble play, construction). Their definition of symbolic play, unlike those used in most other studies, subsumed other types of symbolic representation, such as drawing. (See Tizard et al., 1976a, pp. 252-253, for their categorization of play.) Although this alone would not preclude comparison with other studies, only one of the categories they used for coding play—"dramatic impersonations"—is comparable to those used by other investigators. Here, they found no difference in frequency between the 3- and 4-year-old lower-class and middle-class children.

---

[4] Motor play, exploratory activity, arts and crafts, constructional games, etc.

As part of a study aimed at investigating the developmental changes that take place in young children's symbolic play, Stern, Bragdon, and Gordon (1976) compared the play of middle-class and lower-class 3- and 4-year-old children to determine areas of similarity and difference. Their study differs from those mentioned above in that it examines the play behavior of children who *do* play, and not, as did the others the play of all children in the selected classes. Stern et al. found very few differences between the middle-class and lower-class groups when compared on 23 symbolic play behaviors.[5]

DETAILED PRESENTATION OF FINDINGS OF
THE NINE COMPARATIVE STUDIES
(SEE TABLE 1)

Because the vocabulary of symbolic play varies from study to study, I shall use the terms defined by Stern et al. (1976) in presenting the findings of the comparative studies. Equivalent terms used by other investigators for what appear to be the same or similar play behaviors are given. But first some of the most basic terms must be clarified.

When a child acts as if she/he were another person (a doctor using a stethoscope on a doll), an animal (moving around on all fours and barking like a dog), or even an inanimate object such as an airplane (running swiftly with arms outstretched and making motor sounds), it is clear to most people that she/ he is engaged in role-play—often used as a synonym for symbolic play. This kind of play was called "persig" play by Stern et al. ("persig" standing for *person* as signifier). When a child (who is not a "persig") makes an *object* act as if it were a person, animal, or object (moving a small square block along a curvy block road, saying "beep beep," as if the small square were a car) this is also symbolic play.[6] Stern et al. called this "obsig" play ("obsig" standing for *object* as signifier) to distinguish it form persig play, and because there is no commonly used term for it. Smilansky's term, "imitative role play," and Griffing's "role play" are equivalent to persig play, and apply both to individual and group play, and their sociodramatic play is equivalent to group persig play. Even when the use of objects as signifiers is included in their analyses, none of the other investigators except Tizard et al. (1976a) and Golomb (1975) appears to differentiate between obsig and persig play as Stern et al. (1976) do (but cf. Piaget's definition, 1962; also, Curry and Arnaud, 1974; Halfar, 1970; Huston-Stein, Friedrich-Coffer, & Susman, 1977).

---

[5] The difficulties experienced by Stern et al. (1976) in locating centers attended by lower-class children in which symbolic play could be observed was a clear indication that, whatever the reasons, there was more symbolic play in schools attended by middle-class children than in those attended by lower-class chilren.

[6] That is, the object is not just a signifier in persig play, it is the *major* signifier.

TABLE 1 Comparison of Symbolic Play of Lower-Class and Middle-Class Children: Results of Nine Studies

Categories	Stern, Bragdon & Gordon (1976)[1]	Golomb (1975)	Tizard, Philps & Plewis (1976)[1]	Smith & Dodsworth (1978)	Smilansky (1968)	Griffing (1980)[1]	Rosen (1974)[1]	Rubin, Maioni & Hornung (1976)[1]	Eifermann (1971)[1]
Group Play	(Cooperative Pretense Play)[3] m.c. = l.c.[2]	m.c. = l.c.		m.c. = l.c.	(Interaction) m.c. > l.c.	(Interaction) m.c. > l.c.	(Socio-dramatic play) m.c. > l.c.	(Cooperative dramatic play) m.c. > l.c.	(Symbolic play) l.c. > m.c.
Persig Play	(Role Play) m.c. = l.c.	(Role Play) m.c. = l.c.	(Dramatic impersonations) m.c. = l.c.		(Imitative role play) m.c. > l.c.	(Role Play) m.c. > l.c.	(Role Play) m.c. > l.c.		
Type of Signifier	(Representative)	(Objects as replicas)		(Replica use)	(Toys)	("Make believe with objects" = all types of signifiers)			
				l.c. > m.c.	l.c. > m.c.				
	(Semi-represent.)			(Elaborated use of objects = semi-repres. & imaginary)					
	(Non-repre-sent.)	(Undefined objects)			(Undefined objects)				
	(Imaginary)	(Imaginary)			(Make believe re objects)				
	m.c. = l.c.	m.c. = l.c.		m.c. > l.c.	m.c. > l.c.	m.c. > l.c.			
Emotional Stance	(Affective involvement) m.c. = l.c.				(No specific term) m.c. only				

TABLE 1 (cont.)

Persig Differentiation	Age 3: m.c. = l.c. Age 4: m.c. > l.c.	(Appropriate role division) m.c. = l.c.	(No specific term) m.c. only	
Length of Play Unit	m.c. = l.c.	(Episode duration) m.c. = l.c.	(Persistence 10 min. +) m.c. > l.c.	(Persistence most of 5 min. period) m.c. > l.c.
Themes and Roles	(Play themes and roles) m.c. = l.c.[2]		(Themes and roles) m.c. = l.c.	
Amount of Verbalization	m.c. = l.c.	(Verbalization) m.c. > l.c.	(Amount of speech) m.c. = 2 × l.c. m.c. > l.c.	(Verbal communication) m.c. > l.c.
Persig Language	Age 3: m.c. = l.c. Age 4: l.c. > m.c.		(No specific term) m.c. only	
Labeling of Play	m.c. = l.c.		m.c. only	(Verbal expression of make-believe) m.c. > l.c.)
Socialized Communication	m.c. = l.c.	(Socialized language) m.c. = l.c.		

[1] Statistical tests were used to determine the presence of significant differences between the lower-class and middle-class groups. All differences are statistically significant.
[2] m.c. = middle-class group; l.c. = lower-class group.
[3] Parentheses around a category name indicates that this is the term that the investigator(s) used.

Only the findings on the eleven symbolic play behaviors which are included in two or more studies will be presented here. In order to compare the findings of these studies, it is often necessary to treat as equivalent, categories which are not. The categories used in these studies vary in degree of inclusiveness as well as in consistency of inclusiveness. They may cover group and individual play, group play alone, individual play alone, other play activities as well as symbolic play and, in one case, non-play activities; they may also be composite (combining two or more different play behaviors) or simple (only one).

Group play is included in all but one study (see Table 1). The Stern et al. group play category differs from Smilansky's, Griffing's, Rosen's, and Rubin's et al. in that it includes obsig play, while the others apply only to persig play.[7] Golomb's category is more inclusive than the rest because it covers play activities other than symbolic play. Smilansky, Griffing, Rosen, and Rubin et al. found that the incidence of group symbolic play was greater among the middle-class than the lower-class children. Smith and Dodsworth's group play category includes both associative and cooperative play (Parten's categories, 1971). In estimating the amount of group play, they also included other play activities as well as symbolic play. Although they found more group play in the middle-class group than in the lower-class, the difference was not significant. Neither Golomb nor Stern et al. found any difference between the groups, whereas Eifermann found that at ages 6 and 7 (combined) more lower-class than middle-class children engaged in group symbolic play.

Of the six investigators who compared the lower-class and middle-class children with regard to the incidence of persig play, three (Smilansky, Griffing, and Rosen) found that it occurred more frequently in middle-class than in lower-class groups; three (Stern et al., Golomb, and Tizard et al.) found no difference between the groups. The Stern et al. category applies only to group play, while, in the other studies, it applies to individual play as well. The Golomb category is part of her symbolic play scale.

When children play, they use objects, real or imaginary (called "signifiers") to represent people, other objects, animals, story or TV characters ("the signified"). The degree to which the signifier and the signified resemble each other may vary. For example, a child may use a stick, a pillow, or a very human-like doll to represent a baby. Five studies took account of the type of signifier children use. Stern et al. defined four types of signifiers in terms of the distance between the signifier and the signified with respect to perceptual, functional, and class relationships. *Representative* signifiers closely resemble the signified (a toy car with many details of a real one); *semi-representative*

---

[7] However, in the Stern et al. (1976) study, more than four-fifths of the group symbolic play at ages 3 and 4 consisted of persig play.

signifiers bear some resemblance to the signified (a closet represents a jail); *non-representative* signifiers have little or no resemblance or functional relationship to the signified (a block represents a baby); and an *imaginary* signifier is an imagined object or person of which we become aware because of the child's actions or words.

Stern et al. found no difference between the two groups in the use of the four types of signifiers. They found, moreover, that approximately half the signifiers used by both groups at ages 3 and 4 were *representative*. The child's use of representative, non-representative, and imaginary signifiers serves as one cue for his/her score on Golomb's symbolic play scale. Golomb found no differences between the two groups on this scale. Smilansky's category, "make-believe in regard to objects," refers to the use of actions and verbalization as substitutes for toys, equivalent to imaginary signifiers. She found that middle-class children tend to use imaginary signifiers and also "undefined objects" (non-representative signifiers), while lower-class children tend to use toys (representative signifiers). Smith and Dodsworth found that middle-class children showed more "elaborated use of objects" (i.e., semi-representative and imaginary objects) than lower-class children, while lower-class children were more likely to make "replica use of objects" (i.e., representative objects). Griffing found that middle-class children engage in "make believe with objects" more than lower-class children; i.e., they use more signifiers—representative, non-representative, and imaginary combined.

Emotional stance has to do with the way children express emotional qualities—through their actions, language, or facial expressions. In symbolic play, "mother" may be bossy or loving or punitive, may be concerned with the "baby's" need for food and tenderness, or may ignore it. Stern et al. found no difference between the groups in the incidence of this kind of behavior at ages 3 and 4. Golomb's "affective involvement" is defined similarly to emotional stance.[8] She also found no difference between her groups in this respect. Smilansky describes the middle-class children in similar terms, but states that lower-class children do not behave this way. The middle-class child, she says, "really *plays* the part, imitates tone and gestures, spoils and is spoiled, shouts in mock anger, speaks pompously" (p. 37), while, among the lower-class children, "there is no evidence of dramatic text, verbal identification of the child with this role, or other signs, gestures, and so on, of dramatic involvement" (p. 39).

Persig differentiation[9] refers to the fact that when children play "train" together, one may be the conductor, another the engineer, and others passengers.

---

[8] And was coded separately as well as being part of the symbolic play scale.

[9] Often called role-differentation, and similar to what Piaget (1962) calls collective symbolism.

Smilansky's description of how the middle-class child *"reacts* dramatically to the dramatic image projected by his fellow player, from within his own role" (p. 37) probably refers to similar behavior. Smilansky found that this occurred only in the play of middle-class children. Golomb found no difference in "appropriate role-division" between her two groups, whereas Stern et al. found that, although at age 3 the groups are similar, at age 4 there is a marginally significant difference in the incidence of persig differentiation—more among the middle-class than the lower-class children.

Five studies include a measure of attention span, but the mode of measurement varies somewhat from study to study. Smilansky and Griffing measured children's play attention span in terms of specified time limits. Smilansky defines "persistence" as "the child persists in a play episode for at least 10 minutes," and, therefore, apparently ignores all play lasting a shorter time. Griffing rated the length of the play on the basis of 5-minute play segments. Smith and Dodsworth estimated "length of episode" (within each 5-minute time sample). Stern et al. and Golomb, on the other hand, measured the duration of the play episode, whatever its length. Stern et al. defined *length of play unit* as the number of minutes during which a child stays with a specific play content even though she/he may interrupt it one or more times in response to external or internal stimuli. Golomb also divided the play of each child into episodes (for symbolic play her criterion is change in character of the play resulting, for example, from change in participants) and measured "episode duration." Stern et al. found that, at both age levels, the two groups were similar with respect to length of group play units, in those lasting 20 minutes or less as well as 21 minutes or longer. Smith and Dodsworth report no significant difference between middle-class and lower-class children in the mean length of play episodes. Golomb also found no difference in the length of play episodes. Both Smilansky and Griffing found that middle-class children's sociodramatic play lasted longer than lower-class children's. Only two studies compared the two groups with respect to the content of *play themes and roles*. Both Smilansky and Golomb found no differences.

Five studies were concerned with the use of language in symbolic play— the extent to which it is used, the functions it serves, and the use of socialized language. Comparing the two social-class groups with respect to *amount of verbalization* (average number of symbolic play-related statements per child), Stern et. al. found no difference between the two groups. Griffing, however, found that verbal communication was greater in the middle-class than in the lower-class group. Smith and Dodsworth scored verbalization "for each one-minute period in which the child was seen to make a meaningful statement" (p. 187). They found that middle-class children were more likely to verbalize than lower-class children. They included statements made during both symbolic and non-symbolic play. Smilansky found that the average number of words per child in the middle-class group was twice that of the lower-class group. However, her category is not really equivalent to the categories of other investigators because she not only included language spoken during drawing, painting, and building as well as during symbolic play, but also language that is not play-related. Smilansky states, however, that the differences between the groups would probably be greater if only play-related language was included.

Stern et al. define *persig language* as language spoken by a child when she/he is a signifier (e.g., "All aboard," when a child is a conductor on a train); that is, it is an integral part of the play symbolism. They found no difference between the groups at age 3, but at age 4 the lower-class children surpassed the middle-class children. In contrast, Smilansky found that only middle-class children used persig language. Griffing's "verbal expression of make-believe" combines persig language and verbal descriptions accompanying symbolic actions. She found a highly significant difference between the groups on this variable, the middle-class children greatly exceeding the lower-class children in their verbal expression. The Stern et al. category, *labeling of play,* is similar to Griffing's "verbal expression" category (without persig language), but there was no difference between the groups in frequency of use.

Stern et al. and Golomb found no difference between the two groups in the use of *socialized communication* (the child talks with the intention of communicating with another person). Golomb's category applies to other play activities as well as to symbolic play.

SUMMARY OF FINDINGS

This review of study findings indicates that there is an almost complete split between Smilansky/Griffing/Rosen/Rubin et al. and Golomb/Tizard et al./ Stern et al. Within each of the two groups, the number of studies in which the results are the same for any play category depends almost entirely on the number of studies in which the category was included. Smith and Dodsworth can not be included in either group because two of their findings are in agreement with the Smilansky group and two, with the Golomb group.

Within the Smilansky group, all four studies found that the middle-class children engage in more group play than the lower-class children. Smilansky, Griffing, and Rosen found that middle-class children engage in persig play more than do lower-class children; Smilansky and Griffing found that symbolic play lasts longer, and that there is more verbal communication in the middle-class group than in the lower-class group. Smith and Dodsworth also found more verbal communication in the middle-class group than in the lower-class group. Smilansky found that the middle-class children use non-representative and imaginary signifiers more than the lower-class children, and lower-class children use representative signifiers more than middle-class children, while Griffing found that middle-class children use more of all types of signifiers than do lower-class children. Smith and Dodsworth also reported that middle-class children use semi-representative and imaginary signifiers more than lower-class children, and lower-class children use representative signifiers more than middle-class children. Of the remaining five categories, four (emotional stance, persig differentiation, persig language, and content of themes and roles) were included as distinct categories only in the Smilansky study, and one (labeling of play in combination with persig language) only in the Griffing study. The only exception to the pattern of higher incidence of each play behavior in the middle-class group than in the lower-class group was in relation to content of themes and roles, which Smilansky found to be the same in both groups.

Golomb, Tizard et al., and Stern et al., on the other hand, found no difference between the middle-class and lower-class children in the amount of persig play. Golomb and Stern et al. Also found no differences in the amount of group play, in the use of representative, non-representative, and imaginary signifiers, and in emotional stance, length of play unit, and socialized communication. Smith and Dodsworth also found no significant difference between the middle-class and lower-class children with regard to group play and length of play unit. Golomb found no difference in the amount of persig differentiation, but Stern et al. found no difference only at age 3. The remaining three categories were included only in the Stern et al. study. No difference was found in persig language at age 3, but the lower-class children used persig language more than the middle-class children at age 4; there was no difference in labeling of play or amount of verbalization.

Moreover, similarities between the two groups are minor. Both Smilansky and Golomb, who were the only ones to investigate the content of themes and roles, found no differences between the two groups. Like Smilansky who, however, did not differentiate in terms of age, Stern et al. found that at age 4 there was more persig differentiation in the middle-class than in the lower-class children's play.

DISCUSSION

These contradictory findings bring into clear focus the amount of disarray in this area of research. Findings to date not only make it virtually impossible to answer the questions which prompted this review, but also raise new ones which are equally unanswerable.

The first question raised concerned the ways in which the symbolic play of middle-class children was similar to or different from that of lower-class children. It is evident now that very few general conclusions can be drawn about the relative quality of symbolic play among lower-class and middle-class children. Excluding the findings of Stern et al. and Eifermann[10], for those play categories reported in two or more studies we find the following:

---

[10] Stern et al., because their sample includes only children who engaged in symbolic play and Eifermann, because her sample is not within the age range covered by the other studies.

1. There is agreement that the content of themes and roles is the same among middle-class and lower-class children, and that the amount of verbalization (however defined) is greater among middle-class than lower-class children.

2. More investigators (five as compared to one) report that group play is more prevalent among middle-class than lower-class children; more (three to two), that persig play is more prevalent among middle-class than lower-class children; and more (two to one), that middle-class children are more likely to use semi- and non-representative as well as imaginary signifiers than are lower-class children, and that lower-class children are more likely to use representative signifiers than are middle-class children.

The consistency of these results, despite the many differences in methodology and in the characteristics and backgrounds of the samples, is an indication of their validity. These findings, however, provide little enlightment about the nature and, especially, the quality of the symbolic play of middle-class as compared with lower-class children. Although there is, as yet, no substantiating evidence, the findings of the Stern et al. study suggest that the symbolic play of lower-class and middle-class 3- and 4-year olds is similar in many respects. The findings of Eifermann and of Smith and Dodsworth suggest that there may be a developmental lag in the symbolic play of lower-class children.

The second question was: What inferences, if any, can be made about the relative cognitive maturity of the play of middle-class and lower-class children? In order to make such inferences, there must be evidence of a positive relationship between age and/or intelligence (or some other clearly cognitive characteristic) and the incidence of specific play behaviors.

In five of the nine studies, the relationship between age and specific symbolic play behaviors was investigated. The combined findings of Stern et al., Golomb, and Rubin et al. indicate positive relationship between age and many symbolic play behaviors. All three found a positive relationship between age and incidence of group play, and both Golomb and Stern et al. found relationships with a number of others (e.g., length of of play unit, emotional stance, persig differentiation, the use of imaginary signifiers). Smith and Dodsworth, on the other hand, report that age was not an important factor in influencing the number of samples in which symbolic play was observed.

Smilansky[11] found no relationship between age and scores in her six basic symbolic play categories, including group play, but she does mention some age-related changes in the play of the middle-class children *other* than the six com-

---

[11] Smilansky states that her conclusions about the influence of age were based on "general observations" (p. 40). To determine the effect of chronological age, she checked "the presence or absence of the major elements of sociodramatic play" (p. 39). She found that most of the middle-class children used all six basic components by age 3, whereas the lower-class child "lacks" most of them. No increase in the number of components was observed with the increase in age.

ponents: "The play becomes more complex, more fulfilled, more completed, more sustained, more flexible within expanding limits, and so on" (p. 40). In addition, both Smilansky[12] and Griffing[13] report no relationship between intelligence and symbolic play. It is interesting to note, however, that Smilansky does make assumptions about the relative cognitive maturity of the six basic play behaviors. In all cases, a higher incidence of these play behaviors is assumed to be more advanced. She concludes therefore, that the play of the middle-class children is more advanced than that of the lower-class children.

Thus, there is some evidence from these studies that age influences specific play behaviors,[14] but there is only negative evidence with regard to the relationship between intelligence and symbolic play behaviors. On the basis of age alone, we might conclude that middle-class children are more cognitively advanced than lower-class children with respect to amount of verbalization, incidence of group play, and use of imaginary signifiers in symbolic play. No general conclusions, however, can be drawn from these studies regarding cognitive differences between middle-class and lower-class children.

All these studies started out with the assumption that socioeconomic status could influence the quantity and/or quality of children's symbolic play. Since, in most studies, the differences in socioeconomic background between the comparison groups were very large,[15] the presence of so many contradictory findings implies that socioeconomic status, by itself, is not the overriding influence in the symbolic play of young children. Apparently Smilansky found this to be true. In her experimental study of the effect of teaching on disadvantaged children's play, she combined into one control group both lower-class and middle-class Israeli children of European extraction because "we did not find significant differences in their sociodramatic play" (p. 109). This not only supports the findings of Golomb and Stern et al., but also suggests that cultural factors might be responsible for the dramatic differences Smilansky found in her comparative study.

Smilansky, who stresses cultural differences, describes the home situations of the lower-class Israeli children of Middle Eastern and North African immigrants and those of the middle-class children of European extraction as very different with respect to the nature of the parent-child relationship (particularly

---

[12] Smilansky states that her conclusions about the influence of "I.Q." were based on "general observation" (p. 40). She does not mention which test, if any, was used to measure intelligence.

[13] Griffing, who used the Goodenough-Harris Drawing Test as a measure of mental maturity, pointed out that "the imaginative and cognitive skills involved in socio-dramatic play may represent types of cognitive functioning different from those tested in traditional IQ tests" (1980, p. 27).

[14] There is a considerable amount of support for this finding in other studies, e.g. Halfar (1970); Lunzer (1959); Markey (1935); and Piaget (1962).

[15] Some of Griffing's "high-SES" group are described as "semiskilled" workers, while Smith and Dodsworth characterize their lower-class group as mainly working class, and Tizard et al. characterize theirs as working class. Thus, some of Griffings "high SES" group may be similar to some of Smith and Dodsworth's and Tizard's et al. lower-class group.

the authority relationship); the presence of toys, didactic games, and books in the home; encouragement of and participation in their children's symbolic play; responsiveness to children's needs and attitudes toward play vs. non-play activities. The paucity of information about cultural and family backgrounds in the other studies precludes any comparisons.

It is unlikely, however, that the cultural differences between the lower-class and middle-class populations in the United States, England, and Canada, where the other studies were located, are as vast as those Smilansky describes in her "disadvantaged" and "privileged" populations (see Table 2). Smilansky herself suggests that the culturally deprived children of "Asian-African" extraction in Israel are different from the culturally deprived children of European extraction because of the differences in home experiences as well as in the "different stimuli that the environment (outside the family) affords the culturally deprived child(ren) of European extraction (television, for example)" (p. 62). Yet many American psychologists as well as educators have assumed that her findings apply to American middle-class and lower-class children. At the same time, the contradictory results of the studies reviewed here suggest that the degree to which the comparison groups differ with regard to cultural background is not a primary influencing factor.

We are still faced, therefore, with two related, unanswered questions: If social-class and/or cultural differences cannot be considered responsible for similarities and/or differences in symbolic play, on the basis of these studies, what can? And, what factors are responsible for the contradictory findings?

Information from the studies about the characteristics of the sample, type of school and play situation, data collection procedures, and analytic methods, as well as background factors, were tabulated in order to find out if there were any systematic differences between middle-class and lower-class children which might provide clues. Only those which are reported on by all eight investigators[16] were examined (see Table 2). They are: (1) country in which the study was located; (2) age range of the sample population; (3) socioeconomic status of the families; (4) racial and/or ethnic background; (5) type of educational institution attended by the children; (6) number of schools/centers attended by the children; (7) site of observations; (8) type of data; (9) focus of observation; and (10) analytic measures. Inspection of these data indicated that although there are no systematic differences between the two groups there are many differences within each group, slightly more within the Smilansky study, however, than in the other studies.

There are many possibilities which should not be ignored even though the data from the studies have not provided any clear indicators. It must be

---

[16] What is reported depends partly on the design of the study and partly on where the study is reported—in a book or unpublished report or in a journal where the constraints due to lack of space are considerably greater. (And it is not always possible to distinguish which is the primary reason). Eifermann is not included because her study belongs in neither group.

TABLE 2 Background Factors in Eight Studies

Categories	Stern, Bragdon & Gordon (1976)	Golomb (1975)	Tizard, Philps & Plewis (1976)	Smith & Dodsworth (1978)	Smilansky (1968)	Griffing (1980)	Rosen (1974)	Rubin, Maioni & Hornung (1976)
Location of Study	United States	United States	England	England	Israel	United States	United States	Canada
Age of Sample	3s & 4s	3 to 6	3s & 4s	3s & 4s	3 to 6	5s & 6s	"Kindergarteners"	Mean age-3.88
Socioeconomic Status of Comparison Groups	m.c.[1]-upper-m.c. l.c.[1]-"poverty level"	m.c.-middle- & upper-m.c. l.c.-welfare or low income	m.c.-middle-class l.c.-working class	m.c.-middle-class l.c.-working class	m.c.-high-"sociocultural" l.c.-low "sociocultural"	m.c.-middle-class l.c.-welfare or unskilled labor	m.c.-"culturally advantaged" l.c.-"culturally disadvantaged"	m.c.-upper-m.c. l.c.-welfare
Ethnic and/or Racial Background of Sample	m.c.-white l.c.-80% black, 20% white	m.c.-white l.c.-mostly white, some Puerto Rican	m.c. & l.c. white	Not reported	m.c.-European extraction l.c.-Middle Eastern & North African extraction	m.c. & l.c. black	m.c.-white l.c.-black	m.c. & l.c. white
Type of Educational Institution	m.c.-Independent Schools l.c.-Head Start and Day Care	Nursery School Day care center Kindergarten classes	Traditional nursery schools Trad. Nursery schools with language emphasis Day Care	m.c.-2 state nursery schools l.c.-1 state nursery school 1 state day nursery	Nursery and kindergarten classes	Public School (P.S.) kindergartens	m.c.-P.S. kindergartens l.c.-P.S. kindergartens Day care centers	m.c. & l.c. University Early Childhood Center

TABLE 2 (cont.)

Number of Schools/ Centers/ Classes	m.c.-4 independent schools l.c.-5 Head Start centers, 1 day care center	m.c.-1 nursery school l.c.-1 day care center Kindergarten classes	m.c.-2 of each type l.c.-2 of each type	m.c.-2 l.c.-2	m.c.-18 classes l.c.-18 classes	m.c.-6 "suburban" P.S.s l.c.-3 "inner city" P.S.s	m.c.-1 kindergarten l.c.-2 P.S. kindergarten classes, 2 day care centers	m.c. & l.c. 1 University Center
Site of Observations	Classroom	Classroom	Classroom & Outdoors	Classroom	Classroom & Outdoors	A special Playroom	Classroom	Classroom
Type of Data	Pencil & Paper Narrative records	Narrative records	Pencil & Paper Narrative records	Selected details dictated into tape recorder	Pencil & Paper Detailed records	Pencil & Paper Narrative records	Ratings on "standardized observational schedule"	Play behavior checklist
Focus of Observation	Individual Child & interaction with others	Individual child & interaction with others	Individual child & interaction with others	Individual child & interaction with others	Play	Individual child & interaction with others	Individual child	Individual child
Analytic Measures	1) Presence/ absence during play unit 2) Frequency of occurrence 3) Ratings	1) Content analysis 2) Score on symbolic play scale	1) Frequency	1) Presence during 5 min. time period 2) Frequency of occurrence	1) Content analysis 2) Presence/ absence of play elements 3) Verbal description 4) Average number of words per child	1) Ratings on 4-point scale	1) Frequency	1) Type & duration of social & cognitive play categories

[1] For all studies, m.c. = middle class group; l.c. = lower-class group.

emphasized that many categories of information are not reported in all studies and that the information given frequently lacks the kind of detail that might differentiate between studies. Thus, to infer from such gross data that differences in home or school environments are not responsible in any way for the differences in children's play would be naive, as would be the assumption that any *single* factor is responsible.

The quality of the school environments, for example, cannot be discounted as a contributing source of differences in lower-class and middle-class children's symbolic play, and possibly as a source of difference in results. The comparability of the lower-class and middle-class classrooms/schools was not reported by Smilansky, Rosen, and Rubin et al. The situations reported on by the other five investigations differed from each other. Griffing reports that all schools serving middle-class children, except for a Montessori kindergarten, had space and equipment for symbolic play, and that schools for low-SES children were at least as well-equipped with play materials as were the schools for high-SES children. Golomb reports that there were noticeable differences between the lower- and middle-class classrooms in supplies, open spaces, and provisions for house play, as well as in teacher personality and educational philosophy. She does not, however, specify how they differed. Tizard et al. report that, for each of the three types of schools, the teacher role was similar for lower-class and middle-class children—there was little stimulation of or participation in the children's symbolic play by the teachers.

Stern et al. tried to control for teacher's attitudes and practices in relation to symbolic play. Because of the large number of sample selection criteria, this was not entirely successful. The teachers of two of the six classes of lower-class children (constituting 50% of the lower-class, 4-year-old sample) displayed little interest in the children's symbolic play but scheduled a regular free play period during which many of the children engaged in symbolic play. The other teachers of both lower-class and middle-class children tried to encourage and stimulate play, although not equally or in the same ways. The Head Start and day care classes tended to have more and newer equipment and materials than the independent schools, while the latter tended to have better-trained teachers, who were more sophisticated about symbolic play and child development. That there was symbolic play occurring in all the classes selected suggests that these teachers may have resembled each other in ways that Stern et al. did not take into account, and which are not seen as crucial by investigators in general.

Smith and Dodsworth report that all four nursery schools were similar in design, equipment, and daily routine, but one lower-class school differed from the others in that it was staffed by nursery nurses, while the other three had trained teachers. Except for the amount of teacher-child interaction, which varied from school to school, no further description was given of the nature or quality of the teaching. They found, however, that there was no significant relationship between teacher-child interaction and their findings.

Educators and researchers have suggested that the standard equipment and/

or arrangement of symbolic play areas in preschools are unfamiliar to children who do not come from middle-class homes and/or who are not members of the dominant ethnic group, and these areas, therefore, may not be conducive to symbolic play (see Curry, 1971).

There are other factors which may have affected the study results, not the play itself. One is the underlying approach of the investigator to children's symbolic play. Smilansky and Stern et al. in reporting their studies have articulated their approaches in some detail. One aspect is the value the investigator places on verbalization—the value of verbalization as an indicator of cognitive level as well as the weight given to it in the category system and in coding procedures. Smilansky places very high value on verbalization, seeing it as essential to the development and elaboration of the child's play and also as providing additional sources of satisfaction which are not available to children who engage only in action-oriented play. In comparing the two groups, she points out that for the middle-class children it is sufficient "to record the *verbalization* during play in order to understand fully the unfolding of the theme," while "only a detailed record of the *actions* of the lower-class children will reveal the roles and themes of the play" (1968, p. 39). The implication is, therefore, that middle-class children's play is more advanced. Of her six basic components, only two do not involve verbalization.

Stern et al. on the other hand, view non-verbal behavior as an important component of young children's play. Excluding the categories which are specifically focused on language, there are many which require the recording and coding of symbolic actions and other non-verbal behavior. Detailed directions were given to the observers for recording non-verbal behavior, since this is more difficult to record than verbalization, and the coding of non-verbal behavior is essential. In my view, to equate young children's verbalization during symbolic play with the total meaning of their play is to look at children's play with adult eyes alone. Only if non-verbal and verbal behavior are given equal consideration is it possible to perceive the richness of children's symbolic play as well as the ambiguities.[17] Since, for children, both verbal and non-verbal behavior are essential for expressing their meaning, recognizing both allows the researcher to see play from the child's point of view. This difference in coding method might contribute to differences in results in some categories, such as emotional stance, persig differentiation, or type of signifier.

Another factor is suggested by Schwartzman (1978) in her wide-ranging cross-cultural analysis of children's play. She points out some of the problems in research studies that propose that lower-class children are "imaginatively disadvantaged." She states that "these children are found to be *deficient* in the style of play associated with middle- and upper- middle-class children, which is then taken to indicate (or at least suggest) deficiency in the cognitive, verbal,

---

[17] The ambiguities evident when nonverbal behavior is recorded also makes coding much more difficult than if coding is based on verbalization alone.

and social skills said to be associated with this form of play and these children'' (p. 120). She adds, ''in order to correct this deficit . . . researchers then proceed to train children to play in a 'middle-class' manner, which is then said to produce improved scores in the display of cognitive, verbal and social skills'' (pp. 120–121).

What, then, have we learned, and what can we learn from reviewing these findings? For teachers of children, or future teachers of children, it should be a reminder that there are lower-class children whose symbolic play is similar to that of middle-class children,[18] and that objective observations of the children's behavior should indicate which children, middle- or lower-class, have the capacity to play, as well as those who need special help. It is unfortunate that there has been a tendency to assume that lower-class, minority-group children in the United States are comparable (in their economic and cultural backgrounds) to Smilansky's ''culturally disadvantaged'' and, therefore, that they too are not capable of playing symbolically except on the very lowest level. Since teachers' expectations are likely to influence their behavior in relation to children, and, therefore, the children's behavior, these erroneous assumptions may even have affected study results.

We now know that research in this area has been unproductive in that it has not answered most of the questions; it has not clarified hypotheses about the ways in which the symbolic play of lower-class and middle-class children are the same or different, nor has it provided any clear evidence of the sources of conflicting findings. It has been productive, however, in that we now know that we do not know the answers, and that we must find a way to get more valid results.

We also know that research in this area is in a very primitive state. The relatively small number of studies, as well as the number of categories investigated, is evidence of the impoverished nature of this research. For half the studies, the comparison of the symbolic play of middle-class and lower-class chilren was not the only, nor even the major, focus of investigation. A majority of the investigators focused on four categories—persig play, type of signifier, group play, and length of unit—only the first two of which are intrinsic to symbolic play. Only three studies included as many as eight or nine similar categories. When one thinks of symbolic play in all its fullness and complexity, and the many aspects that could be studied—the content of symbolism, the use of the self versus use of objects as self-signifiers, the use of symbols to represent the child's conscious and unconscious needs and wishes, play as an expression of the child's perception of reality, formal aspects of the play such as degree

---

[18] Griffing points out that ''it would be a mistake to conclude that all high-SES children performed well and all low-SES children performed poorly. Highly imaginative play episodes were observed among lower-class children . . . a number of high-SES children received very low play scores'' (1980, pp. 25–26).

of complexity, coherence, organization—one realizes how little has been done. Only the content and some formal characteristics of the play, represented by the categories I have been discussing, have been explored. Except for Golomb's rating scale, which covers a number of kinds of symbolic play behavior, the categories studied are simple, and the measures used, with the exception of Smilansky, are quantitative. At the same time, it is understandable that most researchers tend to choose the simplest and, therefore, the most easily quantifiable characteristics of play to investigate first.

But, considering the results of this approach, perhaps we should question its usefulness. Although the Stern et al. study included a much larger number of symbolic play behaviors than those with which we have been concerned here, each one was considered separately. Also, the study focused on the conscious, cognitive aspects of play. At its completion I felt that in using this atomistic, relatively simplistic approach, much of what was essential to symbolic play was being ignored and that, perhaps, a more holistic, qualitative approach might be more fruitful.

The need for a more integrative approach to factors influencing children's symbolic play behavior is also indicated. Classifying children grossly in terms of social class or ethnic background has provided little enlightenment. Sophisticated methods for checking relationships between combinations of home and school environmental factors and more complex symbolic play behaviors should be used.

The process of trying to understand exactly what was meant by the various terms used in these studies, and especially to determine the equivalence of different category names across a number of studies, emphasizes the importance of clarification of meaning. Although standardization of symbolic play terms would be most useful, I suspect that people will not easily give up their terms. But, regardless of the words used, they must be defined so that others can understand them, and good, unambiguous examples of each term or category are essential. This will not only improve communication, but also will help researchers clarify for themselves the meaning of the terms they use.

Although the data, data collection procedures, and methods of analysis were fairly well reported in these studies, they are not delineated sufficiently for the reader to understand how the results were obtained.[19] Because symbolic play is considered so important for young children's cognitive and affective development, progress in research on symbolic play is very desirable. It seems

---

[19] Smilansky's study is an extreme example of this. Her observers recorded play episodes in different play areas, not the play of individual children. Since her report is almost entirely descriptive, one does not know whether she actually counted the number of children in each play episode who were engaged in persig play, or just counted the number of persig play episodes, or counted at all. We do not know if her description was based on her impressions from reading the records taken by her observers or from going into some classrooms herself. Nor do we know whether some children in a class participated in more than one of the recorded play episodes.

to me that one way of attaining this would be for researchers to describe the problems encountered in their research, the compromises made (often because of too little time and money), and what they would do differently if they were able to continue research in this field. Researchers need to learn from others' experiences and new understandings as well as from their own. Perhaps the suggestion made by Shulman and Tamir (1973), in relation to research on teaching in the natural sciences, is appropriate here. They emphasize the need "to develop centers of research in which groups of investigators coordinate their efforts in joint attacks on common problems" (p. 1139).

REFERENCES

Bloom, B. S., Davis, A., & Hess, R. *Compensatory education for cultural deprivation.* New York: Holt, Rinehart & Winston, Inc., 1968.

Curry, N. E. Consideration of current basic issues on play. In *The Child Strives for Realization.* Washington, D.C.: National Association for the Education of Young Children, 1971.

Curry, N. E., & Arnaud, S.H. Cognitive implications in children's spontaneous role play. *Theory into Practice,* October 1974, *13,* 273–277.

Eifermann, R. R. Social play in childhood. In R. E. Herron & B. Sutton-Smith (Eds.), *Child's play.* New York: John Wiley & Sons, Inc., 1971.

Feldmann, S. A preschool enrichment program for disadvantaged children. *The New Era,* 1964, *45* (3), 79–82.

Golomb, C. *Pretense play: An examination of its social and cognitive significance.* Paper presented at the Wheelock College Symposium on Symbolization and the Young Child, October 1975.

Griffing, P. The relationship between socioeconomic status and sociodramatic play among black kindergarten children. *Genetic Psychology Monographs,* 1980, *101,* 3–34.

Halfar, C. L. *Developmental trends in sociodramatic play: A naturalistic study of symbolic play.* Unpublished doctoral dissertation, University of Chicago, Chicago, IL, September 1970.

Huston-Stein, A., Friedrich-Cofer, L., & Susman, E. J. The relation of classroom structure to social behavior, imaginative play, and self-regulation of economically disadvantaged children. *Child Development,* 1977, *48,* 908–916.

Lunzer, E. A. Intellectual development in the play of young children. *Educational Review,* 1959, *11,* 205–217.

Markey, F. Imaginative behavior of preschool children. *Child Development Monographs.* New York: Bureau of Publications, Teachers College, Columbia University, 1935.

Parten, M. B. Social play among preschool children. In R. E. Herron & B. Sutton-Smith (Eds.), *Child's play,* New York: John Wiley & Sons, Inc., 1971.

Piaget, J. *Play, dreams and imitation in childhood.* New York: W.W. Norton & Co., 1962. (First published in English in 1951 by W.W. Norton & Co.)

Rosen, C. E. The effects of sociodramatic play on problem-solving behavior among culturally disadvantaged preschool children. *Child Development,* 1974, *45* (4), 920–927.

Rubin, K. H., Maioni, T. L., & Hornung, M. Free play behaviors in middle- and lower-class preschoolers: Parten and Piaget revisited. *Child Development,* 1976, *47,* 414–419.

Schwartzman, H. B. *Transformations: The anthropology of children's play.* New York & London: Plenum Press, 1978.

Shulman, L. S., & Tamir, P. Research on teaching in the natural sciences. In R. M. W. Travers (Ed.), *Second handbook of research on teaching.* Chicago, IL: Rand, McNally & Co., 1973.

Smilansky, S. *The effects of sociodramatic play on disadvantaged preschool children.* New York: John Wiley, & Sons, Inc., 1968.

Smith, K., & Dodsworth, C. Social class differences in the fantasy play of preschool children. *Journal of Genetic Psychology,* 1978, *133,* 183–190.

Stern, V., Bragdon, N., & Gordon, A. Cognitive aspects of children's symbolic play. Unpublished manuscript, Bank Street College of Education, September 1976.

Tizard, B., Philps, J., & Plewis, I. Play in pre-school centres—I. Play measures and their relation to age, sex and I.Q. *Journal of Child Psychology and Psychiatry,* 1976a, *17,* 251–264.

Tizard, B., Philps, J., & Plewis, I. Play in pre-school centres—II. Effects on play of the child's social class and of the educational orientation of the centre. *Journal of Child Psychology and Psychiatry,* 1976b, *17,* 265–274.

7

Developing Cognitive Skills Through Art*

Rawley A. Silver

College of New Rochelle

This chapter presents teaching and testing procedures based on the premise that cognitive skills can be evident in visual as well as verbal conventions, and that these skills, traditionally identified, assessed, and developed through words, can also be identified, assessed, and developed through drawings. Procedures have been developed to form the Silver Test of Cognitive and Creative Skills. In addition to a description of this test and approach to teaching, this chapter provides pertinent literature, the rationale, a summary of six studies which have utilized the test, and implications of the test's uses for the educational practitioner.

BACKGROUND LITERATURE

Cognition

Bruner (1966) explained cognition as a means of organizing the barrage of stimuli from the outside world. We reduce the barrage by constructing models— imaginary representations. We match a few milliseconds of new experience to

---

* Copyright registration for portions of this chapter has previously been obtained by Rawley A. Silver, 1978, 1980, Rye, NY. The author wishes to express her appreciation to John Kleinhans, Ph.D., and Claire Lavin, Ph.D., for their analyses of the statistical data; to Patricia Schachner, Lisa Irving Halprin, Janice Bell, and Norma Ott, for volunteering to administer the test to their students; and to Eldora Boeve, Karen Hayes, Judith Itzler, JoAnn O'Brien, Niru Terner, and Phyllis Wohlberg, for teaching in the five schools in the NIE Project.

a stored model, then predict what will happen next from that model. For example, we may glimpse a shape and a snatch of movement, then respond to the model we happen to match—a night watchman, a burglar. In other words, thought is carried out by representing reality vicariously and economically. As Bruner pointed out, we represent with the aid of "intellectual prosthetic devices," such as language, but there are pictorial devices as well. (Bruner, 1966, pp. 16–19).

Children's drawings are pictorial devices that can represent reality vicariously and economically, and thus reflect their thinking. Children with inadequate language are deprived of many opportunities to represent their experiences. Without language, children lack a major device for constructing models of reality. This alone could account for cognitive deficiency. But if children's visuospatial capacities are intact, they may be able to construct visual models of reality, and represent their experiences nonverbally by drawing images of them.

The Role of Language in Cognition

Language is obviously related to thinking; whether it is essential to thinking has been debated. There is evidence that language and thought develop independently, that language follows rather than precedes logical thinking, and that even though language expands and facilitates thought, high level thinking can and does proceed without it (see for example, Arnheim, 1969; Furth, 1966; Torrance, 1962; Piaget, 1970).

A recurrent theme in the writing of Piaget is that logical thinking exists before the appearance of language, which occurs around the middle of the second year. By the beginning of their second year children are capable of repeating and generalizing their actions. If they have learned to pull a blanket to reach a toy on top of it, they are capable of pulling the blanket to reach anything else. They can also generalize by using a stick to move a distant object or by pulling a string to reach what is attached.

Furth (1966) reviewed over 50 empirical studies comparing performances of deaf and hearing populations on conceptual tasks involving both abstract and concrete material, as well as tasks involving memory and visual perception. He concluded that intellectual ability is largely independent of language.

Sinclair-de-Zwart (1969), a linguist who originally thought that the operational level of children would reflect their linguistic level, performed two experiments to determine the relationships between these levels in children ages 5 to 8. She established two groups: conservers, who realized that when liquid was poured from one glass to a glass of another shape the quantity did not change; and nonconservers, who judged the quantity according to the appearance of the containers. In her first experiment, she asked the children to describe simple objects. She found that the conservers kept in mind both objects at once, while the nonconservers failed to do so. In her second experiment, she taught the nonconservers to describe the objects in the same terms used by the conservers, then examined them to see whether this training had affected their development. In every case there was only minimal progress after linguistic training, and she concluded that language is not the source of logic, but is on the contrary structured by logic. If this conclusion is so, the usual assumption of causal relationships may be reversed. It is usually assumed that improving a child's language will improve his thinking, but higher levels of thinking may be the cause as well as the consequence of improved language skills, and nonverbal procedures may cause levels of language to rise.

The function of language in the thinking of normal children is primarily to pin down their perceptions, organize their experiences, and understand and control their environments, according to Strauss and Kephart (1955). By labeling perceptions with a word, hearing children can make them usable again and again. In addition, language opens up the whole field of vicarious experience. When children cannot obtain a desired result, they can substitute words for the unsuccessful activity, and, by symbolizing it, obtain it imaginatively without having to lift a finger, so to speak. Furthermore, by hearing about the experiences of other people, children can obtain information that otherwise they would have to obtain by themselves. Thus, they can compare themselves with others and use the experiences of others, without having to have the experiences themselves.

Can art symbols serve these same functions of language, not only for normal children but also for children with inadequate language? Like language symbols, art symbols are a way of labeling perceptions and experiences. Art symbols can represent particular subjects or classes of subjects. For example, a painting of a man can represent the painter's father, or authority figures in general, or Man in the abstract, or all three, just as the *word* "man" can represent each or all of these ideas, depending on the verbal context. Children with inadequate language are handicapped in representing their thought effectively, but even though their capacity for language may be impaired, their capacity for symbolizing may be intact. These children may be able to represent their thoughts nonverbally by drawing them.

Left and Right Brain Hemisphere Thinking

A consideration of the different modes of thinking of the left and right hemispheres of the brain would seem relevant to this discussion, for although verbal-analytical thinking (left brain thinking) predominates in our educational system, it may be that this dominance handicaps students (and teachers) whose preferred mode of thinking is visual-spatial (right brain thinking).

The left hemisphere of the brain seems to be specialized not only for language, but also for analytical and sequential thinking. It is associated with concepts and intellect, science and mathematics, logic and history. Talking, writing, reading, and understanding verbal messages are accomplished more effectively through the left hemisphere.

The right hemisphere of the brain seems to be specialized not only for spatial thinking and visual-motor skills, but also for processing information simultaneously or holistically. It is associated with intuition and creativity, art and metaphor, music, poetry, and dance. Manipulating objects and recognizing faces and patterns are accomplished more effectively through the right hemisphere.

Although our society (and thus our education system) values more highly the verbal and analytical skills of left hemisphere thinking, we need and make use of both brain hemispheres. (Physicists, for example, often use graphic methods to simplify complicated mathematical calculations.) Both hemispheres of the brain share much of their information through nerve fibers that cross over from one hemisphere to the other. In this manner, patterns and incoming information are relayed widely throughout the brain.

Studies have shown that people tend to favor one mode of hemispheric thinking over the other. Preferred modes are established early in life and, for some, visual thinking is the preferred mode (Witkin, 1962). Such individuals tend to solve problems through right hemisphere activity while others tend to solve problems through left hemisphere activity. To illustrate, imagine that it is now 3:40 p.m. What time will it be in half an hour? One person translates the problem into arithmetical quantities, another translates it into images in which he or she visualizes the face of a clock (Arnheim, 1969).

According to Lutz (1978), there is evidence that visual thinking is a crucial and central part of the creative process. In reviewing statements by highly creative scientists, she noted that Michael Faraday, the father of field theory, visualized the electric and magnetic lines of force. Einstein reported his reliance on mental imagery rather than language, and Kebule discovered the benzine ring through a vision of a series of atoms linked in a chain and biting its tail like a snake.

Lutz also cited a study by Martindale (1975) of brain wave activity which provides some evidence that creativity is related to activity of the right brain hemisphere. This study found that people classified as "low creative" showed very little brain wave activity in either hemisphere when presented with creative tasks—they seemed to use their brains in the same way regardless of whether or not the task was creative. The alpha brain wave activity of "medium creative" people indicated that they primarily used the left hemisphere. "Creative" individuals were found to produce large amounts of alpha brain waves in both hemispheres when presented with a creative task. The balance of this brain activity between the two hemispheres was near equal, suggesting that creative individuals use both modes of hemispheric thinking.

Moses (1980) recently explored the effects of instruction in visual thinking on performance in mathematics. Students in fifth grade, ninth grade, and in college were tested before and after 12 weeks of instruction in seeing, imagining, and drawing two- and three-dimensional figures. All activities focused on the visual modes of thought rather than on the analytical. Four tests were used to measure spatial visualization, reasoning, problem solving, and cognition. Instruction in visual thinking was found to improve spatial and reasoning abilities: males were better at spatial tasks and females were better at reasoning tasks. Further instruction, however, was found to lessen this difference in abilities between males and females. Problem-solving was also found to correlate significantly with spatial skills, reasoning skills, and degree of visuality. Thus, individuals who were successful at solving problems tended to use visual thinking as one means of solving problems. In conclusion, Moses observed that creative visual thinking "is sorely missed in the typical classroom schedule."

RATIONALE BEHIND THE DEVELOPMENT OF THE SILVER TEST OF COGNITIVE AND CREATIVE SKILLS

The considerations outlined above led us to question whether it might be useful to consider a new mode of teaching and a new type of assessment instrument in which visual-spatial activities, notably art activities, could be used to develop, reinforce, and assess children's cognitive skills. The author reasoned that such a method might more readily develop and assess the cognitive skills of those children who, for one reason or another, rely more on visual-spatial modes of thinking than on verbal-analytical modes of thinking. As noted above, traditional methods of teaching have long been based upon activities favoring the latter mode of thinking. The same would seem true of traditional tests of assessing cognitive skills, such as the Otis Lennon School Ability Test.

Independent Structures

The Silver Test is based upon three independent concepts or structures, identified as fundamental in mathematics by the Bourbaki group of mathematicians (see Piaget, 1970). One structure is based on ideas of space and applies to neighborhoods, borders, points of view, and frames of reference. A second structure is based on the idea of a group and applies to numbers and classifications. The third structure is based on ideas of sequential order and applies to relationships.

Although these ideas are usually developed through language, they can also be perceived and interpreted visually, and, although they may seem highly abstract, Piaget (1970) has found them in primitive form in the thinking of unimpaired children as young as 6 or 7 years of age.

The same three structures appear, in slightly different form, in recent studies by investigators concerned with learning disabilities in reading. One of these investigators, Bannatyne (1971), found that children with dyslexia usually attain higher scores on certain WISC subtests that, as a group, involve manipulating objects in space without sequencing. He suggested that the three subtests—Picture Completion, Block Design, and Object Assembly—formed a special category, which he called Spatial Ability. Bannatyne also found that dyslexic children do reasonably well in the WISC subtests that involve the ability to manipulate spatial images conceptually. These subtests—Similarities, Comprehension, and Vocabulary—form his Conceptual category. In one study, involving 87 learning-disabled children of ages 8 to 11, he found that 70% had Spatial scores greater than their Conceptual scores. Because the WISC test is standardized, only 50% of normal children would have Spatial scores greater than their verbal Conceptual scores. Bannatyne also found that these children almost always do worse on WISC subtests involving ability to sequence (Arithmetic, Coding, and Digit Span subtests—his Sequencing category).

Bannatyne reasoned that it would be useful to regroup the subtests into Spatial, Conceptual, and Sequential categories rather than into the traditional Verbal and Performance categories, and subsequent studies by other investigators have confirmed his findings and supported his hypothesis. Rugel (1974), for example, reviewed 25 studies of WISC subtest scores of disabled readers, reclassifying the subtests into Spatial, Conceptual, and Sequencing categories. He found that disabled readers scored highest in Spatial ability, intermediate in Conceptual ability, and lowest in Sequencing ability, thus supporting Bannatyne's hypothesis.

Smith, Coleman, and Dokecki (1977) administered the WISC-R test to 208 school-verified learning-disabled children, recategorizing the subtests in the manner suggested by Bannatyne. The mean Spatial score obtained was significantly greater than the mean Conceptual score, which, in turn, exceeded the Sequential scores.

These findings suggest that learning-disabled children are characterized by the same pattern of abilities that Bannatyne found for children with dyslexia, and that Rugel found for disabled readers in general (including those with dyslexia, minimal brain dysfunction, emotional disturbance, and cultural deprivation). In their discussion of the significance of finding that these children possess in common high visual-spatial skills, moderate conceptual skills, and low sequential skills, these investigators noted that a cognitive approach to diagnosis and remediation has received little attention compared to perceptual and psycholinguistic approaches. They suggested that the time may now be ripe for serious consideration of the cognitive approach.

The time may also be ripe for serious consideration of the role of art in developing cognitive skills. As Bannatyne (1971) observed, learning-disabled children have intellectual abilities of visual-spatial nature that are not being recognized, allowed for, or trained, since the emphasis is usually on linguistic rather than visual-spatial education.

Creativity

Another concern in the development of the Silver Test was the concept of creativity. Many investigators (e.g., Torrance, 1962) have found that creative individuals share traits such as originality, fluency, flexibility, independence, sensitivity to problems, and playfulness (the ability to toy with ideas and concepts). Originality seems to receive the greatest emphasis. Whereas analytical thinking proceeds inductively or deductively toward a correct, conventional solution, creative thinking proceeds divergently, making unusual associations and perceiving relationships in apparently diverse elements.

THE TEST INSTRUMENT

The Silver Test consists of three main subtests or tasks: drawing from imagination, drawing from observation, and predictive drawing. The test is designed to assess a child's understanding of concepts of space, sequential order, and class inclusion, without the child having to speak or write if need be. One goal is to enable teachers to identify children with cognitive or creative strengths who may do poorly on traditional tests of intelligence or achievement. Another goal is to provide a pre-post test instrument for measuring the progress of individuals or the effectiveness of instructional programs.

Drawing from Imagination

The purpose of this task is to assess ability to represent concepts of class or function and to assess creative skills. The concept of a class or category of objects involves the ability to select and combine into a context, such as selecting words and combining them into sentences. According to linguist Roman Jackobson (1964), selecting and combining are the two fundamental operations underlying verbal behavior. The two fundamental kinds of language disorder— receptive disorders and expressive disorders—are linked with verbal selection and combination. Jackobson defines receptive disorders as a disturbance in ability to make selections and expressive disorders as a disturbance in ability to combine parts into wholes.

Selecting and combining are no less fundamental in the nonverbal behavior of art activities. The painter, for example, selects and combines colors and shapes, and if his work is figurative, he selects and combines images as well. Furthermore, selecting and combining are fundamental in creative thinking. The creative person is often characterized as one who makes unusual leaps in associating experiences and combining them into innovative forms. In other words, the creative person has an unusual capability for selecting and combining, re-

Figure 1:"Watching TV," by Sarah, age 7.

gardless of whether expression is through language, visual art, or other media. Finally, selecting and combining would seem fundamental to emotional adjustment, for impairment of concept formation is one of the main ways in which neurological damage impinges on thinking.

To determine ability in the drawing task, students are asked to select two images (one from each page of stimulus drawings), and to combine them into narrative drawings of their own. A rating scale is used to assess the meaning or content of the drawing response (ability to select), the form of the response (ability to combine), and its creativity (ability to represent).

To illustrate, Sarah, age 7, selected images of a girl and a television set, and titled her drawing "Watching TV" (see Figure 1). Her drawing was scored[1] at the intermediate level for ability to select (on the basis of function rather than class). It received a low score for ability to combine because the subjects in her

---

[1] Further information about scoring the test may be obtained from Dr. Rawley A. Silver, A.T.R., Graduate School, College of New Rochelle, New Rochelle, NY 10580.

drawing were combined on the basis of proximity rather than along a base line, which is scored at the intermediate level and is typical of 7-year-olds. In ability to represent, her drawing received an intermediate score because she changed or elaborated on the stimulus drawings but was not particularly original, expressive, or playful.

Figure 2 was made by Daniel, age 9, who selected images of a bride, refrigerator, and television, and titled his drawing "Wedding Presents." Daniel transformed the stimulus drawing of a bride, creating a full-length frontal view and inventing a remarkable costume. He also gave her an elaborate TV set and either two refrigerators or a refrigerator and freezer. This drawing received an intermediate score for ability to select and combine, and a high score for ability to represent, being highly inventive and imaginative.

In contrast, Betty, age 13, did not, at first, relate the subjects she selected in either size or placement. Then, as she finished her drawing (Figure 3), she added the dog on a leash, thus relating the dog to the girl. Her drawing shows low levels of ability to select, combine, and represent. Betty is learning-disabled.

Drawing from Observation

The purpose of this task is to assess concepts of space. In tracing the development of concepts of space, Piaget and Inhelder (1967) observed that, initially, young children regard each object in isolation from all other objects, but that eventually they arrive at a coordinated system embracing objects in three directions—left-right, before-behind, and above-below. To determine ability in spa-

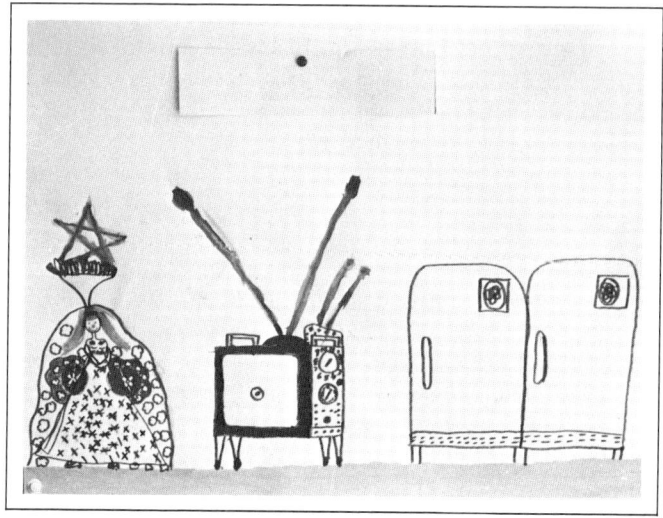

Figure 2: "Wedding presents," by Daniel, age 9.

Figure 3: Untitled drawing by Betty, age 13.

tial concepts, students are asked to draw an arrangement of four objects. Their responses are scored for ability to discern and represent horizontal, vertical, and depth relationships.

Figure 4 is a drawing made from observation by Ben, age 6. In the drawing, objects are represented accurately in height and width. Ben was aware that the narrowest cylinder was in front of and to the right of the widest cylinder, and that the tallest cylinder was farthest to the right. His drawing does not show, however, that the cylinder was actually further forward than the pebble. In contrast, Sarah's drawing (Figure 5), also made from observation, received low scores because none of the objects is represented accurately in terms of the relationships outlined in Figure 4.

Predictive Drawing

The ability to sequence and conserve is assessed in this third task. According to Piaget (1970), up to the age of about 7, children are typically unable to order systematically. Like ability to order, ability to conserve is basic in logical thinking. This ability to recognize constancy in spite of transformations in appearance normally appears around the age of 7. Piaget and Inhelder (1967) have claimed that the first natural system of reference involves horizontals and verticals, the most stable framework of every-day experience, and that it is important to find out if a child can spontaneously use such a system of reference. Piaget and Inhelder further noted that as adults we are so accustomed to think in terms of horizontals and verticals that they may seem self-evident. Children of 4 or 5,

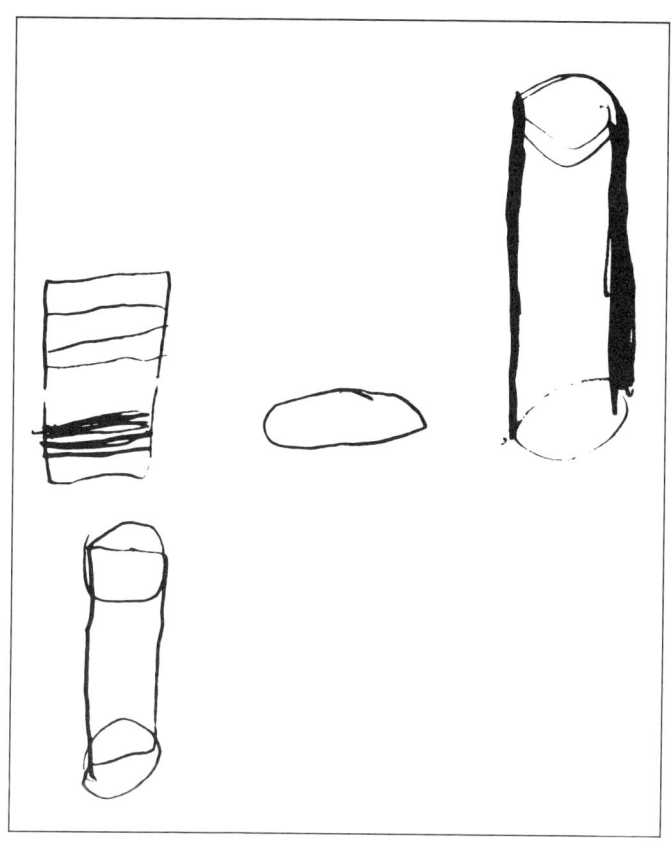

Figure 4: Drawing from observation, by Ben, age 6.

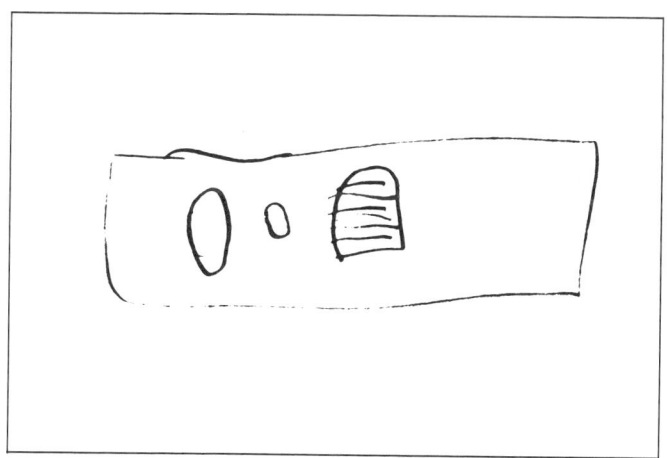

Figure 5: Drawing from observation, by Sarah, age 7.

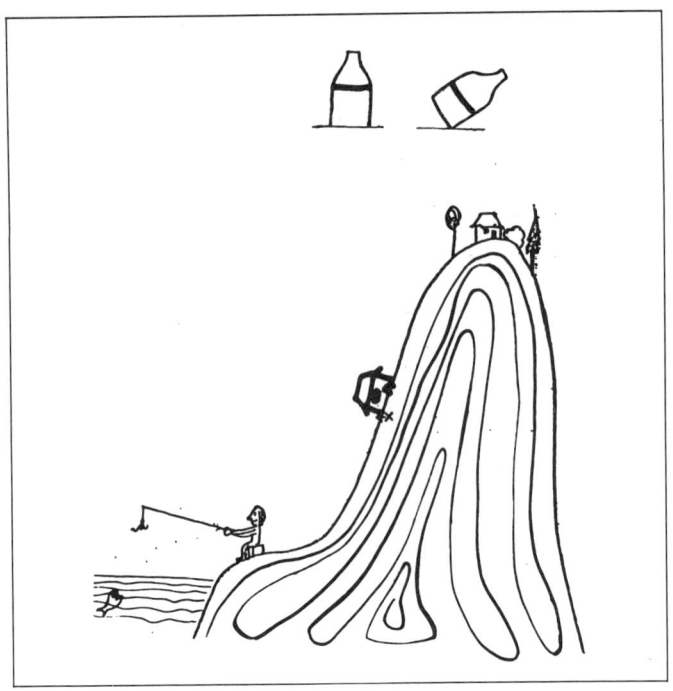

Figure 6: Predictive drawing, by Erin, age 6.

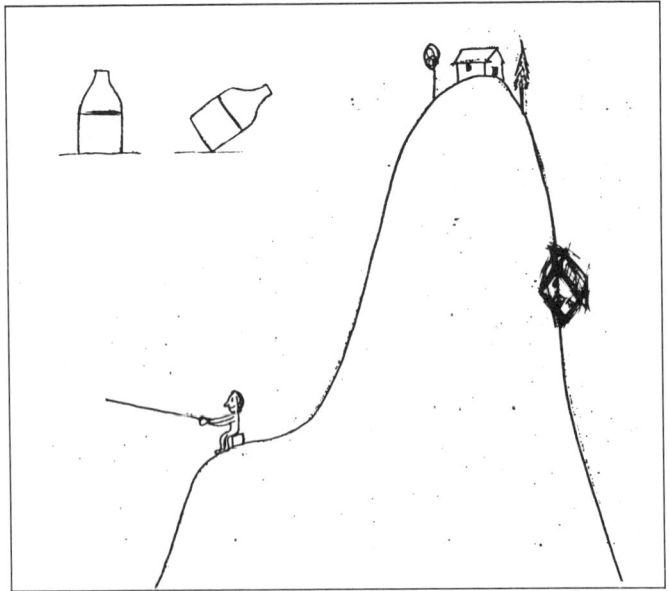

Figure 7: Predictive drawing, by an adult (teacher).

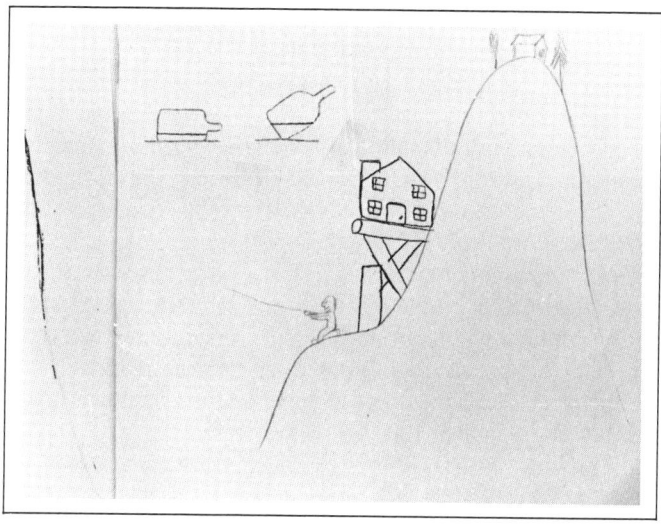

Figure 8: Predictive drawing, by George, age 13.

however, when asked to draw trees and houses on the outline of a mountain, draw them inside the outline. Children of 5 or 6 draw trees perpendicular to the incline, and not until the age of 8 or 9 they do tend to draw them upright. As for horizontal concepts, the 4-year-olds scribble round shapes when asked to draw the way water would look in the outline of a bottle. In the next stage, they draw lines parallel to the base of the bottle, even when the bottle is tilted. At a later stage, these children draw an oblique line in the tilted bottles. Eventually, the lines become less oblique and more horizontal until, at about the age of 9, children immediately draw a horizontal line. Thus, among the tasks in Predictive Drawing, students are asked to draw lines in a glass to show how it would look as it is gradually emptied. This task is used to determine ability to order. To determine ability to predict changes in appearance (conserve), students are asked to draw the way a house would look if moved to a steep slope, and how a half-filled bottle would look if tilted.

Figure 6 is a predictive drawing done by Erin, age 6. In the drawing, the house is drawn perpendicular to the slope and the line inside the tilted bottle is drawn parallel to the base of the bottle. Virtually the same mistakes are evident in Figure 7, which was drawn by an adult in a workshop for teachers. Figure 8 was drawn by George, age 13, a boy with both receptive and expressive language impairment. George's drawing indicates that he knew that water remains horizontal regardless of the tilt of its container, and that a house remains vertical (in this case, supported by posts) even on a steep slope.

TEACHING PROCEDURES

This approach to teaching is related to four goals:

(1) To widen a person's range of communication by extending his or her communication beyond language to include the nonverbal meanings of visual art. In other words, the aim is to provide an additional channel for conveying thoughts and feelings.

(2) To invite exploratory, active learning rather than passive reception of information, by presenting tasks in ways that let students make mistakes and correct them. For example, corrections should not be made by the teacher on a student's work. Instead, suggestions should be offered on a separate sheet of paper and the final decision on what to do with a particular task left to the student.

(3) To provide self-rewarding experiences through work that enables a student to overcome technical difficulties by himself or herself, with minimal help from the teacher when needed. Once a child is absorbed in work, he or she should be protected from interruptions, including those of teachers. The time to intervene is when a child is struggling with a brush that is too large or too small, for example, or whenever the teacher can foresee and prevent discomfort or distraction.

(4) To foster self-confidence. Because of the subjectivity involved, art experience provides special opportunities for both building self-confidence and tearing it down. A drawing is vulnerable to the evaluation of anyone who sees it and feels qualified to judge. Thus, teachers need to provide a classroom atmosphere which fosters self-confidence and mutual respect.

While the tasks used for teaching purposes are based on the same three structures underlying the assessment tasks, media other than pencil and paper are used when teaching. This is particularly so of the tasks designed to develop concepts of sequence and conservation, and which correspond to the Predictive Drawing task of the assessment measure.

Drawing and Painting from Imagination

To develop concepts of class inclusion, stimulus drawings are used.[2] These are 50 drawings on 3×5 cards presented in groups according to category—people, animals, places, things.

In the first lesson, the teacher presents the categories of people and things

---

[2] The stimulus drawings are available from Trillium Books, 1600 Harrison Avenue, Mamaroneck, NY 10543.

in adjacent groups. He or she then asks the children to select one drawing from each group and to draw a narrative picture:

> Make your drawing tell a story about the picture ideas you chose. Show what is happening. Don't just copy these drawings. Change them. Draw your own way. Draw other things too, to have your picture more interesting.

When the drawings are finished, they are discussed in such a way as to reinforce associative thinking. Working with groups of children, the teacher holds up their drawings one at a time and encourages each child to talk about her or his work. Key words are written as titles.

In later lessons, the other categories of stimulus drawings, and other art materials and techniques, are introduced. In most of the art classes, the teacher encourages the children to draw or paint from imagination. The stimulus drawings remain available, but it is not long before most children prefer their own ideas. Of their own work, emphasis is on originality, on appreciation, and on the content or meaning of the work produced, particularly on the interactions between subjects and the content.

Drawing and Painting from Observation

To develop concepts of space, emphasis is placed on the form rather than content of the work produced, particularly the left-right, above-below, and front-back relationships. In the first of the lessons, designed to focus attention on spatial relationships, the teacher asks the children to sketch an orange and a cylinder made by rolling and taping a sheet of green construction paper. The arrangement is presented below eye level, in the center of the room. When the children have finished sketching, the teacher asks them to change seats with classmates on other sides of the arrangement and to sketch it again. To reinforce thinking, the teacher may call attention to spatial relationships. For example, she or he may point out that the orange is on the left when seen from one point of view, and on the right from another. However, the teacher should encourage students to find other spatial relationships themselves. In later lessons, the children draw and paint other subjects from observation.

Painting Used to Develop Concepts of Sequential Order

The teacher demonstrates mixing a series of blue tints by placing a dab of white poster paint on the upper right-hand corner of a sheet of paper and a dab of blue on the upper left-hand corner. With a palette knife (or stick), he or she then mixes a series of tints between the two main colours by adding more and more white to tints of blue. The teacher then asks the children to see how many tints they can mix on their own papers. Later, red and yellow are added to the palette and the teacher encourages the children to invent colors of their own.

Modeling Clay

Modeling clay can be used to develop concepts of space, sequence, and class inclusion. The "brick" technique—forming clay into small blocks and pressing them together—is used to build human, animal, and other forms which can be associated with one another. The "slab" technique—placing lumps of clay between parallel sticks and rolling them flat—is used to build boxes or houses. The "coil" technique—rolling clay into "snakes" or balls of different size—is used to develop abilities to conserve and to sequence.

With all of the above tasks, teachers can keep logs of classroom observations. By dating, numbering, and scoring key drawings or paintings, teachers are able to both assess a child's ability and note changes in that ability.

STUDIES WHICH HAVE USED THE SILVER TEST

The Silver Test has been used in a number of studies, designed both to assess children's cognitive skills and to develop children's cognitive skills. Six of these studies are briefly presented here, two of which were conducted by researchers other than the author and her colleagues.

Handicapped and Normal Children (1972-73)*

In this study, in which the teaching and testing procedures of the Silver Test were initially developed (for a fuller report see Silver, 1973, 1978), one teacher worked with an experimental group of 34 7- to -15 year-old language and hearing impaired chilren, during the school year 1972–73. The children were a randomly selected 50% sample from 12 classses in a school for the language and hearing impaired. The remaining 34 children from these classes served as a control group. Experimental subjects attended art classes once a week for 11 weeks in the fall, and nine weeks in the spring. To compare handicapped with normal (nonhandicapped) children, the test was later administered to 68 normal children in a suburban public school. The test was given to this group once only.

Drawing from Imagination (see Table 1): In this task, the experimental group showed significant improvement ($p < .01$) in the combined abilities of selecting, combining, and representing. They also performed significantly better ($p < .01$) than the control group on the posttest for each of the three tasks.

A comparison of the mean scores of 63 of the normal children with the pretest mean scores of the 34 experimental and 34 control handicapped children revealed no significant differences between the groups. However, posttest scores

---

* The results of this study are presented in Tables 1 to 3.

TABLE 1 Comparing Mean Performance Scores in Drawing from Imagination by Handicapped Experimental and Control Children, and by Normal Children[a]

	Experimental (N = 34)				Control[b] (N = 34)		
Age	Name	Pre	Post	Age	Name	Pre	Post
8	Vi	15	15	7	Ba	9	4
	Je	9	8		Ch		5
	We	3	9	8	Ke	5	4
	Ca	3	15		An	9	10
	Fe	3	10		Jo	13	14
	Ro	3	14		Mi	9	9
	Ev	3	11		Ki	5	5
	Do	5	7	9	Mi		6
	Li	5	4		Di		6
9	Da	11	11		Ro	3	4
	Ra	8	9		Sa	7	14
10	Al	3	12		Ca	3	8
	Ca	5	11		El	7	6
	Ke	15	9	10	Ja		15
11	Ja	9	3		Jo	11	9
	Ru	7	15		Be	3	6
	Je	3	13	11	Pa		9
12	Ep	10	15		He		3
	Ba	3	11		Mi		5
	Ru	5	7		An	12	13
	El	15	13		De		11
	Ra	15	11		Al		7
	Ja	11	14	12	Ma		9
	Ma	13	14		Fe		5
13	Do	9	13		Ga	13	8
	Sh	3	15		Ev	13	14
	Bi	3	15		Ro	9	8
	Ei	14	15	13	Gl		11
	An	7	7		El		15
14	Ca	13	13		Ma		6
	To	13	15		Jo		15
	Ja	11	12	14	An		3
15	Da	6	13		An		15
	Ed	11	11	15	De		5
	Mean	8.0	11.47			8.18[c]	8.44

[a] Scored on basis of 1 to 5 points for level of development: 5 = highest level.
[b] Control children who participated in the Fall program did not have pretests, since teaching and evaluating procedures were developed during the term. Their only test for the ability to select, combine, and represent was the Fall program posttest.
[c] For the Spring program only.

TABLE 1   (cont.)

	Normal children (N = 63)[d]			Normal children (N = 63)[d]	
Age	Name	Score	Age	Name	Score
8	Ni	11		Da	11
	Pa	10		Ji	13
	An	4		To	6
	St	12		Ma	9
	Da	9		Jo	11
	Ca	7		Al	10
	Mi	13	12	La	11
	El	14	13	Ch	7
	Ja	8		Ka	12
	Ja	6		Ro	13
	Da	12		Le	13
	Ch	5		Je	11
	Bo	8		Mi	8
9	Jo	7			
	Li	9		Mi	
	Ho	8		El	7
	Ka	9		Te	8
	Di	10		Er	14
	To	4		Ly	8
	Lo	9		Jo	8
	Al	9		Jo	9
10	Da			We	12
	De	8		An	8
	Ja	8		An	7
	Hu	13		St	
	An	9		Cl	8
	Ma	11		Ju	12
	An	7		Ch	15
11	Th	7	14	Ju	12
	Li	12		An	8
	An	9		Ol	8
	Ma	11		Lo	10
				Mean	9.47

[d] Five children were absent when the test was given.

of the 34 handicapped experimental group children were significantly superior ($p < .05$) to the scores of the normal children.

Drawing from Observation   (see Table 2): The experimental group of handicapped children improved significantly ($p < .01$) on this task. The control group did not improve. No significant difference was found between handicapped and normal children. The handicapped experimental group did have higher mean scores on the posttest, however.

Predictive Drawing (see Table 3): A comparison of the mean scores of the handicapped experimental children before and after the art program showed significant improvement ($p < .01$) on this task in both horizontal and vertical concepts. The handicapped control children did not improve significantly.

Prior to receiving the art program, the mean scores of the handicapped experimental group were found to be significantly lower than the mean scores of the normal children. After the art program, however, while no significant difference was found between the group in horizontal concepts, in vertical concepts the handicapped children improved to a degree that was significantly superior ($p < .05$) to that of the normal children.

During the course of this study, the question of whether art for therapeutic purposes might undermine art education and interfere with aesthetic development arose. A preliminary attempt was made within this study to provide some answers.

TABLE 2 Comparing Mean Performance Scores in Drawing from Observation by Handicapped Experimental and Control Children, and by Normal Children

Experimental group (N = 16)				Control group (N = 16)			
Age	Name	Pre	Post	Age	Name	Pre	Post
8	Je	7	11	7	Ba	0	4
	We	6	12	8	Ke	9	4
	Ca	8	11		An	6	4
	Fe	8	7		Jo	6	6
	Ro	10	15		Mi	13	14
	Ev	12	12		Ki	7	8
	Do	10	14	9	Ro	3	7
	Li	10	7		Sa	6	10
10	Al	3	10		Ca	13	10
	Ca	10	12	10	Jo	11	13
	Ke	9	12		Be	13	9
11	Ja	12	10	12	Ga	14	13
12	Ja	12	14		Ev	13	8
	Ma	15	15		Ro	5	9
13	An	6	12	13	El	4	4
14	Ja	12	9		An	14	13
	Mean:	9.37	11.43			8.56	8.50

[a] Scored on the basis of 1 to 4 points for number of correct representations of left-right, above-below, front-back and proportional relationships in drawing from observation.

TABLE 2   (cont.)

Unimpaired children (N = 63)[b]			Unimpaired children (N = 63)[b]		
Age	Name	Score	Age	Name	Score
8	Ni	13		Da	5
	Pa	8		Ji	8
	An	7		To	10
	St	11		Ma	9
	Da	7		Jo	7
	Ca	6		Al	7
	Mi	10	12	La	16
	El	12	13	Ch	11
	Ja	6		Ka	13
	Ja	16		Ro	15
	Da	10		Le	9
	Ch	4	13	Je	13
	Bo	5		Mi	8
9	Jo	12		Mi	8
	Li	12		El	15
	Ho	5		Te	10
	Ka	14		Er	12
	Di	10		Ly	10
	To	4		Jo	13
	Lo	8		Jo	10
	Al	4		We	14
10	Da	4		An	4
	De	16		An	8
	Ja	13		St	5
	Hu	4		Ci	13
	An	13		Ju	10
	Ma	15		Ch	5
	An	10	14	Ju	8
11	Th	11		An	5
	Li	8		Ol	7
	Ar	12		Lo	16
	Ma	13		Mean:	9.63

[b] Five children were absent when the test was given.

To determine whether emphasis on cognitive skills interferes with the development of art skills, two judges were asked to evaluate drawings and paintings produced by the children in the fall program experimental group. The judges were a college instructor of art and an art therapist registered by the American Art Therapy Association.

For each of the 18 children in the experimental group, the judges evaluated three drawings or paintings: the child's first work, last work, and a work produced midway in the art program. The 54 works were identified only by number

TABLE 3: Comparing Mean Performance Scores in Predictive Drawing by Handicapped Experimental and Control Children, and by Normal Children[a]

Experimental group

Fall program (_N_ = 18)

Name	Sex	Age	Diagnosis	IQ	Horizontal		Vertical	
					Pre	Post	Pre	Post
Do	F	13	ER	Av	3	5	2	3
Sh	F	13	ER	Av	3	5	3	5
Ca	F	14	R	95	4	5	3	4
To	M	14	ER	97	3	4	5	5
Bu	M	13	ER	56	2	5	4	5
Da	M	15	E	100	4	5	4	5
Ed	M	15	E	65	3	4	2	5
Ep	M	12	E	85	3	4	4	5
Ev	F	13	ER	90	2	2	2	5
Ba	F	12	R	86	4	3	3	4
Je	F	11	ER	72	3	5	3	5
El	F	12	ER	140	5	5	5	5
Ro	M	12	E	DN	2	3	5	2
Ri	M	12	ER	77	5	5	5	5
Ru	M	11	R	87	5	3	2	5
Vi	M	8	R	ab AV	3	5	3	4
Da	M	9	ER	DN	2	5	2	5
Ru	F	9	ER	75	1	1	2	3

Spring program (_N_ = 16)

Name	Sex	Age	Diagnosis	IQ	Horizontal		Vertical	
					Pre	Post	Pre	Post
Je	M	8	ER	68	2	2	1	5
We	M	8	E	94	1	2	2	5
Ca	M	8	ER	94	2	4	3	5
Fe	M	8	E	104	2	2	2	4
Al	M	10	E	Av	3	5	1	3
Ro	F	8	R	66	2	4	3	3
Ca	M	10	R	87	5	5	5	5
Ev	M	8	R	96	5	5	2	5
An	M	13	R	72	2	2	2	3
Ja	F	12	E	83	2	2	2	3
Je	F	14	E	100	2	2	3	3
Ma	M	12	ER	50	5	5	5	5
Ja	M	11	ER		3	4	2	2
Ke	M	10	ER	DN	1	2	2	3
Do	F	8	ER	97	2	3	3	3
Li	F	8	ER	86	2	5	2	3
					2.88	3.76	2.91	1
					1.55	1.76	1.47	1.08

[a] Scored on the basis of 1 to 5 points for level of development.

TABLE 3 (cont.)

Control group

Fall program (N = 18)

Name	Sex	Age	Diagnosis	IQ	Horizontal score	Vertical score
Gl	F	13	ER	99	2	1
El	F	13	ER	Av	2	2
De	F	15	ER	65	5	4
An	M	14	ER	79	3	2
Pa	M	11	ER	94	5	5
Ma	M	13	E	74	2	2
Jo	M	13	E	70	5	5
Mi	M	11	E	75	5	4
He	F	11	ER		2	4
Ma	F	12	E		1	2
An	F	11	ER	Av	2	2
De	F	11	ER	73	2	2
Al	M	11	E	Def	2	3
Fe	M	12	E	87	5	5
Mi	M	9	E	92	2	4
Di	M	9	ER	77	2	4
Ja	M	10	E	83	5	2
Ch	F	7	E	57	2	4

Spring program (N = 16)

Name	Sex	Age	Diagnosis	IQ	Horizontal Pre	Horizontal Post	Vertical Pre	Vertical Post
Ro	M	9	ER	65	2	2	1	3
Ke	M	8	ER	Av	2	2	2	4
Ah	M	8	ER	100	5	5	2	3
Jo	M	8	ER	94	3	4	2	5
Sa	M	9	ER	77	2	2	3	3
Ba	F	7	R		1	2	3	3
Ca	M	9	R	99	5	3	2	5
Ki	M	8	R	Av	2	4	2	5
Ga	M	12	ER	110	5	5	5	5
Ev	F	13	E	65	2	2	3	5
An	F	14	ER	89	2	2	5	2
Mi	M	8	E		5	3	2	2
Ro	M	12	ER	72	2	2	2	3
Jo	M	10	ER	bd	2	2	2	3
El	F	9	R	73	2	2	1	1
De	F	10	ER		2	2	2	5
Combined mean:					2.88	2.75	2.82	3.44
Combined (sd)^2:					2.05	1.27	1.60	1.75

TABLE 3   (cont.)

Normal children (*N* = 68)

tested once

Age	Name	Horizontal	Vertical	Age	Name	Horizontal	Vertical
8	Ni	4	0		Ma	1	2
	Pa	5	0		Jo	5	5
	An	4	5		Al	1	4
	St	5	4		El	5	4
	Da	4	1		Su	3	2
	Ca	1	0		Jo	3	1
	Mi	1	2		Di	5	1
	El	4	0		Je	4	2
	Ja	4	1		Jo	1	1
	Ja	4	0		Da	3	1
	Da	1	0		Am	4	1
	Ch	5	4	12	La	5	5
	Bo	4	1		Pa	4	4
9	Jo	3	1		Ti	3	2
	Li	4	4		Da	3	4
	Ho	5	5		To	4	1
	Ka	5	0		Ma	2	4
	Di	4	3		Ga	4	5
	To	5	0	13	Ch	5	5
	Lo	5	0		Jo	5	5
	Al	4	0		Mi	3	5
10	Da	1	1		Pa	5	5
	De	4	4		Bo	5	4
	Ja	4	1		Th	4	4
	Hu	1	5		Ma	5	1
	An	4	3		Ro	4	5
	Ma	5	3		Ka	5	2
	An	5	2		Le	3	3
11	Th	1	3		Je	5	5
	Li	4	4	14	Ju	1	1
	An	3	3		An	5	5
	Ma	5	1		Ol	5	5
	Da	1	1		Lu	5	5
	Ja	5	0				
	To	1	3		Mean scores	3.68	2.56

and were shown in random order to conceal the sequence in which they had been produced.

Working independently, the judges rated each drawing or painting on a 5 point scale ranging from "commonplace form or content" to "highly skillful, exploratory, or sensitive." They also scored for creative and expressive qualities ranging from "imitative, learned, impersonal" to "highly personal and imaginative."

Both judges found improvements that were significant ($p < .01$). As rated by the art therapist, the mean score for work produced in the first class was 4.44, and the mean score for work produced in the last class was 7.27 ($t = 3.13$). As rated by the college instructor of art, the mean score for work produced in the first class was 3.66 and the mean score for the work produced in the last class, 6.33 ($t = 3.29$). Thus the children's art skills improved even though the main purpose of the project was to develop their cognitive skills.
NY 10543.

Learning Disabled Children (1975)

This second study (see Silver & Lavin, 1977; Silver, 1978) explored whether the teaching and testing procedures of the Silver Test would be useful for children who had an opposite constellation of skills—that is, auditory and language strengths rather than visual-motor strengths—and whether the procedures could be used effectively by others (in particular, teachers). Eleven graduate students, who had registered for an elective course in using the procedures, worked under faculty supervision with 11 children with visual-motor weaknesses. The children were not systematically selected but were enrolled as their applications were received. There was no control group.

After 10 weekly 1-hour art classes, the chilren improved significantly in the three areas of cognition: drawing from imagination ($p < .01$), drawing from observation ($p < .05$), and sequencing ($p < .01$). These results suggest that the teaching and testing procedures are useful for such children and that they can be successfully used by practitioners initially unfamiliar with them.

Normal Children (1978)

In this third study (unpublished), the question of whether the Silver Test could be used successfully with normal children who had special educational needs was investigated. Another group of 11 graduate students worked under faculty supervision with 11 children selected by school administrators as achieving below grade level academically for a variety of reasons. Again, there was no control group. These children made significant gains in the three areas of cognition: drawing from imagination ($p < .01$), predictive drawing ($p < .05$), and drawing from observation ($p < .05$). Thus, these results again would seem to verify the usefulness of the teaching and testing procedures.

Normal and Learning-Disabled Children in a Variety of Schools (1979–80)

This study, which was supported by a grant from the National Institute of Education, had two aims: (1) to explore the degree to which the Silver Test measures cognitive skills by examining the relationship between this test and six traditional tests of intelligence or achievement; and (2) to attempt verification of the results of previous studies which used the Silver Test by using a more controlled research design, a more diverse population, and a wider variety of settings. (A fuller report of this study is given in Silver, Lavin, Boeve, Hayes, Itzler, O'Brien, Terner, & Wohlberg, 1980.)

Otis Lennon School Ability Test: The Silver Test and the Otis Lennon School Ability Test were administered by researchers in the study to 99 normal second and third grade children, drawn from two of the schools included in the project. The tests were also administered (in a third school) by a teacher who volunteered to take part in the study. Significant relationships were found between two of the Silver subtests—Drawing from Imagination and Predictive Drawing—and the Otis Lennon scores. There was no significant relationship between Drawing from Observation and the Otis Lennon Test.

WISC Performance IQ Scores: The sample in this study was drawn from two schools for deaf children and a school for children with language and learning disabilities. In two of the schools, the test was administered by volunteer teachers. Significant correlations were found between the WISC Performance IQ scores of 65 children and their total and subtest scores on the Silver Test.

Metropolitan Achievement Test (MAT): A significant relationship was found between MAT Reading scores and total Silver Test scores of 79 normal children drawn from (i.e. 5 schools had been involved) two schools involved in the study. Significant relationships were also found between MAT Reading scores and two subtests of the Silver Test—Drawing from Imagination and Predictive Drawing. There was no significant relationship between MAT Math scores and total Silver Test scores.

SRA Math Achievement Scores: Significant relationships were found between SRA Math scores of 65 normal children and their scores on the Drawing from Imagination and Predictive Drawing subtests of the Silver Test. There was no significant relationship between the total Silver Test scores and the SRA Math scores, or between the Drawing from Observation subtests and the SRA Math scores.

Iowa Test of Basic Skills: While significant correlations were found between the scores of 20 normal children on the Iowa Composite and Math Tests and the Total Silver Test, Drawing from Imagination, and Drawing from Observation subtests, no significant correlations were found for Predictive Drawing.

Canadian Cognitive Abilities Test (CCAT): The Silver Test was administered to a class of normal second grade Canadian children, and these scores were compared to their scores on the CCAT. Significant correlations were found between the CCAT and Drawing from Imagination. No significant correlations were found between scores on the CCAT and scores on the Drawing from Observation and Predictive Drawing subtests.

As noted above, the second part of this study examined the effectiveness of the Silver Test with a more diverse population. This part of the study involved a sample of 84 children, ages 7 to 11, who had been nominated by school administrators on the basis of being at least one year below grade level in reading or mathematics. The children were drawn from five schools: one school for learning-disabled children, and four schools for both normal children and children with special educational needs. From this population, the participants were selected on the basis of their scores on the Silver Test. A matched control group received no special treatment. During the course of the program, a number of children were lost for various reason. Consequently, additional children were randomly removed to equate the number in each group for statistical analysis.

Five art specialists, one from each school, worked with two groups, each comprising five children, for approximately 40 minutes a week for 12 weeks. During the first 6-week period, all teachers used the same procedures. During the second 6-week period, these teachers adapted the procedures to meet the needs of individual children, and devised procedures of their own. The Silver Test was administered before and after the art program.

As in the earlier studies, the posttest scores of the experimental group showed significant gains over the pretest scores; however, there was no significant difference between posttest scores of experimental and control groups (see Figure 9).

After the program ended, the scoring guidelines of the Silver Test were modified and tightened, and all test booklets were rescored blindly. The scores were then re-analyzed, but essentially the same results as those obtained previously were found. However, a school by school analysis of net change scores (the pretest minus the posttest scores) showed significant differences between pre- and posttest scores in the school for learning-disabled children. In this school, the experimental group gains were significantly higher than the control group gains. In the four other schools, the experimental groups gained significantly, but their gains were not significantly higher than control group gains. In each school, however, there were individual children who made dramatic gains in all test scores.

Hayes Study: Normal Children, Grades 1–3 (1978)

Hayes (1978) examined whether a correlation exists between children's drawings and reading achievement. Hayes administered the Silver Test to 75 first, second, and third grade normal children from lower to middle income backgrounds and compared these scores to the children's scores on the Informal Reading Inventory

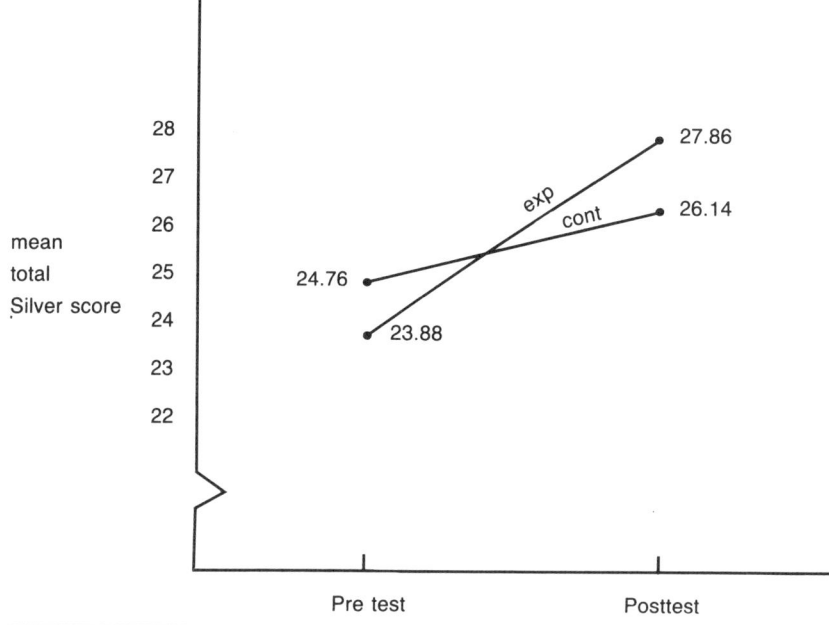

[a] Both posttest scores differed significantly from pretest scores ($p < .05$). In addition, the experimental group's posttest scores differed significantly from the combination of the other three groups of scores. Analysis and Fiqure 9 prepared by John Kleinhans. PhD

Figure 9: Mean Scores for Experimental and Control Groups on Pre and posttests in Five Schools in the 1980 Project[a]

for first graders, and the SRA Reading Form *F*/Primary II for second and third graders.

Significant correlations were found between the Drawing from Imagination subtest of the Silver Test and reading achievement for the three grades. Correlations between Drawing from Observation and reading achievement were significant for the third grade only, while Predictive Drawing correlated significantly with reading for the first grade only.

Moser Study: Learning Disabled Young Adults (1980)

Moser (1980) examined the reliability and validity of the Silver Test. In order to assess reliability, Moser administered the test twice to 12 learning-disabled subjects and computed separate reliability coefficients for each of the subtests. To assess validity, she administered the test to 35 normal subjects and 38 learning-disabled subjects and compared the mean scores. Moser also compared the scores of her 38 subjects on the Wechsler Adult Intelligence Scale (WAIS), the Bender Test, the Draw-A-Man-Test, and the Silver Test.

Moser's results give credence to the reliability and validity of the Silver Test. All of the test-retest correlations were significant ($p < .05$). The learning-disabled group scored lower than the normal control group on the Silver Test ($p < .001$), and on the draw-a-Man Test ($p < .05$). Significant correlations were found between total and subtest Silver scores and scores on the Draw-A-Man, Bender, and WAIS tests a the $p < .01$ and $p < .001$ levels.

CONCLUDING OBSERVATIONS

Positive correlations were found in the above studies between scores on the Silver Test and 10 traditional tests of intelligence or achievement. The correlations were of moderate strength significance with the language-oriented tests, and of high significance with the spatially-oriented tests.[3] These findings seem to indicate that the Silver Test is measuring, through the medium of drawing, aspects of cognition that are also measured to some extent by the traditional tests. As such, the Silver Test would seem useful as an instrument for evaluating learning and creativity and for identifying children who have cognitive strengths that may escape detection on language oriented tests. The Silver Test also seems to offer some explanation as to why some children do well on the Silver Test but not on traditional tests of intelligence—the latter use a different medium from that of the Silver Test to tap cognitive skills. Classroom teachers need to be aware that some of their pupils may have capabilities and potentialities easily overlooked by conventional tests. Also, teachers need to be aware that all pupils can benefit from nonverbal activities that call for right brain hemisphere functioning. Thus, children can visualize, imagine, invent, observe, predict, and solve problems through the media of drawing, painting, and modeling. Tasks that are open-ended with many possible correct solutions invite children to discover solutions for themselves, thus facilitating their learning. The tasks can be a particularly helpful means of working with children who rely on right brain hemisphere functioning as a matter of preference or necessity (such as deaf, learning-disabled, or language-impaired children), or any child who has difficulty putting thoughts into words or in understanding what is said.

The findings of studies to date with the Silver Test also suggest that teachers may be able to stimulate cognitive growth without neglecting the usual goals of teaching art, such as developing sensitivity to aesthetic values and the skills required in drawing, painting, and modeling. For example, college instructors who judged children's drawings and paintings in the 1972–73 study with handicapped and normal children found improvements in skill and creativity to a degree that was statistically significant, even though the main purpose of

---

[3] The Silver Test is scheduled for publication in September, 1982, by Special Child Publications, P.O. Box 33548 Seattle Washington 98133.

the project was to develop the children's cognitive skills. This suggests that different educational goals can be pursued concurrently, and that we do not have to sacrifice one developmental need for another. Art therapists can include aesthetic goals without sacrificing spontaneity, and art educators can stimulate cognitive growth without abandoning the traditional goals of art education. Much still remains to be done in the area of developing children's cognitive skills through art. It is hoped that the discussion and the findings of studies using the Silver Test presented here will encourage others to do further research.

REFERENCES

Arnheim, R. *Visual thinking.* Berkeley, CA: University of California Press, 1969.

Bannatyne, A. *Language, reading, and learning disabilities.* Springfield, IL: Charles C. Thomas, 1971.

Bruner, J. S. *Studies in cognitive growth.* New York: John Wiley & Sons, 1966.

Furth, H. Research with the deaf. *Volta Review,* 1966, *68,* 34–56.

Hayes, K. *The relationship between drawing ability and reading scores.* Unpublished masters dissertation, College of New Rochelle, New York, 1978.

Jakobson, R. In A. V. S. de Reuck & M. O'Connor (Eds.), *Disorders of Language.* Boston, MA: Little, Brown & Co., 1964.

Lutz, K. *The implications of brain research for learning strategies and educational practice.* 1978. (ED 163 068, 30 pp.)

Moser, J. *Drawing and painting and learning disabilities.* Unpublished doctoral dissertation, New York University, New York, 1980.

Moses, B. *The relationship between visual thinking tasks and problem-solving performance.* Bowling Green, OH: Bowling Green State University, Ohio, 1980. (ED 187 734, 25 pp.)

Piaget, J. *Genetic epistemology.* New York: Columbia University Press, 1970.

Piaget, J., & Inhelder, B. *The child's conception of space.* New York: W. W. Norton & Co., 1967.

Rugel, R. P. WISC subtest scores of disabled readers. *Journal of Learning Disabilities,* 1974, *10*(7), 57–64.

Silver, R. A. *Cognitive skills development through art activities.* NY State Urban Education Project Report #147232101, 1973.

Silver, R. A. *Developing cognitive and creative skills through art.* Baltimore, MD: University Park Press, 1978.

Silver, R. A., & Lavin, C. The role of art in developing and evaluating cognitive skills. *Journal of Learning Disabilities,* 1977, *10*(7), 27–35.

Silver, R. A., Lavin, C., Boeve, E., Hayes, K., Itzler, J., O'Brien, J., Terner, N., & Wohlberg, P. *Assessing and developing cognitive skills in handicapped children through art.* NIE Project #G 79 0081, 1980. Available from Graduate School, College of New Rochelle, New Rochelle, NY 10801. ERIC Document Reproduct Service (EC #140–395)

Sinclair-de-Zwart, H. Developmental psycholinguistics. In D. Elkind & J. H. Flavell (Eds.), *Studies in cognitive development.* London: Oxford University Press, 1969.

Smith, M. D., Coleman, J. M., Dokecki, P. R., & Davis, E. E. Intellectual characteristics of school labeled learning disabled children. *Exceptional Children,* March 1977, *43,* (6), 352–357.

Strauss, A. A., & Kephart, N. C. *Psychopathology and education of the brain-injured child* (Vol. 2). New York: Grune & Stratton, 1955.

Torrance, E. P. *Guiding creative talent.* Englewood Cliffs, NJ: Prentice-Hall, Inc., 1962.

Witkin, H. A. Psychological differentiation. New York: John Wiley & Sons, Inc., 1962.

8

The Kindergarten: A Retrospective and Contemporary View

Bernard Spodek

University of Illinois at Urbana-Champaign

About 125 years have passed since the kindergarten was introduced in the United States. During this time, there have been a number of changes in conceptions of kindergarten education. The first kindergartens were based upon the philosophy and pedagogy of Friedrich Froebel; the first major change from that early conception modified kindergarten practice to make it more consistent with principles derived from progressive education and from the emerging field of child development. Also during this time, kindergartens slowly became integrated into the American public school system. More recently, newer conceptions of kindergarten education appear to be evolving. With the almost universal acceptance of kindergarten education as a legitimate part of public schooling, the distinction between the kindergarten and the primary grades seems to be disappearing in American schools. This chapter will explore these changes and some of the reasons underlying them.

FROEBELIAN KINDERGARTENS

The kindergarten was designed by Friedrich Froebel as a child-centered educational institution. Froebel viewed education as supporting development and as resulting from self-activity. His kindergarten theory unified man, God, and nature, presenting this unity to young children through a series of symbolic materials and activities. Each child constructed his or her conception of unity as a result of active involvement in the kindergarten (Lilley, 1967).

Central also was the conception of man as *Gliedganzes,* a word coined by Froebel himself.

> The word *Gliedganzes* means a member of a whole who is potentially commensurate with the whole to which as member he belongs, but who can make his potentiality actual only in and through active membership (Blow, 1913, p. 9). The concept of *Gliedganzes* contains three distinct implications. The first, that which is generic or the reproducers of the species in lower forms of life, becomes Ego in man. The second implication is that this generic Ego or universal self is not only the ideal Human, but the divine. . . . The third and final implication is that this immanent-transcendent God is one with the absolute first principle through which is given its being. (Blow, 1913, p. 10)

The major vehicles of Froebel's curriculum were the *gifts,* sets of manipulative materials to be used in prescribed ways demonstrated by the kindergarten teacher, and the *occupations,* a series of craft activities (Froebel, 1887).

Gifts

Solids

First gift: 6 colored worsted balls about 1½" in diameter
Second gift: Wooden ball, cylinder, cube, 1½" in diameter
Third gift: 8 1" cubes, forming a 2" cube
Fourth gift: 8 brick-shaped blocks, 2" × 1" × ½"
Fifth gift: 27 1" cubes, three bisected, three quadrisected diagonally, forming a 3" cube
Sixth gift: 27 brick-shaped blocks, 3 bisected longitudinally, 6 bisected transversely

Surfaces

Seventh gift: Squares, entire and bisected
Equilateral triangles, entire, halves, thirds

Lines

Eighth gift: Straight, splints of various lengths

Points

Ninth gift: Circular, metal or paper rings

Reconstruction

Tenth gift: Softened peas or wax pellets and sharpened sticks or straws.

Occupations

Solids: Plastic clay, cardboard work, woodcarving
Surfaces: Paper folding, paper cutting, parquetry, painting
Lines: Interlacing, intertwining, weaving, embroidery, drawing
Points: Stringing beads, perforating

The sphere, represented in the balls of the first gift, with its single external surface, symbolized unity. A ball appears again in the second gift, along with a cube, a 6-sided solid representing diversity. A cylinder with attributes of both the sphere and the cube was included to represent the mediation of opposites. The other gifts followed and, with songs, games, movement activities, stories, poetry, nature study, and gardening, rounded out the curriculum.

During this general period, others were experimenting with Froebelian ideas and sponsoring kindergarten programs of their own. Margarethe Schurz established the first kindergarten in the United States in Watertown, Wisconsin, in 1856. Her major contribution may have been in introducing the idea of the kindergarten to Elizabeth Peabody, who became a tireless advocate of kindergarten education, not only establishing the first English-speaking kindergarten in Boston, but also travelling extensively throughout the United States carrying the message of kindergarten education wherever she was invited and helping individuals and groups establish kindergartens (Snyder, 1972).

The first public school kindergarten, taught by Susan Blow, was established in St. Louis in 1873. It was a long time, however, before kindergartens were to receive widespread acceptance within the public schools. Conflict existed between the educational philosophy underlying elementary education and that underlying the kindergarten. The problems of articulation between the two types of school programs required a solution before the two systems could operate comfortably side by side. As Benjamin C. Gregory wrote in the yearbook of the National Society for the Scientific Study of Education (1908):

> In passing from the kindergarten to the primary school, there is a break. Do what you will to soften the change, to modify the break, it still remains a break. Three general methods of dealing with the difficulty have been employed: (1) To provide a connecting class to take the child out of his kindergarten habits and introduce him to those of the primary school: in the words of some teachers, "to make him over." (2) To modify the kindergarten and made it more nearly resemble the primary schools. (3) To modify the primary school to make it more nearly resemble the kindergarten. To these might be added a fourth: To do a little bit of each. (p. 22)

Nina Vanderwalker (1907), writing just a year earlier, had suggested that the introduction of kindergartens into the elementary school had already influenced the primary curriculum in numerous ways. Art, music, nature study, and games had been introduced into the grades as a result of this contact. The process of curriculum diffusion that operated probably went both ways, with elements of the primary curriculum also introduced into the kindergarten.

The kindergartens of that era were a part of private as well as public schools, including German-language schools developed to serve the German-speaking communities, where the acceptance of the Froebelian kindergarten had been carried over from abroad. Many English-language schools adopted kindergartens as well. Frequently, kindergartens were used to serve other than secular educational purposes: a number of churches considered the kindergarten a valuable means for carrying on religious work, and incorporated kindergartens into their activities. In addition, church missionaries used kindergartens to reach socially isolated minority groups in America, as well as foreign groups abroad. Kindergartens were also established by American missionaries in many less-developed countries.

Among yet other sponsors of kindergartens in the United States was the Women's Christian Temperence Union, which provided aid to families plagued by problems of alcoholism. Programs were also incorporated into many of the early settlement houses established in slum areas, to provide social services to poor and immigrant families. Labor unions and private businesses also sponsored kindergartens during this era.

This variety of sponsors caused some confusion between the idea of the kindergarten as an educational institution and the concept of the creche or day nursery, which served a child-caring function. In addition, while many kindergarten sponsors maintained programs of high quality, others stretched their resources to serve as many children as possible and to provide that service as a labor of love, with less well-prepared teachers often providing the staffing (Vanderwalker, 1908). As kindergartens became diversified, their practices often reflected the purposes of the sponsors. Church-related kindergartens taught religious precepts, while settlement house kindergartens were concerned with meeting broad social needs. Confusion between education and philanthropy was evident (see Spodek, 1982).

THE KINDERGARTEN AND PROGRESSIVISM

In the early years of kindergarten development in the United States, good practice was determined by adherence to Froebel's writings. However, kindergarten practitioners soon began to modify their classroom activities, revising and transforming Froebel's prescriptions. Paper dolls were added to the beds constructed from the blocks in Froebel's gifts, along with sand tables, doll-houses, and other materials which promoted free social interaction among children (Weber, 1969). Prior to the end of the nineteenth century, the evolving field of child study came to the attention of kindergarten educators through the writings and lectures of scholars such as G. Stanley Hall. In addition, the progressive education movement—which was to address issues related to the education of younger as well as older children—was evolving.

The child-study movement originated in the United States under the leadership of G. Stanley Hall. Hall's method of studying children was to observe them directly, analyze their products, and query those who worked in close contact with children through interviews and questionnaires. These techniques were a major change from the traditional use of introspective recall to study childhood. Hall suggested that education be consistent with children's minds, rather than reflect adult thought, and he believed that the emotional rather than the intellectual life of the young child was of greatest value. Hall criticized Froebelian kindergarten theory as being superficial and fantastic—he considered that young children needed large, bold movements rather than the sedentary activities of the gifts and occupations and asserted that free play could serve their developmental needs (Hall, 1901).

John Dewey, whose ideas provided one of the important bases for progressive education, also suggested a form of education for young children which was quite different from that of Froebel. In establishing a sub-primary class in the University of Chicago Laboratory School, Dewey called for educational activities that would support continuity in children's growth and would be connected to their everyday lives. The child's life in the home and the community, rather than a set of abstract ideas symbolized in manipulative materials, was to be the basis for school activities (Dewey, 1900).

Both Dewey and Hall lauded the philosophy underlying Froebelian kindergarten while criticizing the limitations of its practice. Dewey admired the fact that Froebel had rooted the education of children in their activities, valued social learning, and believed that children gained knowledge through productive and creative activities. Hall credited Froebel with developing a form of education based on children's play and with pointing to recapitulation theory as the basis for understanding the development of children (Ross, 1976). Thus, for many kindergarten educators, the introduction into the kindergarten of educational ideas from such scholars as these was seen as an extension of Froebelian ideals rather than as a rejection of them.

During the early years of the twentieth century, the number of kindergarten educators attracted to these newer ideas about early childhood education continued to increase. Some suggested a break from traditional kindergarten education and the development of a kindergarten curriculum that was responsive to the nature and the life of the child; others suggested a reconciliation of newer ideas about children's learning and development with traditional Froebelian ideals. The International Kindergarten Union, representing kindergarten educators of the time, established a committee to study these conflicting educational ideologies and to devise a set of recommendations for some clear policy on kindergarten education. Rather than author a single report, this Committee of Nineteen, as they were called, issued a book containing three separate ones. The first report, written by Susan Blow, was a statement of Froebelian philosophy and an endorsement of traditional kindergarten practices; it was approved by a number of committee members. The second report, written by Patty Smith Hill and endorsed by other committee members, was a statement of progressive kindergarten principles and practices reflecting the philosophy of John Dewey.

The third report, written by Elizabeth Harrison, presented a compromise position and recommended a reconciliation of the other two opposing positions (Committee of Nineteen, 1913).

Kindergarten practice in the United States went through a complete reconstruction during the first third of the twentieth century. Froebelian principles in a general sense remained, along with vestiges of Froebelian practices, such as Circle Time and the use of finger plays. But kindergartens became more reflective of children's lives at home and in the community, and their methods reflected the knowledge that was being generated about how children learn and develop. By the 1930s the transformation was virtually complete.

In their description of the Horace Mann Kindergarten—a demonstration kindergarten at Teacher's College, Columbia University—Garrison, Sheehy, and Dalgleish (1937) describe an exemplary program for 5-year-olds. This program was viewed as a model of what kindergarten education ought to be. The teachers were seen as being responsible for creating an environment filled with worthwhile activities and for developing a growing classroom organization rooted in the experience and needs of the children. Experiences were organized around the social sciences, the natural and physical sciences, the creative arts, and the "tool subjects" of reading, writing, spelling, and arithmetic. Materials for physical play, manipulative play, dramatic play, art, and woodworking were provided. The large Patty Hill blocks and the smaller Pratt unit blocks found in this kindergarten were a far cry from the one-inch cube blocks of the Froebelian gifts.

The general plan of this program was a flexible one, building on as well as creating interests in children. The social science program was designed to clarify children's social experiences and to provide for their adjustment to social life. Work in the natural and physical sciences was designed to give children an opportunity to observe, experience, and experiment with phenomena, to gain scientific information, and to enjoy nature. The creative arts helped children develop skills and enjoy and appreciate art experiences utilizing a range of media, including language. The academic skill areas were presented only in informal ways.

It is difficult to determine to what extent the kindergartens of this era reflected the exemplary practices of the progressives. There are few descriptive studies of practice in the period, but where studies do exist they are of ideal rather than representative programs (e.g., DeLima, 1925; Pratt & Stanton, 1926). The pattern of the Horace Mann Kindergarten is also reflected in early childhood textbooks published during that era (e.g., Foster & Headley, 1948; Gans, Stendler, & Almy, 1952). In addition, reform kindergarten practices were suggested as being just as appropriate for the primary grades:

> A modern progressive primary grade room does not look unlike a kindergarten room. . . . The same informal organization is carried on with the

children gradually assuming more and more responsibility for the conduct of the room. Children are given the opportunity to carry out their own aims and purposes and to judge their results. . . . As in the kindergarten, the children move freely, work individually or in small self-organized groups. . . . The subject matter of the first grade is related to and grows out of the activities. . . . While acquiring information and developing skills are not overlooked, the emphasis is on social living and the development of character. (Whipple, 1929, pp. 260–261)

CONTEMPORARY KINDERGARTEN PRACTICES

During the past decade or so, we have seen another major shift in kindergarten practices. The concern for young children's development and for the creation of programs reflecting their needs and interests seems to be lessening. In its place can be found a concern for the achievement of specific learning goals. It seems as though the kindergarten is again being reconstituted, this time essentially as a downward extension of primary education. Thus, the change is from a concern for continuity of development to a concern for continuity of achievement.

A number of strategies have been used to alter the kindergarten to make it more responsive to primary education. One is to adopt prescribed, commercially prepared educational programs, often extensions of textbook series in academic areas. Such adoptions, it is suggested, ensure the continuity of learning through the elementary school. Prescriptive programs have also been suggested and adopted; these have been designed to provide children with the prerequisites for success in later school learning. Many such programs are based upon "nationally validated" early childhood curricula originally created for handicapped or potentially handicapped young children (Fallon, 1973; Far West Laboratory, 1976). While a range of program alternatives are suggested, in many cases the activities prescribed are tied to a screening or evaluation instrument, so that success or failure on a specific test item determines the child's sequence of learning activities. In both cases, once programs are selected, teachers function less as decision-makers and more as technicians who implement predetermined activities.

A number of influences seem to have led to the present situation. Among these are the following:

1. Kindergarten attendance has become the rule rather than the exception.
2. Major shifts in the orientations of early childhood curricula have taken place.
3. Parallel shifts in developmental theories used to justify early childhood curriculum have occurred.

4. Social pressures to offer academic instruction at an early age have been exerted.
5. The use of standardized achievement tests in evaluating the education progress of young children has increased.
6. Many kindergarten teachers are inadequately prepared to be effective early childhood curriculum makers.

Kindergarten the Rule

Kindergartens were first introduced in the public schools in 1873, with kindergarten children representing only slightly over 1% of the elementary school student population (K-8) at the turn of the century (42% of these attended private schools). It was estimated that, in 1922, only about 12% of 5-year-olds attended kindergartens. Even by 1964, less than half of the 5-year-olds attended kindergartens, while in 1978 the numbers exceeded 80%. Enrollment seems to have become stabilized at slightly over 82% in 1977 and 1978 (Grant & Eiden, 1980). The table presented here (Table 1) summarizes kindergarten attendance in the United States in the decades since the turn of the century, identifies the proportion of those in attendance in public and private institutions, and compares kindergarten attendance to total elementary school attendance during this period. (Since some 5-year-olds are enrolled in first grade, the actual percentage of attendance in kindergarten is somewhat less than this chart would suggest.)

Only in recent years could elementary program designers expect that children entering the primary grades would first have been in kindergarten. Once attendance became the norm, kindergartens received much more attention from those who develop elementary programs and educational materials. Kindergarten education then became the expected beginning point for children in schools and thus a focus for building educational continuity into school programs.

Shift in Curriculum Orientation

During the past 145 years that kindergartens have been in existence, they have been used to achieve a range of different goals, including teaching philosophical idealism, Americanizing children, building proper habits, providing emotional prophylaxis for children, serving as a vestibule for the primary grades, presenting the content of school subjects to young children, and helping to develop learning-to-learn skills (Spodek, 1973). This period of curriculum development can be characterized by both its continuities and discontinuities. The continuities can be seen in the persistent concern for two types of goals for young children: the support or stimulation of growth or development, and the achievement of specific learning (Spodek, 1977). Concern for growth can be found in the original Froebelian kindergarten. This same concern was articulated in a different

TABLE 1 Elementary School and Kindergarten Enrollment

Level	1899–1900	1909–10	1919–20	1929–30	1939–40	1949–50	1959–60	Fall 1969	Fall 1978
				Year					
Kindergarten-Grade 8	16,261,846	18,528,535	20,963,722	23,739,840	21,127,021	22,207,241	32,412,266	37,011,390	32,242,000
Kindergarten	225,394	346,189	510,949	786,463	660,909	1,175,312	2,293,492	2,821,213	2,861,000
Public	131,657	293,970	481,266	723,443	594,647	1,034,203	1,922,712	2,601,242	2,642,000
Nonpublic	93,737	52,219	29,683	54,456	57,341	133,000	354,000	200,000	200,000
Percent of Enrollment									
Five-year-olds enrolled in public school	58	85	94	91	90	88	84	92	92
Elementary children enrolled in kindergarten	1.3	1.8	2.4	3.3	3.1	5.2	7.0	7.6	8.9

From *Digest of educational statistics 1980* by W. V. Grant and L. J. Eiden. Washington, DC: National Center for Educational Statistics, 1980.

way in the progressive kindergarten, as well as in the development of nursery education.

The alliance of the reform kindergarten with the progressive primary school was supported by a mutual concern for the growth of the child. The idea of "development as the aim of education" (Kohlberg & Mayer, 1972), a basic progressive education concept, provided the connection between early childhood educators and developmental psychologists. "Growth" or "development," used in a metaphorical sense by progressive educators, seemed to take on a literal meaning in early childhood education. As the progressive education movement waned, there was a general lessening of concern for development and an increase in the concern for achieving specific learning outcomes. This concern for learning was imposed upon the kindergarten as well, with the kindergarten conceived of as preparing children for the learning they will achieve in later school years. Gans, Stendler, and Almy (1952) characterized this "readiness" view of the kindergarten as the *3Rs Curriculum* some 30 years ago:

> The 3Rs approach has not only prevailed in the primary grades, but it has reached down into the five-year-old kindergarten. Counting, some writing and reading readiness activities chiefly in the form of workbook exercises have been typical experiences in kindergarten where this curriculum has been in operation. Under such a setup the kindergarten is seen as a year of settling down for children, of adjusting to sitting still and following directions, so that they will be better prepared for a more rigorous attack on the 3Rs during first grade. (p. 80-81)

The difference between the concerns of kindergartens of 30 years ago and those of today is with the intensity of academic instruction in the kindergarten. Instead of being concerned with using the kindergarten year to get children prepared for the organization of the primary grades, both the organization and the content of these grades seem to have been introduced into the kindergarten.

Shifting Developmental Theories

The advent of the Head Start Program has been characterized as resulting from the joining of new views of human development with new concerns for social justice. At the time that educators seemed to be increasing their concerns for the problems of educating disadvantaged children, new ideas relating to cognitive development—and especially to the importance of the early years on this development—seemed to be coming to the fore. The work of Jean Piaget, which had been accumulating for decades, began to receive the attention of American psychologists and educators. Piaget's theories described children's cognitive development as moving through a series of stages with achievement at later stages dependent upon successful progress through earlier stages. The early experiences of the child were seen as having significant impact on total intellectual development, even though direct instruction was not viewed as effective in moving children through these stages. Hunt, in his classic formulation *Intel-*

ligence and Experience (1961), brought together a wealth of theory and research from many sources in support of the idea that these early experiences could have a major impact on the developing intellect. Bloom's (1964) analysis of test data on intelligence suggested that a great deal of the variance in later tests of intelligence could be accounted for by the variance in tests taken by children before 5 years of age. Thus, it was demonstrated that what children learn early in life could affect their continued learning.

In addition to this awareness, behavioral psychologists were demonstrating that by manipulating the motivational sets of children, and by analyzing complex tasks in terms of simpler components to be taught separately and later integrated, many specific skills could be learned by children at an early age. Behavioral principles were used to understand development and to provide the basis for systematic programs to teach young children (Bijou & Baer, 1961).

While each of the developmental theories briefly described above is different from the others, and none of the theories directly translates into the kindergarten program, all have been used to support the notion that intellectual development begins early in life and that what one learns in the early childhood years can have serious consequences for later learning. Growing out of the empirical research and the theory generation that took place in child development during this period, a number of educational programs arose for young children at the kindergarten and pre-kindergarten level. While these programs were originally designed for poor children, and many became the bases of the planned variations of Head Start and Follow-Through, a number of these programs or their variants have been broadly generalized to other early childhood populations.

While the evidence accumulated that there was much that young children could learn prior to first grade, there was no unanimity on the issue of what young children ought to learn during that period—what priorities ought to be given to the different learnings that are possible—and what the long-term consequences of particular learnings are. As kindergartens moved under the influences of the elementary school, it was felt in many cases that those learnings most consistent with what is taught later in school, or which seemed to be preparatory to later school learning, ought to be supported in the kindergarten. Yet there is no evidence that there are greater long-term payoffs for these kinds of learning activities than there are for activities more consistent with the growth ideology of the progressive kindergarten.

Early Instruction in Academic Skills

The introduction of reading and writing into the kindergarten is certainly not a new phenomenon. An exhibit at the 1876 Philadelphia Centennial Exposition labeled ''The American Kindergarten'' was criticized for encouraging such activities as reading and writing. This intrusion of academics into the Froebelian kindergarten was defended by citing a need to ''Americanize the kindergarten idea" (Ross, 1976). Formal reading instruction was never considered a part of the Froebelian kindergarten, nor did the progressive kindergarten offer more than informal activities related to basic academic skills.

A number of pressures have led to the increased concern for teaching academic skills in the kindergarten. On the one hand, there seem always to have been parents who wished their children to be involved in academic instruction as early as possible. Many of these parents have gifted children, or at least view their children as gifted. Montessori preschool programs have been attractive to these parents because of the promise made that their children would learn the three R's significantly earlier than they would have traditionally. Books have been made similarly available, detailing instructions for parents to engage in activities which promise to give their young children superior minds, or at least early access to school learning. These parents may strive to enroll their children early in school and/or to influence the school to make academics available to their children at the earliest possible moment. Wagner (1977) describes Alice Beck, an exemplary kindergarten teacher whose classroom is characterized as providing child-centered education through individualization and project learning. She deals with parental pressure to teach academics in kindergarten by meeting with parents early in the year to find out what they want for their children from kindergarten. She explains her goals to parents, encourages classroom visits, solicits help on projects, and informs the parents regularly and honestly about their child's activities.

A greater pressure to offer early instruction in academic skills, however, has resulted from the concern that the public schools may not be adequately preparing all children in the area of basic academic skills. The perceived failure of the public school system to provide adequate basic skills instruction has led to a number of suggested solutions, including the use of minimum competency tests and instruction in the academic skills at the earliest possible moment. The logic of this latter position seems inviolate. When the teaching of academic skills has begun in first grade, there have been failures. Some of these failures could be overcome by providing additional instructional time well before the initial assessment of success.

A number of concerns might be raised with this approach. To add instructional time for academic skills within the kindergarten requires that the time be taken from some other activities, activities which are also educational. Thus, there are no absolute gains in learning, but rather there are trade-offs; at best, achievement is gained in one area at the expense of achievement in other areas. With the addition of instruction in academics in the kindergarten, losses have been those activities that traditionally have been highly prized: art, music, science (including nature study), as well as opportunities for expression and play. These were the very activities kindergartens were applauded for having introduced into the elementary school in years past.

While articles on kindergarten cooking (Placek, 1976), block building

(Liedke, 1975), art (Warfield, 1973), environmental values (Bryant & Hunger-ford, 1977) and science (David, 1977) can still be found in the professional literature, often the justification for their inclusion in the kindergarten is related to the academic outcomes that can be derived. The use of blocks, for example, is advocated for teaching mathematical concepts of grouping, comparing, one-to-one correspondence, and ordering, as well as for familiarizing children with numbers and number names (Liedke, 1975). Thus, the academic values are used to justify the inclusion of these program activities. In addition, one can question what is actually taught in kindergartens in relation to academics. Durkin (1978) has criticized current kindergarten reading practices for sometimes being offered prematurely to children; when offered, the programs may themselves be poor.

In moving academics downwards into the kindergarten, too often the focus has been on mechanical learning. While mechanics are not the most critical aspects of academic learning, they are the ones that are most often assessed by standardized tests.

Increased Use of Standardized Tests

Directly related to the concern for instruction in the basic skills has been the call for the increased use of standardized achievement tests to periodically and regularly assess the achievement of these skills in children. While in the past educators often advocated postponing administration of standardized achieve-ment tests, assessment instruments are now being presented to children at earlier and earlier ages. These tests also influence what is taught.

A number of states have developed their own testing programs, while others have used commercially available standardized tests. Brickon and Roeber (1978) describe the development of a state kindergarten assessment program in Michigan. Teachers were able to use the formal instruments developed by the state education agency, other standardized tests, or other informal assessment techniques in their pilot program. Interestingly, most assessment was done in the area of cognitive and psychomotor skills, areas most easily assessed using the state-developed instruments. When the areas of music and art were assessed, evaluation was most often done through teacher observation.

An example of the relationship of testing to the teaching of basic skills can be found in *The National Conference on Achievement Testing and Basic Skills* (National Institute for Education of the Department of Health, Education and Welfare, 1978). The call at that conference, by educators and politicians alike, was for the improvement of instruction in basic academic skills and, beginning early, for the regular and continued administration of standardized achievement tests as a way of improving instruction in basic academic skills.

Since the content of most standardized achievement tests in the early grades is on the mechanics of reading, language, and arithmetic, and since programs at these grades are assessed by children's achievement on these tests, the focus on instruction more often leans toward teaching letter-sound associations, computation skills, spelling, punctuation, and the like, rather than toward higher-order academic processes such as comprehension, problem solving, and the application of principles to real problems.

One of the issues raised in the recent evaluation of the program models in Follow-Through was that the instruments used to evaluate achievement were more appropriate for some areas than for others. Since most tests used focused on achievement in the mechanics of reading, language, and arithmetic, those models that emphasized instruction in these skills were strongly favored in the evaluation (House, Glass, McLean, & Walker, 1977). Because program elements that are evaluated tend to receive greater attention from school personnel, especially when schools are being criticized, program goals such as social competence, for which there are no adequate standardized measures, tend to receive lower priorities.

The view that standardized tests are best for evaluating kindergarten programs becomes an issue in that academic goals alone, rather than a broad range of educational/developmental goals, become the basis for judging the program. Kindergarten programs can become totally academically oriented if they only seek to achieve those goals that can be assessed through standardized achievement tests. Lesiak and Wait (1974) describe how a traditional kindergarten program was modified into a "diagnostically oriented" program through the intervention of school psychologists. Prescriptive activities were provided to children in three program domains, based upon a profile developed for each child using objective assessment techniques (tests).

Hutchins (1981) found that the adoption of a preschool screening program contributed to the valuing of more measurable education objectives and the use of more direct instructional methods in a kindergarten. In addition, the pace, sequence, and quantity of learning offered each child was often governed by the screening test, and the program itself was legitimated in the community in relation to that test. Thus, a cyclical pattern was established whereby a set of tests not only determined a child's educational experiences but also legitimated those experiences.

Inadequate Preparation of Kindergarten Teachers

Within the early childhood tradition, the teacher is seen as the individual responsible for the development and modification of the curriculum. Teachers must know a great deal in order to create and choose appropriate educational activities for young children. This knowledge is provided in programs of teacher preparation and is attested to by state teacher certification. The area of teacher preparation and certification in early childhood education has recently been surveyed (Spodek & Saracho, 1982). Generally, programs require that teachers have knowledge of principles of learning and of child growth and development, as well as of foundations and general education. Most important is the knowledge of curriculum and teaching methods appropriate to the age level of the children to be taught. Opportunities to practice this knowledge are provided in practicum situations.

The last survey of teacher certification programs related to early childhood education in the United States indicated that even though kindergarten teachers may have completed teacher education programs and become certified, they might not necessarily know a great deal about early childhood education. Of the 44 states responding to a survey and requiring that kindergarten teachers be certified, 35 required certification in elementary education. In only 8 of these was a kindergarten or early childhood endorsement available. Thus, in the majority of states, anyone prepared to be an elementary school teacher has been considered competent to teach kindergarten (Education Commission of the States, 1975). Another recent study of college programs preparing early childhood teachers revealed that a majority of students in most of the programs take a double major and/or prepare for dual certification. The other certificate in most instances was in elementary teaching (Spodek & Davis, 1981).

In some states, kindergarten teachers are certified in early childhood education. In other cases, they receive a kindergarten endorsement on an elementary certificate. In still other cases (Illinois, for example), an elementary teaching certificate is all that is required for teaching in the kindergarten as well as in the elementary grades. Thus, while some teachers may have been provided with an in-depth program in early childhood education, others will have a course or two in addition to their elementary curriculum and methods courses, and many will have no preparation specifically related to kindergarten teaching. Yet all will be considered prepared to teach kindergarten.

Given this range of preparation for teaching kindergarten, it is reasonable to assume that many teachers responsible for making educational decisions in the kindergarten will not have been adequately prepared to make those decisions. These teachers will have knowledge of elementary education methods and curriculum, but not necessarily of early childhood methods and curriculum. It would be reasonable to expect those teachers to view the inclusion of elementary programs in the kindergarten as appropriate.

Even those teachers prepared in an early childhood tradition may not be adequately prepared to cope with program decisions for the kindergarten. The child development point of view in the latter tradition more often than not reflects a ''growth'' mentality and avoids a concern for achievement. This orientation may be inadequate for assimilating the demands of teaching academic subjects. Teachers trained in this tradition might only have their own experience in elementary school to rely on as the basis for decisions, and thus may be ignorant of developmentally appropriate methods of approaching academics.

CONCLUSIONS

The field of early childhood education has changed dramatically during the past two decades. Much of the change is related to increases in the field—greater numbers of children served, more programs in existence, and more practitioners employed. Much of the focus of the field has been determined by changes at the prekindergarten level—the development of Head Start and other similar federally funded educational programs, increases in the number of children in day care centers as well as changes in the sponsorship of these centers, and the availability of programs for preschool handicapped children. Such changes reflect new federal policies which have channelled increasing amounts of federal money into the field. These policies have an impact on the kindergarten as well, even though kindergartens are primarily supported by state and local funds. A spill-over effect has occurred, leading to increased acceptance for kindergartens (Tanner, 1973).

Because kindergartens are within the states' domains, they have been shaped by different influences than have prekindergarten programs. Political influences at the state level have led to dramatic increases in the availability of kindergartens and the parallel increases in kindergarten attendance already described. Prior early childhood initiatives have served to provide a base for kindergarten initiatives. In addition, state budget surpluses and new federal revenue sharing funds in the 1970s have allowed state legislatures to establish such new services as public school kindergartens (Forgione, 1975).

In any one community, a number of influences in addition to the six discussed here may affect decisions about what to offer children in the kindergarten. With the demands for teaching academic skills early, with greater reliance on standardized tests for assessing instruction, and with the unsureness that kindergarten teachers might feel about the nature of the programs they have been offering, decisions are often delegated to others. Packaged programs coupled with assessment procedures or integrated into a total textbook adoption package may be difficult to resist. The process of program development at the school level may be giving way in many communities to more general district-wide program adoptions. The idea of tailoring programs to meet individual children's needs and interests may be giving way to providing programs that will lead children to score well on tests or that will fit more comfortably with later instructional offerings.

Sadly, early childhood educators have had relatively little impact on recent early childhood policies. Consensus does not exist within the field as to the value of different kinds of programs or even as to the value of any early childhood program. Available research is equivocal and tends to be used by policy makers to support predetermined positions (Forgione, 1975).

Most often, the policy concerns of early childhood educators have been to increase the availability of early childhood programs for children. Perhaps it is time now to look beyond the quantitative aspect of early childhood education to its qualitative aspects. As things now stand, most children will attend kindergarten at age 5. But what kind of kindergarten will it be? Will the program be broadly developmental? Will it be designed to achieve objectively measurable academic outcomes? Will teachers be adequately prepared to provide appropriate educational experiences for young children? Will the program reflect a commitment to developmental as well as to academic continuity?

As we attempt to influence the directions that kindergartens take, we need to develop an understanding of the factors that have shaped and continued to shape kindergarten practices, including influences within individual teachers, within the profession, within school systems, and within communities. We need also to learn how to use that knowledge to influence practice. This might require that we become politically as well as pedagogically astute.

REFERENCES

Bijou, S. W., & Baer, D. M. *Child development I: A systematic and empirical theory.* New York: Appleton–Century–Croft, 1961.

Bloom, B. *Stability and change in human characteristics.* New York: Wiley, 1964.

Blow, S. E. (First report). In Committee of Nineteen, *The kindergarten.* Boston, MA: Houghton Mifflin Company, 1913.

Brickon, P. T., & Roeber, E. D. The role of the state agency in local assessment programs. Paper presented at the Annual Meeting of the National Council on Measurement in Education, Toronto, Canada, March 1978.

Bryant, C. K., & Hungerford, H. R. An analysis of strategies for teaching environmental concepts and values clarification in kindergarten. *Journal of Environmental Education,* 1977, *9,* 44–49.

Committee of Nineteen. *The kindergarten.* Boston: Houghton Mifflin Company, 1913.

David, A. R. Science for fives. *Childhood Education,* 1977, *53,* 206–210.

DeLima, A. *Our enemy, the child.* New York: New Republic, 1925.

Dewey, J. Froebel's educational principles. *Elementary School Record,* 1900, *1*(5), 143–151.

Durkin, D. Pre-first grade starts in reading: Where do we stand? *Educational Leadership,* 1978, *36,* 174–177.

Education Commission of the States. *Early childhood programs: A state survey, 1974–75.* Denver, CO: Education Commission of the States, 1975.

Fallon, B. J. *Forty innovative programs in early childhood education.* Belmont, CA: Fearon, 1973.

Far West Laboratory. *Educational programs that work.* San Francisco, CA: Far West Laboratory for Educational Research and Development, 1976.

Forgione, P. D., Jr. Rationales for early childhood policy making: The role of five SEA's in early childhood education policy making. Paper presented at the Annual Meeting of the American Educational Research Association, Washington, DC, March 1975.

Froebel, F. (W. H. Hartmann, trans.) *The education of man.* New York: Appleton, 1887.

Foster, G., & Headley, M. *Education in the kindergarten.* New York: American Book Co., 1948.

Gans, R., Stendler, C. B., & Almy, M. *Teaching young children in nursery school, kindergarten and the primary grades.* Yonkers-on-Hudson, NY: World Book Co., 1952.

Garrison, C. G., Sheehy, E. D., & Dalgliesh, A. *The Horace Mann Kindergarten for five-year-*

old children. New York: Columbia University Teachers College, Bureau of Publications, 1937.

Grant, W. V., & Eiden, L. J. *Digest of educational statistics, 1980.* Washington, DC: National Center for Education Statistics, 1980.

Gregory, B. C. The necessity of continuity between the kindergarten and the elementary school: The present status, illogical and unFroebelian. In B. C. Gregory, J. B. Merrill, B. Payne, & M. Giddings (Eds.), *The coordination of the kindergarten and the elementary school.* 7th Yearbook of the National Society for the Scientific Study of Education, Pt. 2. Chicago: University of Chicago Press, 1908.

Hall, G. S. The ideal school as based on child study. *Journal of Proceedings and Addresses of the National Education Association,* 1901, 474–490.

House, E. R., Glass, G. V., McLean, L. D., & Walker, D. F., *No simple answer: Critique of the "Follow Through" evaluation.* Urbana, IL: University of Illinois, 1977.

Hunt, J. M. *Intelligence and experience.* New York: Ronald Press, 1961.

Hutchins, E. J. A preschool screening examination and a public school. Paper presented at the Annual Meeting of the American Educational Research Association, Los Angeles, CA, April 1981.

Kohlberg, L., & Mayer, R. Development as the aim of education. *Harvard Educational Review,* 1972, *42,* 449–496.

Lesiak, W. J., & Wait, J. A. The diagnostic kindergarten: Initial step in the identification and programming of children with learning problems. *Psychology in the Schools,* 1974, *11,* 282–289.

Liedtke, W. Experiences with blocks in kindergarten. *Arithmetic Teacher,* 1975, *22,* 406–412.

Lilley, I., *Friedrich Froebel: A selection from his writings.* Cambridge, MA: Cambridge University Press, 1967.

National Institute of Education (DHEW). *The national conference on achievement testing and basic skills. March 1–3, 1978. Conference proceedings,* 1978. (ED 171 784, 38 pp.)

Placek, C. Kindergarten cooks. *Day Care and Early Education.* 1976, *4,* 23–25.

Pratt, C., & Stanton, J. *Before books.* New York: Adelphi Co., 1926.

Ross, E. D. *The kindergarten crusade: The estabishment of preschool education in the United States.* Athens, OH: Ohio University Press, 1976.

Synder, A. *Dauntless women in childhood education.* Washington, DC: Association for Childhood Education International, 1972.

Spodek, B. Needed: A new view of kindergarten education. *Childhood Education,* 1973, *49,* 191–197.

Spodek, B. Early childhood education: A synoptic view. In N. Nir-Janiv, B. Spodek, & D. Steg (Eds.), *Early child education International perspectives.* New York: Plenum, 1982.

Spodek, B. Early childhood education: A synoptic view. In N. Nir-Janiv, B. Spodek, & D. Steg (Eds.), *Early child education: international perspectives.* New York: Plenum, 1982.

Spodek, B., & Davis, M. C. The changing nature of early childhood teacher education programs. Paper presented at annual conference of the National Association for the Education of Young Children, Detroit, MI, November 1981.

Spodek, B., & Saracho. O. N. The preparation and certification of early childhood personnel. In B. Spodek (Ed.), *Handbook of research in early childhood education.* New York: Free Press, 1982.

Tanner, L. N. Unanticipated effects of federal policy: The kindergarten. *Educational Leadership,* 1973, *31,* 49–52.

Vanderwalker, N. C. History of kindergarten influences in elementary education. In M. J. Holmes (Ed.), *The kindergarten and its relation to elementary education.* 6th Yearbook of the National Society for the Study of Education, *Pt. 2.* Bloomington, IL: Public School Publishing Co., 1907.

Vanderwalker, N. C., *The kindergarten in American education.* New York: Macmillan, 1908.

Wagner, B. J. Alice Beck of Hubbard Woods: Portrait of a kindergarten teacher. *Elementary School Journal,* 1977, *77,* 343–349.

Warfield, J. A. A visit to the world of the four-year-old: Implications for the kindergarten art program. *Art Teacher,* 1973, *3,* 3–5.

Weber, E. *The kindergarten: Its encounter with educational thought in America.* New York: Teachers College Press, 1969.

Whipple, G. M. (Ed.), *Preschool and parental education.* 28th Yearbook of the National Society for the Study of Education. Bloomington, IL: Public School Publishing Co., 1929.

9

A Comparison of Multi-Age and Homogeneous Age Grouping in Early Childhood Centers

Paula Freedman

Syracuse University

When parents leave their child at the day center or nursery school door, they want to feel that they are *giving* their child something, that she or he will have the best possible experience—an experience that enriches what the family already provides. At the same time, the staff at a good center want to feel that they have designed and implemented the best possible program for young children that their interpretation of research data and familiarity with child development and the curriculum will allow, given the usual constraints of time and money. Thus, in an era when the demand, if not the supply, for day care and preschool is growing, both parents and teachers want to know what is best for the young child. A considerable amount of research and writing has been done which explores the nature and needs of the infant and preschool child, but it falls to the educator to use this information to design a good program appropriate to the children and the community.

One of the earliest decisions to be made in this respect concerns grouping of children. Whether the center serves 0- to 6-year-old children all day or 3- to 5-year-old children for 2½ hours, a number of alternative choices in grouping the children are possible. The choice of what ages to group together is fundamental, for many other decisions flow from this choice. Children may either be in homogeneous age groups with no more than 12 to 18 months difference between the oldest and youngest, in multi-age groups where the spread may be as wide as 5 or 6 years, or somewhere in between. Several kinds of questions need to be answered when deciding on group composition with respect to age. What difference does it make how one groups children? If there is a difference, which aspects of the child's development are affected by age grouping? How does age grouping affect the achievement of preschool goals?

Surprisingly, little research has been specifically directed toward these questions. Researchers have not looked at a multi-age group facility and a homogeneous group facility and systematically explored the differences in terms of a wide range of variables. Certainly this is true for preschool groups, and also for many authors (e.g., Goodlad and Anderson, 1963), who deplore this lack of concrete data for elementary schools as well. Perhaps this is because teachers and other in-house and direct service staff write and publish little, while psychologists and researchers tend to look at more narrow, specific, and scientifically testable issues, such as the frequency and complexity of language or the degree of interaction in a controlled environment involving same-age or different age children. Although such investigations have not directly addressed the question of what kind of classroom is best for the young child—with whom can she or he most profitably and happily spend the hours away from home— they do enable one to draw inferences about grouping.

AGE TERMS AND PROGRAM TERMS

In exploring the questions raised earlier, terms will be used which have no standard definition in the literature and which must, therefore, be stipulated here. A *homogeneous age group* refers to a group of children who spend all or almost all of their school or center day in a group in which the youngest child is *no more* than 18 months younger than the oldest. Other terms for homogeneous age groups include horizontal group or single age group. A *heterogeneous age group* is one in which the age difference between the oldest and youngest child is not *less* than two years. Other terms commonly found in the literature for the heterogeneous age group include multi-age, inter-age, family group, or vertical group.

An interesting mix of terms occurs in the relevant research literature. Apart from a scarcity of data dealing with age rather than ability grouping, *program* terms are sometimes used as if they were interchangeable with *age* terms. Thus, one often finds an investigator talking about a heterogeneous or multi-age group in one part of a report, and about an open or unstructured group in another part. It is essential to observe a distinction between terms based on *age* and age grouping (heterogeneous, homogeneous, multi-age, vertical group, or sibling group) and terms based on program, class, or curriculum organization (open, integrated, unstructured, or closed structured).

HISTORICAL PERSPECTIVE

For school-age children, the one room schoolhouse was the norm until large concentrations of people in one area (urbanization) made separation into many classes by age demographically feasible. For preschool children, *group* care outside the home has been a fairly recent innovation and at the outset was more often seen to have a health or welfare function than an educational one. (For a thorough discussion of historical trends, see Auerbach, 1979; Breitbart, 1974; Joffe, 1977; Marver & Larson, 1978; Robins & Weiner, 1978; Stevens & King, 1976; Takanishi, 1976.) Additionally, as child development theories evolved, so too did a picture of children growing by stages in all their capacities (physical, cognitive, emotional and social). This view has reinforced a pattern of homogeneous grouping in which children of the same age, and presumably stage of development, are kept together. Lists or displays of the developmental characteristics typically found at each age and the developmental levels a child needs to reach before he or she can proceed to following stages (such as one finds in Gesell, Piaget, and Erikson) have strengthened the view of some educators that mixing age groups hinders children's social, cognitive, and emotional growth. This view is, however, open to question. Satterly (1975), for example, argues that stages in the Piagetian or Eriksonian sense should be seen as a logical model rather than as an actual description of how children think at each age. He points to the large variation of development within any age group and argues that such models should not be taken as literal principles for organizing classrooms.

Two recent texts (Broman, 1978; Lay & Dopyera, 1977), both intended for use in teachers training courses, also reveal differing views of child development with respect to stages, as reflected in their chapter headings. Lay and Dopyera organize their text topically around children's affective, social, and cognitive behavior into two categories: before age 3 (infants and toddlers), and ages 3 to 7. Broman, on the other hand, devotes separate sections to the 3-year-old, 4-year-old, and 5-year-old, subsuming developmental questions under more rigid age categories. In short, the preschool staff is faced with an array of research reports and discussions reflecting differing approaches to the education and care of the young child. In deciding between homogeneous and multi-age grouping, educators must rely on their ability to intelligently interpret available data and to be sensitive to the needs and values of the client population.

THE EXPERIENCE OF OTHER COUNTRIES

While the United States has been most innovative in developing early education programs, it has lagged behind other countries in financially supporting such programs. Kahn and Kamerman (1976), in a study of child care programs in nine countries (France, the United States, Canada, Germany, Israel, Poland, Sweden, the United Kingdom, and Yugoslavia), report that with the exception of the United States and Canada, these countries are moving towards public voluntary preschool education for all children over the age of 3 years.

Austin (1976), in his examination of early child care in other countries, notes that "in most countries, children are grouped by single year of age; some countries allow two year age groups such as 3 and 4 year old children in the same class'' (p. 48). In France, the day care center is generally restricted to infants and toddlers. These children are usually divided into four groups: 2 to 8 months, 8 to 18 months, and 24 to 36 months. The older preschoolers (ages 2 to 6) attend age graded nursery schools (see Kamerman, 1977).

In Sweden, note Bergstrom and Gold, there is the usual separation of infants from older children. ''Grouping of children according to age is a state regulation. The state, at the urging of the medical profession, has required age grouping in an attempt to avoid the spread of diseases and epidemics among the younger children in the day nurseries'' (Bergstrom & Gold, 1974, p. 26). Austin reports, however, that Sweden ''is experimenting with sibling groups which span the ages of 2½ to 7 years. The older children are taught responsibility for the younger ones'' (1976, p. 48). A report published by the Swedish Ministry of Education and Social Affairs (1979) describes an experiment conducted since 1976, in which children 7 months to 12 years of age are grouped together with older children joining the younger ones after school. These heterogeneous groups are described as very successful; conflict among the children is reduced because children of different ages make different demands on the teachers, there is less fighting for the same toys, and younger children see the way the older ones resolve conflicts. In addition, the older children seem to enjoy responsibility for the care of the younger children. The advantages for parents of these widely mixed age groups include dealing with the same staff throughout the child's time at the center, opportunities for parents to get to know each other, and opportunities for parents of older children to reassure parents of younger children. According to the report, staff find these groups more stimulating, and they have more incentive to be involved with children and parents they expect to work with for a long time. Staff also find this situation helpful because they come to know the children well as they develop over the years.

In Denmark, the government supports not only services for children below school age but also after-school groups for all youngsters through high school. Generally, such centers house everyone in one facility—infants as well as adolescents who are in the after-school group. As Wagner and Wagner (1976), in their study of the Danish national child care system observe, ''Danish day-care programs seem to recognize the importance of another type of social interaction for children—that of older and younger children together'' (p. 78). Hjartarson (1979) also notes that in recent years Denmark, like Sweden, has encouraged family day care groups that include children ranging in age from infants to 12-year-olds.

Despite emphasis on collectivization and social interdependence, preschoolers in the Soviet Union are placed in homogeneous age groups: one is responsible for one's peer, not older for younger (see Educational Testing Service, 1969).

Cuba provides an interesting case history well chronicled by Leiner (1974). A state system of child care is available on a voluntary basis for children 45 days to 6 years of age. Facilities include provisions for day care, boarding, mixed boarding and home care, depending on family need and availability of space. (As in other countries, Cuba is unable to provide sufficient places for children to meet the demand.) Groups are multi-age in the sense that they cover more than a year's range. Four distinct groups are apparent: 45 days to 18 months (although usually these infants are further divided into 3-month units), 18 months to 30 months, 30 months to 5 years (the widest range and most analogous to the child care age range in the United States), and 5 to 6 years. For a brief time in Cuba, day care centers called *jardins* were available. These centers were less regimented than the traditional centers, had open planning, and were largely outdoors. They accommodated children 18 months to 5 years in a multi-age group. As one *jardin* psychologist explained, "We believe in inter-aged mixing. The little ones learn from the big ones and the big ones learn from the little ones—in play, in responsibility, they all learn" (Leiner, 1974, p. 111). Lela Sanchez, one of the founders of the *jardin* system, stated, "We feel that from the age of 1½ to the age of 4 it is a very positive thing for children to be grouped together . . . it seems to us that at this early stage it is easier for a child to learn from other children than from an adult" (Leiner, 1976, p. 111). However, by 1971 the *jardin* experiment was phased out. The *jardins* were merged with traditional programs and the two leaders of the *jardin* program were assigned other social welfare work. The official position is that the *jardins* did not promote sufficient discipline, which in turn could prevent children from learning as much as they should in their early years.

A point to be raised here and returned to later is that age grouping appears to reflect the goals, even the national goals, of a program. Where the primary goal is to produce open, sociable children who are able to accept and give help, heterogeneous grouping is preferred. Where the goal is to teach a set body of material and to formalize the relationship between dependents and caregivers, homogeneous grouping is favored.

COMMON GOALS AND CONCERNS IN PRESCHOOL PROGRAMS

While different programs stress different things and have different approaches, there are some common concerns—such as acquisition and elaboration of language. Expanding a child's general knowledge is another concern. Many programs stress development of logical thinking. Most are concerned with the socialization of the young child, that is, his or her ability to get along with others and to be a contributing member of the group. All programs seem to emphasize that children meet their goals while emerging with strong, positive self-concepts.

Language Development

Language development is an obvious target of comparison in same-age and multi-age groups. If young children are with same-age peers, will they not tend to have "collective monologues" with limited vocabulary, infrequent verbal exchanges, and dependence on adults for language expansion? On the other hand, in a heterogeneous group with more child-to-child interaction, won't the younger children become an audience for the older, and be unable to get a word in edgewise?

Conversation between two children requires, minimally, three things: sufficient vocabulary to express thoughts, sufficiently developed syntax to communicate without the listener having to depend on contextual clues or to make a large number of suppositions,[1] and a decrease in egocentrism to allow for judging whether a sentence is understood by another and for understanding the perspective from which another is speaking. Given these three requirements, will children expand vocabulary, develop syntactical skills, and decrease egocentrism more in homogeneous or heterogeneous groups? Hamilton and Stewart (1977) found that children learn vocabulary from each other in settings with a variety of age groups. While they imitate adults more in terms of complexity and sentence length, they learn vocabulary rapidly and easily from other children, even when the vocabulary is completely foreign. These authors also point to the language gains frequently made when a child is promoted to the next older age group in a center. They speculate that adult language may be too complex for a child to absorb all the nuances, while the language of the next oldest group of children may be "just right." As children in Hamilton and Stewart's study became older, they imitated adults more and peers less. One might conclude from this study that, in terms of language development, the greatest benefit of heterogeneous grouping is in the very early years of rapid language expansion. In support of this, Mueller (1972) indicated that the processes important for verbal exchanges develop by age 3½, and that thereafter there is no significant difference in effective communication between older and younger children.

With respect to syntax, a study by Bates (1975) offers a somewhat contradictory finding to that of Hamilton and Stewart (1977). Bates found that children's utterances are longer when they speak to adults than when they speak to other children. Perhaps the adult conveys an expectation of more complete

---

[1] In child-adult exchange, particularly parent-child, the adult is able to compensate for lack of verbs and generally "thin" syntax by making a number of suppositions or assumptions. For example, when a child says "Juice," the adult can infer that the child means "I want some juice" or "That can on the shelf contains juice," depending on context. Similarly, "Susie see" may mean "I (Susie) see it," "I (Susie) want to see it," "Susie, (other child) look at this." The point is, an adult or older child can fill in the missing syntax to understand the child's meaningful utterance; same-age peers may not.

utterances, perhaps the child imitates the adult speaker, perhaps the adult is more patient or throws in more cues to encourage and facilitate longer sentences. Bates does not say, although she observes that "there must be something about child-child speech—other than its grammatical simplicity—that is qualitatively different from conversations between children and adults, rendering peer input less useful for the child acquiring his native language" (1975, p. 267). Perhaps there is less of a conflict between Bates, and Hamilton and Stewart, if one sees the former as addressing sentence length and complexity only and the latter as addressing vocabulary and ease of communication with a peer.

Bates does make an interesting observation about young children's egocentric speech, which is usually assumed by Piagetians to reflect their generally egocentric mental outlook. She suggests that the child's egocentric speech may be more a reflection of the child's insensitivity to cues from the listener that he or she has not understood than to failure in the child's ability to role take or decenter. In support of this idea, she cites a study by Peterson, Danner, and Flavel (1972) with 4- and 7-year-olds. These researchers found that, when children were told that the listener did not understand their first utterance and were asked to repeat it, they had no difficulty in augmenting and elaborating. Furthermore, Bates suggests that the reason children respond less to cues that the listener has not understood is that *other* children produce fewer such cues than do adults. Dittman (1972) confirms this for first, third, and fifth graders. Adults are more likely to indicate understanding through such cues as nodding, or saying "uh huh," or indicating misunderstanding through such cues as saying "what?" or looking clearly puzzled. The ability to acknowledge understanding or misunderstanding of the speaker increases dramatically between ages 2 and 4 (Bates, 1971), signifying that, in heterogeneous groupings, older children may contribute to a decrease in the "egocentric" speech of young children by asking them for clarification of their statements.

The significance of the above studies for grouping, as with most of the available research, must be inferred but would seem to point to some advantages in multi-age grouping for children's language development.

Social Development

When one turns to social development, the advantage of heterogeneous grouping is more clear. Charlesworth and Hartup (1967) looked at the amount and kind of positive social reinforcement preschool children gave each other, and found that 4-year-olds gave more reinforcement to other children than did 3-year-olds. Further, 4-year-olds distributed this reinforcement to more children than did 3-year-olds. The advantage for the 3-year-olds is unmistakable. Hartup (1977) studied positive social interactions in same-age and mixed-age pairs of preschool children. (Same-age pairs differed by an average of only 2 months in age, while mixed-age pairs differed by an average of 16 months.) Hartup found that the greatest positive social interaction occurred in same-age older pairs, the least in same-age younger pairs, with mixed-age pairs falling in between. He observes, "The study only established the fact that both younger and older preschool children make behavioral adjustments to the cross-age situation. In each case, behavior differs from the same-age situation" (p. 11). Hartup also points to studies which indicate that older preschool children (particularly those 2 or 3 years older) act as peer models for the younger children.

Much of the research on cross-age social interaction has been done with older children, but it probably has validity for younger children as well. Mobley (1976) studied leadership in grades 1 to 3 in homogeneous and multi-age settings, and found that the self-concepts of students in the multi-age group improved while those of the children in the homogeneous group did not. Buckholdt and Wodarski (1974) reviewed a number of studies, conducted at CEMREL, which examined how different reinforcement systems affect 3- to 11-year-old children's cooperative, competitive, and learning behaviors. Among the results was the fact that preschool children who acted as tutors for each other, and who were given intermittent rewards by an adult, were found to be very good at helping each other: they innovated effective teaching techniques and seemed to enjoy learning from and teaching one another. Buckholdt and Wodarski conclude that, when preschool children of varying ages are grouped together, allowing each to serve as a teacher to some other at some time, group interaction may be enhanced by improving interpersonal and cooperative skills; by improving social perspectives, role-taking, and empathy; by reducing anxiety caused by status, age, and background differences between adults and children; by increasing individualized instruction in the group with the further reward of immediate feedback for the learner; by improving the "child-tutor's" communication skills; and finally, by providing motivation for a task that may be lacking when a child is working alone.

Turning to very young children, Lewis, Young, Brooks, and Michalson (1975) studied the different kinds of interaction behaviors evident when children were paired either with same-age children (1-year-olds with 1-year-olds), or with older children (1-year-olds with 15- to 20-month-olds), or with younger children (1-year-olds with 7-month-olds). The authors found that:

> . . . imitation occurs more frequently with unequal age mates; body contact is more frequent between age mates. This suggests that different behaviors are in the service of various functions, which are at this point unexplicated. However, that various functions are facilitated or retarded by the age composition of peer relationships cannot be denied. Therefore the function as well as the age composition of relationships must be considered (p. 59).

Konner (1975) also reports that cross-age child interactions have less physical and more face-to-face contact than a young child has with his mother. In short, infants may get more genuine social interaction with older children. If sociability in infants is sought, many parents can point to the particular interest and joy a young infant expresses in an older child.

Hammack (1975) compared self-concept in 3-, 4-, and 5-year-old children. Ninety-six children (48 boys and 48 girls) were placed in same-age and multi-age groups matched for informal teaching methods and curriculum. An equal number of boys and girls were in each group. Hammack found that, regardless of group, the higher the child's chronological age, the higher the self-concept score. However, a comparison of pretest scores (at entrance into the group) with posttest scores (after several months in the group) revealed the self-concept scores of boys in the multi-age groups to be significantly higher than the scores of boys in the homogeneous groups. There was no significant difference between groups in the girls' self-concept scores—an interesting observation which invites further exploration.

In general, as with language development, there does not seem to be a good argument for strict, homogeneous grouping.

Cognitive Development

Finally, turning to cognivitve development, the picture becomes more cloudy. It is clear that many children learn much from other children. However, it also seems to be true that where a goal is exclusively academic, homogeneous groups (in which there is probably a concomitant narrowing of ability levels) are successful. Although Mobley (1976) found that the social skills of first and third graders improved in multi-age groups, this was not true for reading scores, which remained the same between the two groups. Math gains were markedly greater in homogeneous groups. On the other hand, Mycock (1966) found no significant difference in reading or math skills between vertically or homogeneously grouped infant school classes (ages 5 to 7). However, she reports that slow learners did better in vertical groups, while the brightest children made greater gains in homogeneous groups.

Preschool programs with predominantly cognitive or skill acquisition goals, such as DISTAR or DARCEE, are ability grouped within classes that generally contain same-age children. Programs with broader or more social goals, such as Bank Street, are more likely to have children of wider age ranges. Montessori schools explicitly call for putting 3-, 4-, and 5-year-olds together. "One reason for the mixture of ages in the [Montessori] preschool class is that younger children are expected to imitate older children in their behavior" (Miller & Dyer, 1975, p. 27). However, Miller and Dyer add that the multi-age group does not appear to be a significant variable with respect to learning.

In summary, research on homogeneous versus heterogeneous groups in preschools is very limited. However, from studies on the language, social, and cognitive development of young children, it appears that many benefits flow from multi-age grouping in preschools where the goals are not so exclusively cognitive as they later become in elementary school. (A significant exception to the general elementary school pattern is the modern informal British infant school, further discussed below.)

PRACTICAL CONSIDERATIONS

Single-age Groups

The most common arrangement for preschool grouping is the homogenerous group. This prevalence of, if not preference for, homogeneous grouping in preschools must be explained, since research evidence alone cannot support it. Through a historical coincidence, larger numbers of children needed group care at a time when maturationist and stage theories of development were also on the ascent, thus providing a rationale for keeping children of the same supposed stage together. There are also practical reasons for such an arrangement: for example, younger children tend to use materials differently than do older ones. A large tray of macaroni set out for the 3- or 4-year-old to string is a great attraction for the 2-year-old to dump or eat. A 5-year-old's elaborate block construction invites the 2-year-old to explore what will happen if he or she pushes it. The patience required in waiting for a turn at a game, or in solving a cognitive problem, may be easily manageable for the 5-year-old but beyond the limit of frustration for the 3-year-old. Thus, in planning activities, it is easier for the teacher and for some of the children if a similar response to an activity can be anticipated from most of the children in the group.

A related problem is that accomodating in a small space, equipment suitable for children of all ages, may be difficult. If a center has limited room, a choice may have to be made between climbing equipment for the 4-year-olds and a small slide for the 2-year-olds. Little direct research is available on the amount and kind of space needed by children of different ages. Loo (1976) studied the effect of high and low spatial density on 5-year-olds and found that aggression increased with density, particularly for boys. Increased "onlooking" behavior from others also occurred, causing a passivity that reduced interaction and learning. Loo observes that, in a high density situation, children may become "catatonically immobile." The low density condition produced more self-involved behavior and more toy play. This study raises the question of whether younger children may be more sensitive to density than older children, and may thus do more onlooking than participating in a room shared with active 5-year-olds. Many teachers have observed that older children seem to need more space than younger children, and that noise and confusion is harder on the 2- or 3-year-old than on the 4- or 5-year-old. From a teacher's point of view, she or he may prefer, when working with younger children, a smaller space in which it is easier to provide close supervision unobtrusively. In sum, the physical setting of a room-space, equipment, material—may be easier to arrange appropriately if the children are likely to use it in the same way, and teachers may perceive this as an argument favoring homogenerous grouping.

Planning the program is a matter of paramount concern to staff. Most teachers believe (and have been taught) that certain activities are appropriate to certain ages and that children must master one set of skills before going on to the next. Generally speaking, it seems simpler to plan for one age group. It is probably most efficient to teach a body of knowledge all at once to a group of children who are ready to learn it and not yet beyond it. In mixed-age groups, whole group activities must be more carefully chosen and small groups more carefully arranged.

With respect to social development, homogeneous grouping can best be defended if one believes that young children under age 3 are capable of parallel play only. If this is so, children older than 3 years in a mixed-age group would have fewer playmates at their level with whom to interact. In fact, it may be that younger children are happier in a smaller group than are older ones, and that the optimum group size at each age may vary sufficiently to argue for homogeneous grouping. All this remains speculative in the absence of research. What is more certain is that tradition and habit are hard to break and most teachers seem to believe that homogeneous grouping is better because it is familiar to them.

Multi-age Groups

While homogeneous grouping refers to one kind of class arrangement, multi-age grouping opens the door to a wide range of arrangements. In a day care center serving 0- to 5-year-olds, decisions must be made not only about combining the 3-, 4-, and 5-year olds, but also about where to place those over 12 to 18 months. Infants under that age are always kept separate for health, safety, and obvious program, scheduling, and staffing reasons. But what about the toddlers? Should they too be kept separate from their more verbal and mobile schoolmates?

Konner (1975), surveying evidence from preindustrial societies, argues strongly for the multi-age group to include toddlers. He points out that throughout human history (and even today in kin-based and small group societies) the play group has always included infants and juveniles because the number of same-age peers was small. Responsibility for the care of infants was shared in these play groups, allowing for modeling of child care among the juveniles. From the younger child's point of view, Konner argues:

> . . . the benefit to any play group member for whom there are older individuals around is greater than that which would accrue to him in a peer

group, since the things that need to be learned are learned more easily from those a little ahead of oneself than those, so to speak, in the same quagmire (1975, p. 103).

Further, Konner contends that peer relations in infants are a product of

laboratory investigations and of child care conditions in advanced industrial states. In this context we can begin to understand the bizarrely inept forms of social behavior which we know in the laboratory and nursery as 'parallel play' and 'collective monologue'. Infants are inept in relating to one another for the simple reason that they were never called on to do so during millions of years of evolution, consequently they could not have been selected for an ability to do this (1975, p. 122).

Obviously, a preschool with teachers and a program focused on the child's development is not the same as a band of infants and juveniles in which infants can learn only from the example of the older children. Nevertheless, Konner's points should be considered by those who see the homogeneous age group as the "natural" order of things.

There is a wealth of literature on peers as models, and there would seem to be little question that children learn from each other. With a wider age range, there is presumably a wider range of behaviors to model, and while younger children may imitate older ones in the classroom, perhaps the older children will imitate their younger peers in the nap room!

From a sociological viewpoint, the multi-age group more closely reflects life at home and, in fact, everywhere except at the traditional school. People do not usually group themselves in narrowly horizontal age groups. Family day care (as opposed to center care) frequently includes infants and older children, and good family day care seems to be an effective model for children's development. Similarly, play groups or small cooperative groups are usually multi-age; separate groups are a luxury of the larger centers, where there are enough children to allow for separation.

Before turning to specific classroom management issues in heterogeneous groups, the mainstreaming of handicapped children should be considered. That handicapped children have a right to develop to their fullest potential in a normal setting, and that "normal" children grow in important ways when accommodating special classmates, no longer seem to be issues. Preschools are especially easy and successful places to mainstream handicapped children, and multi-age classes further facilitate this. When there are children with a wide range of verbal, manipulative, physical, social, and cognitive skills in the room, the handicapped child is simply another variation.

In regard to classroom management, a number of arguments favoring heterogeneous groupings are evident. Research has been cited above which indicates that children can be effective teachers of other children, both through direct tutoring and through example. Although a heterogeneous class can be more difficult for the teacher to manage, in that all instruction must be individualized, allowing older children to help younger children will probably facilitate that individualization. In addition, the ''student'' is provided with immediate feedback on his or her performance, while the ''tutor'' solidifies mastery of a skill by having to explain it. In these situations, older children may also improve their social skills, and both older and younger children may more readily learn to decenter and take the perspective of others when brought frequently into contact with children who see things from a different perspective. Wakefield (1979) cites Zajonc and Markus' (1975) finding that intelligence scores are inverse to birth order and speculates that the explanation for this finding may partially be that younger children have less opportunity to teach others. Thus, Wakefield argues that the teaching of younger children by older not only facilitates classroom management for the teacher, but also is a valuable learning activity for older children in itself.

While multi-age groups make special demands on the teacher in terms of planning, programming, and keeping track of each child's progress, there are advantages. Any one group is made up of children both familiar and unfamiliar with the program, thus aiding continuity. Teachers may gain a stronger sense of sharing with colleagues when each teacher has children of approximately the same age range. Additionally, some teachers may find the challenge of planning activities for the multi-age class intellectually stimulating. For the director, staffing may become more flexible if every teacher is used to working with all ages. The risk of course, is that multi-age groups call for good teachers who are sensitive to children, knowledgeable about child development, and skillful at planning. However, staff of heterogeneous groups may require more extensive training than staff in a homogeneous setting.

The informal British infant school is the most often cited example of multi-age classes. While these schools serve children from 5 to 8, their guiding philosophy and practice seem applicable to younger children as well. Some of the advantages that may apply equally well to preschools are reflected in the observations of Ridgway and Lawton (1968), who note that infant school teachers stated that they found working with children of all ages to be intellectually stimulating. The teachers also commented that older children were given a chance to be responsible for other children, and that a ''family-like'' spirit developed in which everyone helped each other. Ridgway and Lawton write that ''. . . where teachers have had no experience of family grouping, opposition to the idea stems from lack of conviction about informal methods of teaching rather than the actual mixing of age-group'' (1968, p. 162).

Not to be overlooked is the children's preference in grouping. Leiner (1974) recounts an amusing observation that suggests that even young children prefer to be with older ones rather than to be separated from them. In reference to a group of 18- to 24-month-old babies he writes:

While the day care worker tried to lead the children in a song . . . [the children] were continually distracted by a group of older children across the field. Even after the *assistente* adjusted the seating arrangements to allow more children into the circle in order to hold their attention, the youngsters failed to respond; their interest in the activities across the field never flagged (1974, p. 79).

Lewis and Rosenblum (1975) suggest that the heterogeneous, single-room schoolhouse of the past in which the teacher taught the older children, who in turn taught the younger children, may "not be as far-fetched as has been suggested by some . . ." and that "models in which children teach other children need to be considered" (p. 8). Annabelle Dixon (1978, p. 19), best summarizes the position of proponents of multi-age grouping:

The evolution and adoption of vertical grouping, in which children of different ages . . . are in the same class is interesting in that the practice appears to have preceded theoretical justification. Necessity, while mothering invention, also appears to have given birth to vertical grouping . . . Where is the research it is asked, the supporting theories, the hard data? As far as I have been able to ascertain, research support is negligible, there are no specific theories and even the evangelical literature, though detailed and comprehensive in itself, is surprisingly sparse. Yet many schools have quietly changed to a system of vertical grouping even if the majority use a two year span rather than three . . . I believe that it is possible to justify vertical grouping by reference to research but *only if it is accepted that emphasis is given to certain underlying values.*

CONCLUSION

The decision on whether to age-group children homogeneously or heterogeneously depends on the goals of a program, the client population, the resources of the building, and the training and inclination of teachers and administrators. Some multi-age classes have foundered because the teacher failed to individualize the program. Some homogeneous classes have been less successful than they might have been because the teacher planned a program which depended on the children having a range of skills which they did not, in fact, have.

Although this chapter has not directly addressed program structure and content (i.e., either open and individual, or structured and large group oriented), the most successful combination of age grouping and program structure may be multi-age in an open program. Palmer (1971) suggests that a good solution is to have multi-age classes with "working groups," where children come together of their own choice, and "teaching groups," where the teacher organizes the participants to accomplish a specific purpose. Both kinds of groups are temporary, lasting for the duration of the task or the children's interest. Finally, what answers emerge to the questions raised at the beginning of this article?

1. What difference does it make how one groups children?

   It may make a profound difference to children and staff and, by extension, to parents. For children, group composition seems to affect their social environment, their learning environment, their expectations about program stability, and their sense of self, self-esteem, and self-competence. For staff, group composition may have major implications for curriculum design, classroom management, relations with colleagues, and relationships to children and their families. For parents, grouping may affect their child's comfort and success at school, and their relationships with teachers and the support group of other parents.

2. Which aspects of the child's development are affected by age grouping choice?

   Generally speaking, research appears to give some support to multi-age groups with respect to their social and emotional development, as well as to some aspects of their learning. Homogeneous groups appear to be most effective for mastery of specific academic skills. However, it is essential to remember that grouping practices should not be used as a *substitute* for a program—children are grouped in particular ways in order to achieve particular ends. Homogeneous grouping does not necessarily impoverish a well-balanced program, nor will vertical grouping *in and of itself* improve a rigid and unimaginative one. The success or failure of a program rests with staff and their particular skills and inclinations. Grouping offers an opportunity for children to maximize certain kinds of experiences. What those experiences will be reflects staff values, preferences, and abilities.

3. How does age grouping affect the achievement of preschool goals?

   Ultimately, this is the crucial question, and it can only be answered by the center staff and the families they serve. The very process of clarifying values through a discussion of grouping choices is undoubtedly beneficial in itself.

Until much more research is done on the effects of grouping children under 6 years of age in heterogeneous and homogeneous groups in preschool centers, the choice would seem to be a matter of style and goals. However, because the preschool is a child's first sustained out-of-home experience, conditioning his or her expectations about teachers and peers, and because it is so uniquely suited to humanistic education, encouraging social and moral growth, as well as cognitive growth, educators should think critically before making any decision on age grouping of children.

REFERENCES

Auerback, S. *The child care crisis*. Boston, MA: Beacon Press, 1979.

Austin, G. R. *Early childhood education: An international perspective*. New York: Academic Press, 1976.

Bates, E. Peer relations and the acquisition of language. In M. Lewis & L. Rosenblum (Eds.), *Friendship and peer relations*. New York: John Wiley & Sons, 1975.

Bergstrom, J. L., & Gold, J. K. *Sweden's day nurseries: Focus on programs for infants and toddlers*. Washington, DC: The Day Care and Child Development Council of America, 1974.

Breitbart, V. *The day care book*. New York: Alfred A. Knopf, 1974.

Broman, B. L. *The early years in childhood education*. Chicago, IL: Rand McNally, 1978.

Buckholdt, D. S., & Wodarski, J. *Effects of differential reinforcement systems on cooperative behavior exhibited by children in classroom contexts*. Paper presented at the annual meeting of the American Psychological Association, 1974. (ED 100 497, 40 pp.)

Charlesworth, R., & Hartup, W. W. Positive social reinforcement in the nursery school peer group. *Child Development*, 1967, *38*, 993–1002.

Coonrod, D. *Administering the admission and grouping policies of the preschool*. Bloomington, IN: Debcon, Inc., 1979. (ED 192 879, 19 pp.)

Dittman, A. Developmental factors in conversational behavior. *Journal of Communication*, 1972, *22*, 404–433.

Dixon, A. Vertical grouping: A practice or a principle? *Forum for the Discussion of New Trends in Education*, 1978, *21* (1), 19–21.

Educational Testing Service. *Soviet preschool education* (Vol. 1). New York: Holt, Rinehart & Winston, 1969.

Goodlad, J., & Anderson, A. *The non-graded elementary school*. New York: Harcourt, Brace & World, 1963.

Hamilton, M. L., & Stewart D. M. Peer models and language acquisition. *Merrill-Palmer Quarterly*, 1977, *23*(1), 45–55.

Hammack, B. G. Self-concept: Evaluation of preschool children in single and multi-age classroom settings. *Dissertation Abstracts International*, 1975, *35*, 6572–6573.

Hartup, W. W. Peer relations: Developmental implications and interaction in same and mixed age situations. *Young Children*, 1977, *32*(3), 4–13.

Hjartarson, F. *Day care: Other countries*. Canada: Dept. of Health & Welfare, 1979. (ED 160 199, 46 pp.) Available in micro fiche only.

Joffe, G. *Friendly intruders*. Berkeley, CA: University of California Press, 1977.

Kahn, A., & Kamerman, S. *Child care programs in nine countries: A report prepared for the OECD working party on the role of women in the economy*. New York: Columbia University School of Social Work, 1976. (ED 121 428, 87 pp.)

Kamerman, S. *Licensing, standards and regulations in child care programs in Europe, Canada, and Israel. Final report of cross national studies of social services and family policy*. 1977. (ED 156 342, 81 pp.)

Konner, M. 1977. Relations among infants and juveniles in comparative perspective. In M. Lewis & L. Rosenblum (Eds.), *Friendship and peer relations*. New York: John Wiley & Sons, 1975.

Lay, M., & Dopyera, J. *Becoming a teacher of young children*. Lexington, KY: D. C. Heath & Co., 1977.

Leiner, M. *Children are the revolution: Day care in Cuba*. New York: Viking, 1974.

Lewis, M., Young, G., Brooks, J., & Michalson, L. The beginning of friendship. In M. Lewis & L. Rosenblum (Eds.), *Friendship and peer relations*. New York: John Wiley & Sons, 1975.

Lewis, M., & Rosenblum, L. (Eds.), *Friendship and peer relations.* New York: John Wiley & Sons, 1975.

Loo, C. *Effects of spatial density on behavior styles of children.* Paper presented at the annual meeting of the American Psychological Association. Santa Cruz, CA: University of California, 1976. (ED 133 047, 6 pp.)

Marver, J. D., & Larson, M. Public policy towards child care in America: A historical perspective. In P. Robins & S. Weiner (Eds.), *Child care and public policy.* Lexington, KY: D. C. Heath & Co., 1978.

Miller, L. B., & Dyer, J. L. Four preschool programs: Their dimensions and effects. *Monographs of the Society for Research in Child Development,* 1975, *40,* 5-6 (Serial No. 162).

Mobley, C. *A comparison of the effects of multi-age grouping vs. homogeneous age grouping in primary school classes of reading and mathematics achievement.* Unpublished doctoral thesis, 1976. (ED 128, 102, 114 pp.)

Mueller, E. The maintenance of verbal exchanges between young children. *Child Development,* 1972, *43,* 930-938.

Mycock, M. A. A comparison of vertical grouping and horizontal grouping in the infant school. *British Journal of Psychology,* February 1967, *37,* 133.

Palmer, R. *Space, time and grouping.* New York: Citation, 1971.

Peterson, C., Danner, F., & Flavell, J. Developmental changes in children's response to three indications of communicative failure. *Child Development,* 1972, *43,* 1463-69.

Ridgway, L., & Lawton, I. *Family grouping in the primary school.* New York: Agathon, 1968.

Robins, P., & Weiner, S. *Child care and public policy.* Lexington, KY: D. C. Heath & Co., 1978.

Satterly, D. Stages of development: Help or hindrance in educating young children. *Universities Quarterly,* Autumn 1975, *29*(4), 379-388.

Stevens, J. Jr., & King, E. W. *Administering early childhood education programs.* Boston, MA: Little, Brown & Co., 1976.

Swedish Ministry of Education and Social Affairs, Stockholm, Sweden. *Daycare for small children. A debate report by the family aid commission: A summary.* 1979. (ED 180 669, 34 pp.)

Takanishi, R. *Early childhood education in urban America, Parts I & II.* Overview papers presented at IMTEC/DECD Bicentennial Seminar on Managing Change in Urban Education, October 11, 1976. (ED 135 452, 48 pp., & ED 135 453, 17 pp.)

Wagner, M., & Wagner, M. *The Danish national child care system.* Boulder, CO: Westview, 1976.

Wakefield, A. P. Multi-age grouping in day care. *Children Today,* 1979, *8*(3), 26-28.

Way, J. W. Verbal interaction in multi-age classrooms. *Elementary School Journal,* 1979, *79,* 178-186.

10

Caring for the Caregivers: Staff Burnout in Child Care

Marcy Whitebook, Carollee Howes,

Rory Darrah and Jane Friedman

Child Care Staff Education Project,
Berkeley, California[1]

Since the 1960s there has been a tremendous increase in the number of women working outside the home. The greatest increase has been among mothers of young children. In the United States, 7.5 million children under 6 years of age have working mothers (U.S. Dept. of Labor, 1981). The supply of adult supervised, affordable care for these children is woefully inadequate, particularly

[1] The *Child Care Staff Education Project* is a nonprofit organization formed to study issues and to share information affecting child care workers. The current project began in 1977, when individuals from a variety of disciplines, including early childhood education, developmental psychology, social work, and environmental planning formulated a questionnaire which sought to directly reveal the experiences and opinions of child care workers about their jobs.

Several local groups and many individuals encouraged this study through their contribution of energy, skills, supplies, and use of equipment. Without their assistance, the study would not have been possible. Thanks to East Bay Workers in Child Care, Interview Committee of the Child Care Staff Education Project, San Francisco Child Care Switchboard, Bananas, Parents and Workers United for Child Care, Bay Area Staff of the National Jury Project, and the University of California, Davis. There are many individuals in the groups mentioned above who deserve personal thanks, but space does not permit listing them all.

Special thanks to Bob Fitzgerald for his help with statistical problems, to Harry Chotiner for his editing and encouragement, to Charlotte Watkins for her editorial suggestions, and to the child care workers who shared their experiences with us.

The project has recently received a grant from the Rosenberg Foundation to develop a handbook, a newsletter, and to carry out other activities (such as workshops) for child care staff.

For more information about the Child Care Staff Education Project, write to P.O. Box 5603, Berkeley, California, 94705.

for children 2 years old and younger (AIRBS, 1979; SDE, 1978).[2] This lack of sufficient services has been the focus of much agitation and advocacy.

In addressing the need for more child care, many advocates stress the importance of providing good quality services for the crucial early years. Discussions concerning quality child care among early childhood personnel, parents, and legislators commonly focus on such issues as curriculum, parent involvement, and staff training (e.g., Panetta, 1975.)[3] Although varied and difficult to evaluate, educational curricula that enhance cognitive, physical, social, and emotional growth are accepted as the major ingredient of high quality care. Parent involvement programs that respect the cultural background of families are also labeled as a key aspect of good care. Finally, specific child care related training for staff appears to enhance adult-child interaction, and thus has been considered a critical variable of quality services (Abt Associates, 1979; Grotberg, Chapman, & Lazar, 1971; Morgan, 1975; Oyemade & Chargois, 1978; Pettygrove, 1981; Prescott, 1972).

Rarely is the caregiver's job satisfaction considered an important component of quality care. Yet the impact of adults' experiences on children's lives is assumed by most people. Tense, overworked, or ill parents, it is argued, will be hampered in their ability to care for children. Although the relationship between child care staff and children is different in many ways from the parent-child relationship, the interrelationship between adult and child experience is nevertheless important (Katz, 1980; Whitmarsh, 1966). As Freudenberger (1977), Maslach and Pines (1977), Reed (1977), and Sutton (1977) note, a stressed child care worker will likely be hampered in his or her ability to provide good care.

Little research has been conducted so far which reveals exactly who child care workers are and how they experience their work.[4] The National Day Care

---

[2] While some opponents of child care (e.g. Woolsey, 1978) contend there is enough care presently available, evidence of unmet need in many communities is apparent in the existence of long waiting lists for services. Child Care Information and Referral groups report that infant care, family day care homes, care during special hours such as evenings and weekends, and subsidized care are in very short supply in their communities. Approximately one-fourth of the agencies indicated that certain kinds of care did have enough spaces; this was usually preschool care (AIRBS, 1980).

[3] A low ratio of children to adults which allows for individualized attention for children is also considered a critical variable of high quality services. However, the National Day Care Study (Abt, 1979) found that group size appears to influence quality more than ratios within certain limits. Thus, the role of ratios is currently being debated.

[4] The focus of this article will be on center providers as opposed to family day care or home providers. The authors, however, recognize the importance of family day care providers, who constitute a much greater portion of the workforce which provides care outside of the child's home. Indeed, there are an estimated 1.85 million family day care providers, 6% of whom are licensed (West, 1980). The vast majority of family day care providers are self-employed and usually work independently of other people. Thus, their work structures and environments vary significantly from those of center staff. However, many of the problems discussed in this article, particularly those of low pay and status, apply to family day care providers as well (Howes, 1980; Hubner, 1981; Rubin, 1975; Prescott, 1972).

Study (Abt, 1979) profiles the approximately 200,000 workers in child care centers in the United States. They are primarily female and under 40 years of age. Despite considerable education and training, child care workers earn close to or less than the minimum wage. The turnover at most child care centers is 15 to 30% a year, which exceeds the national average of 10% for most human services fields (Seiderman, 1978).

Informal observations reveal even more disturbing facts. Many child care staff appear to be stressed and overworked. Burnout, the phenomenon whereby one loses interest in and energy for one's work, is the current focus of much debate:

> The mention of "burn-out" in most gatherings of child care workers pro-
> vokes immediate and intense discussion. Staff meetings, parties and after-
> work bull sessions abound with both symptoms of and conversation about
> burn-out. It is a term that is intuitively grasped and accepted and at the
> same time a phenomenon about which there is little precise understanding.
> Freudenberger recently described the "burn-out syndrome" as exhaustion
> resulting from excessive demands on energy, strength or resources. It is a
> painful and debilitating response to work pressures, which child care work-
> ers immediately find familiar (Mattingly, 1977).

Burnout, and the turnover of staff it fuels, is not just an inconvenience—it results in a lack of trained, experienced workers and creates morale problems for those left behind. Centers must constantly orient new staff even though limited budgets allow no resources for such "non-essential" line items. Most importantly, continual changes in staffing limit efforts to build consistent, creative, and responsive environments for children and their families. The quality of care children receive is in effect victimized by burnout.

CAUSES OF BURNOUT

Burnout is a complicated phenomenon, undoubtedly caused by the interplay of several factors. Those who have written about it often identify more than one cause. But despite the variety of interpretations, their analyses generally consist of some combination of the following three sources of burnout: 1) the nature of the work; 2) the personality types of child care workers; and 3) the structural components of centers.

Freudenberger (1977) and Mattingly (1977) suggest that it is the nature of the work itself that causes the conditions. As with other human services, the necessarily intensive interaction between worker and client (adult and child) is thought to become more draining and less gratifying over time. In this view, a solution to burnout involves diversifying the type of work people in centers perform so that there are breaks from constant direct work with children.

Freudenberger (1977), Reed (1977), and Sutton (1977) contend that those who enter the field have personality types which lead them to burnout. Staff are seen as people with unconscious needs to come to terms with their own troubled childhood experiences. When unsuccessful, they "burn out." A variation of this position suggests that people who engage in this work are idealistic and highly motivated to improve conditions for young children. They "burn out," however, because they do not have a realistic sense of their own limits to create positive change (Nida, 1979). The cure, based on this analysis, involves a new emphasis on self-awareness and counseling in training programs.

Maslach and Pines (1977) identify the structural components of day care centers that are influential in causing or alleviating burnout. They find that lower ratios of adults to children, more dependable breaks and substitute policies, and better communication between staff can positively affect workers' experience and therefore their ability to perform the job with less stress.[5]

Although each of the views articulated above contributes to an understanding of burnout, there appears to be more to the story. Our experience as child care staff suggests that working conditions, other than those mentioned above, such as low pay, lack of benefits, and unpaid overtime contribute significantly to one's job dissatisfaction.[6] Furthermore, these working conditions in most occupations appear closely tied to one's job title as well as to the source of funding. In this light, we wondered whether the phenomena of burnout and turnover occur at different rates among staff of different levels and at different centers.

To deepen our understanding of these issues, we questioned child care workers about their jobs. We found that their responses, which are described in the following pages, raised new perspectives in the burnout debate, and led to suggestions of alternative strategies for addressing the problem of child care worker morale.

SAN FRANCISCO STAFF SURVEY

Sample and Method

During the fall of 1978 and the winter of 1979, 95 staff people working in 32 child care centers in San Francisco were interviewed. One-fifth of the total centers in the city were represented. Included were both half-day and full-day programs. Public centers included those run by the school district as well as

---

[5] These structural factors appear to influence adult-child interaction. Howes (1980) found that caregivers with fewer children in their care, who worked shorter hours and had fewer housework responsibilities, engaged in more facilitative social stimulation, expressed more positive affect, were more responsive, and were less restrictive and negative toward children in their care.

[6] Concern with low salaries has been growing within the field as inflation and costs soar (Gaines, 1979). Teachers of early childhood students at the two and four year college level are noticing a drop in enrollment. In some cases, students are using the child development background as a basis for a career in counseling or another more lucrative human service. (This information come from the authors' personal experience.)

those receiving other public monies such as Head Start. Private centers included both non profit and proprietary programs. Each funding category was proportionately represented, and centers were randomly selected within each category.

Initial contacts with the selected centers were made by letter. If the response to the letter was positive, a visit was made to the center. During a staff meeting, the purpose of the survey was explained and appointments were made for interviews. As many staff persons were wary of participating if there was any possibility of their superiors having access to their responses, we guaranteed confidentiality. For this reason, interviews were conducted over the phone, after working hours.

The interview consisted of open-ended and scaled items. Scaled items were used to ascertain information about the following topics: training, experience and education of staff, job responsibilities, wages, hours of paid and unpaid work, benefits, center structure, adult to child ratio, break and substitute policy, frequency of meetings and topics discussed, and decision-making processes in centers. Open-ended questions sought to ascertain sources of tension and satisfaction, frequency and reasons for turnover, and changes staff would like to see in their centers. Information about center budgets and sources of funding was solicited separately from center administrators.

One-third of the staff interviewed were head teachers/directors, one-third were teachers, and one-third were aides or teaching assistants. Although the head teacher/directors did perform some administrative functions, all spent a considerable time with children.

Staff Characteristics. Eighty-nine percent (89%) of the people interviewed were female—a percentage slightly lower than that of females performing the work nationally (Abt, 1979). Half of those interviewed were ethnic minorities, most of whom held aide or assistant positions.

The Final Report of the National Day Care Study (NDCS), published in 1979, found that 54% of child care staff had completed some post secondary education. In contrast, as is evident in Table 1, 96% of our sample had completed some college work. Seventy percent (70%) had earned a bachelor's degree, with 45% completing some coursework beyond their degree. Seventeen percent (17%) had earned a Master's degree. A high level of experience had also been accumulated by our subjects. Seventy percent (70%) had worked in the field for three years or more, and 56% had been working in child care for over five years. Only 5% had been in the field for less than a year.

Wages. Another finding of the NDCS was that average wages for child care staff were low. In 1978, head teachers and teacher's aides were reported to earn $7,180 and $4,940 a year respectively for full-time work. We predicted that our sample would earn considerably more than the national average for several reasons. First, our sample was exclusively from an urban California community, a setting known for a considerable degree of public financial support for child care. Second, our sample included more highly educated subjects than

TABLE 1   Relation Between Job Title and Educational Level

Group	n	Educational Level			
		High School Diploma, No College %	**Some College, No Degree** %	**Bachelor's Degree, No Advanced Work** %	**Bachelor's Degree Plus Some Advanced Work**[a] %
Head Teachers/ Directors	22	0	9	23	68
Teachers	34	0	3	50	47
Aides	32	12.5	44	31	12.5
TOTAL STAFF	88	4	21	36	39

[a] Seventeen percent (17%) of all staff had completed their Master's Degree.

those in the NCDS. Finally, we anticipated higher earnings due to our subjects' experience in the field.

While our data did reveal higher wages than the national average, the results placed the workers in our sample at the lower 10% of adult wage earners. Since San Francisco has one of the highest standards of living in the country, the higher than national average wage may have been less a reflection of high educational and experiential level and more a result of regional salary schedules. Over twenty-nine percent (29.4%) of staff grossed $500 or less per month. About thirty-two percent (32.6%) earned between $500 and $800 per month. Almost

TABLE 2   Relation Between Center Funding Type and Wages

Group	n	Gross Earnings			
		under $500 per month %	**$500–800 per month** %	**$800–1,000 per month** %	**over $1,000 per month** %
Private Proprietary Staff	18	39	39	17	5
Private Non-profit Staff	27	41	48	11	0
Public School Staff	25	28	12	12	48
Other Public Staff	21	14	38	43	5
TOTAL STAFF	91	31	34	20	15

nineteen percent (18.9%) were salaried at $800 and $1,000 per month. Only fourteen percent (14%) grossed over $1,000 per month.

The bases for salary differentials emerged in a clear pattern. As is shown in Table 2, two-fifths of staff in privately funded centers—as compared to one-fifth of staff in publicly funded centers—had gross earnings of $500 or less per month. Staff in publicly funded centers were most likely to earn the highest wages.

However, publicly funded programs were not all the same. The only staff to net over $800 a month were found in public school centers. Through unionization those staff classified as teachers had won parity with elementary school teachers in pay and benefits. These public school employees were the only unionized employees in our sample and are among the few currently unionized child care personnel nationwide.[7]

Job classifications further served as a basis for wage differentials in our sample (see Table 3). Whereas approximately a quarter (24% and 27% respectively) of teachers and head teacher/directors took home $500 or less each month, two-thirds of aides and teaching assistants earned $500 or less per month. Although aides had less less formal education than teachers and head teacher/directors, 88% of aides in our sample has taken some college courses. Thus, their low wages are particularly noteworthy.

A curious result with respect to hours further underscores the wage difference between public and private programs. There was no significat difference in the monthly earnings of people working in full- or part-day programs, even though part-day programs required a shorter work day (six hours as compared to eight hours). The majority of our sample working in part-day programs worked in public facilities, such as community colleges, which tended to pay a relatively high salary.

Finally, compensation was reduced by the recurring and informal process of workers personally purchasing supplies for their centers. Over half of those

---

[7] Much of the union activity among child care employees has involved those working in public school programs. In San Francisco, the American Federation of Teachers was effective in winning better working conditions for child care staff until the cutbacks of the late seventies and eighties. Generally however, child care personnel do not appear to be a union priority, even when they are faced with a crisis. Child care positions—particularly those equal in pay to elementary positions—were given to tenured elementary teachers. Early childhood trained personnel were laid off or demoted to lower paying positions.

Unionization has been occuring outside of the public schools. In Southern California, co-operative nursery school teachers formed a union over 20 years ago and affiliated with OPEIU (Office and Professional Employees International Union). During the sixties, Head Start personnel joined their ranks, and eventually they affiliated with AFT (American Federation of Teachers). This Early Childhood Federation, Local 1475, represents workers in 14 different non-profit child care agencies. SEIU (Service Employees International Union) is currently organizing among child care workers in private programs, both non-profit and proprietary. District 65 of the UAW (United Auto Workers) continues to address both groups as well.

TABLE 3 Relation Between Job Title and Wages

		Gross Earnings		
		under $500 per month	$500–700 per month	over $700 per month
Group	n	%	%	%
Head Teachers/ Directors	22	18	36	46
Teachers	34	18	38	44
Aides	30	53	30	17

interviewed reported that their center supply budget was inadequate; 60% said they contributed from one to ten dollars of their own money each month for supplies.

Hours.   The low pay and minimal benefits of child care do not reflect a short work week. On the contrary, most of the staff in our sample worked several hours without pay each week in addition to the full-time schedule for which they were paid. Almost half of those interviewed stated there was no method of compensation for the extra hours they worked, and many reported that even when there was a method for compensation—such as taking off time at a later date or extra pay—it was often impossible to actualize.

We asked people to estimate how much time they spent in curriculum preparation and planning, meetings, parent contact, and center support/maintenance. We then asked them to estimate the amount of time for which they were paid. Seventy-two percent (72%) reported spending time outside of regular paid hours, with 58% reporting that they spend 30 minutes or more of outside time each work day. This was true in spite of the fact that almost three-quarters received some daily paid preparation time.

Much communication between parents and staff appeared to occur during unpaid hours. Only 39% of staff were paid for work with parents. Forty-five percent (45%) reported spending unpaid extra time. Communication between staff also occurred during nonpaid hours. Only 48% of staff in our sample reported being paid for staff meetings, although 98% were required to attend them.

There are numerous chores that are essential to center operation but which are hard to classify. These include thorough cleanings, rearranging or building new equipment, and fundraising. Forty-four percent (44%) of those interviewed reported spending between 1 to 15 hours of unpaid time a month in performing such duties. Twenty-six, percent (26%) reported that their job and/or its quality mandated such participation. For example, the only way to ensure a thorough center cleaning or building improvements for the play-yard was through staff performing the necessary labor. In extreme cases, fundraising by staff was necessary to meet the payroll.

Benefits. Benefits are a major vehicle for supplementing wages. (The relationship between center funding type and benefits received, and the relationship between job title and benefits received, are shown in Tables 4 and 5 respectively.) We anticipated not only that staff would receive limited benefits, but also that those with the lowest wages would receive the fewest benefits. Benefits were least likely to be received by aides and staff in privately funded centers— in effect, those staff most needing additional income. Almost half of our sample received no medical coverage through their job. Two-thirds of the sample who received medical benefits received only partial coverage. Public employees were most likely to receive medical coverage as well as to have a choice of medical plan. Public school staff were even more likely to receive a choice than staff from other public programs. The majority of staff in our sample (71%) received no dental coverage through their jobs. The few who did receive coverage were most likely to be teachers in the public centers, especially the public school centers. In over 70% of the cases, dependents were not covered for either medical or dental expenses.

TABLE 4 Relation Between Center Funding Type and Benefits Received

	Benefits Received				
Group	Medical coverage[b] (n[a] = 93)	Dental coverage (n = 92)	Nine plus sick days a year (n = 90)	Two weeks plus paid vacation a year (n = 85)	More than one other benefit[c] (n = 90)
	%	%	%	%	%
Private Proprietary Staff	28	0	35	43	41
Private Non-profit Staff	46	7	50	48	76
Public School Staff	64	65	81	64	70
Other Public Staff	90	28	100	58	86
TOTAL STAFF	58	27	67	54	70

[a] Numbers in parentheses indicate the number of staff who answered each of these questions.
[b] Forty percent (40%) received coverage upon onset of employment, while others had waiting period to establish eligibility. Only 37% of those receiving coverage had employers who paid total cost. In over 70% of cases, coverage was not extended to dependents.
[c] These include worker's compensation, social security, unemployment, and retirement.

TABLE 5   Relation Between Job Title and Benefits Received

	Benefits Received				
Group	Medical coverage[b] (n[a] = 93)	Dental coverage (n = 92)	Nine plus sick days a year (n = 90)	Two Weeks plus paid vacation a year (n = 85)	More than one other benefit[c] (n = 90)
	%	%	%	%	%
Head Teachers/ Directors	54	18	70	61	89
Teachers	73	51	75	70	72
Aides	43	10	59	50	63

[a] Numbers in parentheses indicate the number of staff who answered each of these questions.
[b] Forty percent (40%) received coverage upon onset of employment, while others had waiting period to establish eligibility. Only 37% of those receiving coverage had employers who paid total cost. In over 70% of cases, coverage was not extended to dependents.
[c] These include worker's compensation, social security, unemployment, and retirement.

Paid sick time, holidays, vacations, or professional enrichment days constitute other forms of benefit. Again we anticipated that the lowest paid staff would receive the fewest paid days off. As the examples that follow indicate, this was the case. Staff in public centers received more paid holidays than staff in private centers. However, not all private centers were the same. Staff in proprietary centers were even less likely than staff in nonprofit private centers to receive paid days off. The average number of paid holidays fell between seven and twelve a year for our sample. Two to four weeks of paid vacation were granted to slightly less than half of our sample. Longer vacations were most likely to be received by public center staff.

Leaves of absence can be used by workers for emergencies or to supplement vacations. Staff in our sample were largely unaware of the policy of their center in this regard. Leaves were available for about two-fifths of the staff. People working in public programs, head teacher/directors, and teachers as compared to aides were most likely to have this option. Maternity leave was available to 49% of female staff interviewed. Sixty-four percent (64%) of this group received some pay while on leave. Paternity leave was available to 50% of men interviewed. Only one man reported that he could be paid for this leave. Barely a third of staff interviewed received paid professional enrichment days. Aides were least likely to be included in that grouping.

Child care workers are constantly exposed to colds, the flu, and other minor illnesses. Thus, paid sick days are of critical importance if staff are to stay home while ill. Sixteen percent (16%) of the staff in our survey did not receive any paid sick days. Sixty-five percent (65%) received nine to twelve sick days a year, and 16% received more than one sick day a month. Employees in proprietary centers were least likely to receive paid sick days.

Breaks. By law, California workers are entitled to a 15-minute paid break for every four hours of work (U.S. Dept. of Labor, 1976). In actuality, the situation is quite different. More than a third (37%) of the staff in our study failed to receive a paid break. A small number (5%) received an unpaid break. Thus, over a quarter of staff received no paid or umpaid break for every four hours of work. Staff employed in privately funded centers were most likely to be in this category. Moreover, 39% of those entitled to paid breaks found them inadequate, either because there was no time to take them or because there were not enough staff to cover them. In only two-fifths of the cases did staff feel there were always enough staff to cover for breaks.

Adult-Child Ratio. The National Day Care Study found optimal adult-child ratios in groups of 3- to 5-year-olds to range from 1 to 5 to 1 to 10. Quality of care differences noted within this range were judged to be a function of total group size rather than of ratio. However, poorer quality care was identified in groups with ratios greater than 1 to 10. In our sample, 35% of staff worked in centers with a ratio of over 1 to 10. The majority of private proprietary centers in our sample (78%) had ratios of 1 to 11 or more. Although two-thirds of the staff in our sample worked in centers with so-called high ratios of adults to children, 57% felt that their center ratio only occasionally allowed for individual work with children.

Job Responsibilities and Decision Making. It is not uncommon to en-counter a great deal of bitterness in centers concerning the division of labor.[8] Many centers do not have formal, written policies outlining responsibilities. But even where formal policies exist, often they are not a true indicator of who performs which tasks and of how policies are determined. Thus, we decided to ask staff their perceptions of what was included in their job responsibilities and how much time they spent performing these responsibilities. We also asked staff about their role in a variety of decision-making situations in order to ascertain power and authority lines. We understood we would be getting results from only one vantage point, but we hoped this particular perspective would give insight into much of the tension which impedes the successful operation of many centers.

Our results with respect to job responsibilities by job title suggest one possible explanation for the frequent bitterness encountered in centers around

---

[8] While preparing the questionnaire, we had numerous discussions with child care staff about the sources of job tension. Story after story was recounted about staff tensions connected to unclear or unfair job title distinctions. For example, many aides felt they did as much curriculum planning as the teachers. Yet they received no paid preparation time, while the teacher did. Or the teaching staff believed that they were being included in a hiring decision, only to find their input disregarded.

questions of the division of labor. Although job title did reflect differences in pay, benefits, and education, it gave very little information about the types of tasks performed by staff. There were no differences in the range of duties reported by aides, teachers, or teachers/directors. All engaged to some degree in the following activities: curriculum planning and implementation, meal preparation, maintenance, parent communications, and clerical and administrative tasks. There were differences in how much time staff with different titles spent performing each task: teachers/directors were more likely to spend time in clerical and administrative chores and parent communications. However, job title reflected no differences in paid or unpaid time spent in curriculum planning and implementation, maintenance, and meal preparation. Job title was also likely to give concrete information about involvement in major policy making, as well as in day-to-day decisions. Major policy decisions dealt with hiring and firing, center enrollment, budget, relations with parents and community, administrative structure, and determination of working conditions. Day-to-day decisions (those needed for the actual work with children) included setting-up and cleaning-up activities, grouping of children, determination of appropriate discipline, daily communication with parents, indoor and outdoor supervision, scheduling, and a procedure for division of staff responsibilities. All staff had significantly less power and control in the former set of decisions than did center administrators. Only 18% of teaching staff (aides, teachers, and head teachers/directors) were included in major decision-making. However, one-third of head teachers/directors were included in governing bodies, while less than one-quarter of teachers and fewer than one-fifth of aides were included. Thus, the majority of child care staff were employed within a hierarchical decision-making structure. Over half said they were dissatisfied with their arrangement because they found decision-makers often ill informed and/or insensitive to the ramifications of their decisions.

In contrast to major policy decision-making, teachers tended to have much more involvement in day-to-day decisions. Seventy percent (70%) of teachers and 66% of head teachers/directors made these decisions. The decreased involvement of of head teachers/directors in this area probably reflects their increased involvement with tasks which removed them from direct work with children. However, although teachers and aides spent equal time with children, only 37% of the aides were involved in making day-to-day decisions. Aides were dissatisfied with this procedure, because their opinions were disregarded despite their perceived parity in responsibility. Teachers, however, were pleased with their autonomy in this area of their jobs.

Job Satisfaction. Job satisfaction would appear to be located in the domains of pay and benefits rather than in the nature of the work performed. For child care workers, low pay and poor benefits are unlikely to be a major source of satisfaction. Instead, there must be something about the work itself which serves to satisfy those who work with young children.

This was true for the majority of staff in our sample. Seventy-eight percent (78%) reported that the direct work with children was what most engaged and pleased them about their jobs. Several aspects of this work were mentioned, including immediate feedback, physical contact, facilitating and observing growth and change, and related opportunities for self-reflection. These findings are particularly interesting given the assertion that intense work with children and adults, the essence of child care work, fuels the turnover rate in the field (Freudenberger, 1977; Mattingly, 1977).

Staff mentioned other reasons relating to the nature of the work as sources of job satisfaction. In order of frequency these were staff relations, flexibility, and autonomy of job, and opportunity to learn and develop personal skills while working. Learning how to communicate with and depend on other staff members was encouraged, because of the many opportunities to solve problems within a context of shared purpose. Flexibility and autonomy were linked to the fact that no two days are alike in child care, and to the the degree of control over day-to-day decision-making. Staff gained a sense of competence and felt that they were learning from dealing with continually arising issues. Aides, who were less involved in decision-making, were, not surprisingly, the least likely to state this as a reason for satisfaction. Staff working in proprietary centers were least likely to claim they were learning and acquiring new personal skills on the job.

But what of the considerable dissatisfaction which is reflected in the high rate of turnover and the urgency with which discussions of burnout are conducted in child care circles? In order to identify the reasons behind job dissatisfaction, we asked people to state both what they liked least about their job and what the sources of tension were. In both cases, one cluster of responses emerged—low pay and unpaid hours what (we label overwork and underpayment).

There were other, if less pressing, reasons for job dissatisfaction. These were staff relations, managing children, and maintenance and division of responsibilities. While staff relations were also cited as a source of satisfaction, close working conditions sometimes served to exacerbate differences in educational philosophy and/or personal values. Those who were lower on center hierarchies (i.e., teachers and aides), were twice as likely as head teachers/directors to state that staff relations were a distasteful part of their jobs. This may reflect the former's relative lack of power and input in determining staff policies.

Maslach and Pines (1977) found that job structure greatly affects child care staff in terms of job satisfaction and/or the tendency to burn out. In our sample, staff-child ratio, hours of direct work with children, breaks, mechanisms for input, and flexibility of center structure all were correlated with staff perception of job satisfaction. If would also appear that the perception of children as tension producing is somehow linked to center structure and working conditions. Only five percent (5%) of staff in part-day programs mentioned children as a source of tension, whereas 22% of staff in full-day programs made this statement. Public center staff were least likely to list children as a source of tension, with private proprietary staff most likely to do so.

Maintenance was frequently mentioned as a distasteful aspect of child care work. Perhaps this reflects a conflict in job expectations for those with relatively high levels of education. They had not expected that, after college, their work would involve cleaning, washing dishes, and preparing food.

Private center employees were more likely than public center employees to feel some tension on their jobs, while proprietary center staff were even more likely than private nonprofit staff to experience tension. Full-day program staff were more likely than half-day staff to say they experienced tension.

Head teachers/directors stated more often than aides or teachers that they experienced tension in relation to their jobs. The reasons for this are hard to pinpoint. One hint comes from the tendency of head teachers/directors to list diversity of responsibility as a source of tension. This suggests that it may be tied to the additional responsibilities that accompany increased power. If something went wrong, they were likely to be held accountable. Furthermore, in many cases, their pay and benefits were not significantly higher than those of the teachers, though they often had more training and experience. Thus, their tensions may reflect conflict about career expectations. Although head teachers/directors had more input into major policy making than other staff, they were frequently excluded from decision-making bodies, such as center boards or advisory groups.

Job Security and Turnover. The final report of the *National Day Care Study* stated that the turnover rate at centers averaged 15% a year. We were unsure whether the rate for our sample would be higher or lower, due to the interplay of conflicting forces such as high educational levels coupled with cutbacks.

Staff in our sample tended to switch centers often. More than two-thirds (70%) of staff in our sample had been in the field for three years or more. Yet over a third (37%) of the total sample had been at their jobs for less than a year. While fifty-four percent (54%) of the total group had been in the field for five years or more, only 17% of the total group had been in their centers that long. One fifth of staff interviewed had been at their jobs for less than six months.

Job structure and working conditions appear to be associated with turnover. As indicated in Table 6, turnover rates were lowest for staff in part-time programs, which in our sample tended to be staff with higher wages, better adult-child ratios, and less tense work environments. Turnover rates were highest for staff in private proprietary centers, which are the ones with the highest ratios, worst reported working conditions, fewest benefits and most stated tension. The high degree of tension in proprietary centers may well be a response to the high turnover rate as well as a cause of it.

TABLE 6 Relation Between Center Funding Type and Years in Current Job

| | | Number of Years at Current Job | | | |
		1 year or less	1–3 years	3–5 years	5 or more years
Group	n	%	%	%	%
Private Proprietary Staff	18	44	33	17	6
Private Non-profit Staff	28	39	29	25	7
Public School Staff	23	29	21	14	36
Other Public Staff	21	38	43	0	19
TOTAL STAFF	90	37	30	15	18

Staff perception of the causes of turnover confirms the above contention. Low pay and upaid overtime were the most frequently cited reasons for high turnover. Also cited frequently was lack of mobility: 58% agreed with the statement that there was no opportunity of advancement in the job. Another related reason commonly given for turnover was the relative insecurity of the field in general. Cutbacks or threats of such were seen as undercutting people's ability to stay at any one job.

These data suggest that the field is filled with educated, trained, and experienced people who have very little opportunity for securing better jobs. Thus, it is hardly surprising to find that 20% of those interviewed said they expected to leave the field in the next year. Only 24% see themselves as making a lifetime commitment to work in the field.

Changes Desired. When people were asked what changes they would make in their work situation, one cluster of responses again emerged as overwhelmingly important: higher pay, more benefits, increased job security, and career mobility. Other commonly desired changes included better staff/child ratios and more control over policy and day-to-day decision making.

CONCLUSIONS

The data generated by this study revealed information about working conditions and job structure as well as job satisfaction and job classifications. Essentially, our data confirmed the commonly held assumption that child care staff are underpaid and overworked. Furthermore, it indicated that differences in working conditions and job satisfaction are most often related to differences in job title, funding source, and length of program day. The data suggest that the frequently cited high rate of turnover and burnout of child care personnel is intimately tied to these working conditions.

The results of our study suggest a new understanding of how an enthusiastic and hopeful worker gradually loses her or his eagerness and becomes fatigued, irritable, and likely to quit. We recognize burnout as a complex process influenced by the interplay of many factors, including the intense nature of the work, the personality tendencies of people attracted to the field, and the specific structure of child care centers. However, our research indicates that burnout is less an intrinsic element of the child care worker's personality or activity, and more a function of the *context* in which the work itself is performed. By context we include not only the particular structure of a given institution, but also the larger social forces affecting institutional policy. These social forces include available monies, resources, and prevailing attitudes toward programs and caregivers.

Staff in our sample consistently raised these contextual issues as a key to their understanding of burnout and efforts to reduce it. They repeatedly labeled their working conditions—long hours, low pay, lack of benefits, mobility, and job security—as responsible for their dissatisfaction, frustration, and inability to make long term commitments to their jobs. The constant threat of cutbacks for public employees and the high unemployment rate for teachers were also mentioned as feeding feelings of hopelessness.

The nature of child care work may aggravate the tendency to burn out in low paying and low status jobs. Our sample, however, found the nature of the work to be very satisfying. Child care attracts and engages people who otherwise would seek higher status and better salaried employment. We are not suggesting that higher wages, more benefits, and better adult-child ratios will alone eliminate burnout and turnover in the field, but in view of the responses of those we interviewed, as well as our own experience, we think it is the area in which to begin making changes.

RECOMMENDATIONS FOR IMPROVEMENT

Many who read this may agree that working conditions need to be improved, but will argue that in time of economic recession such improvements are not possible. We agree that, given limited resources, it is necessary to differentiate between those changes that can be made in working conditions within current budget constraints or with only minimal additional funds versus those which require substantial new monies. The suggestions that follow are made with acknowledgement that more money is both needed and hard to obtain.

Changes Within Existing Resources

Previously cited studies of burnout in child care have made valuable suggestions for changes that would alleviate some stress currently experienced by staff.[9] These include such measures as introducing a greater variety of tasks, reducing the number of hours working directly with children, increasing vehicles for peer support and communication between staff, and establishing small ''familial groups'' within larger centers. Three additional changes are suggested by our survey:

1) *Increasing Staff Involvement in Decision-Making:* Our results confirm the observations of Freudenberger (1977), Seiderman (1978), and Neugebauer (1975) that staff with more involvement in decision-making appear to be more satisfied with their jobs. Being able to make suggestions and to use one's skills to solve problems is a potentially positive aspect of child care work. Staff participation is needed on policy making bodies and in such decisions as hiring. Ongoing evaluation for staff and administration, including mechanisms to inform administrators of the implications of their decisions, should be developed. A well functioning grievance policy, written into staff contracts, is basic to developing this involvement. However, lower level staff must be guaranteed ''immunity'' from future sanctions when sharing their ideas, reactions, and grievances with superiors.

2) *Examining Job Title Distinctions:* In our study we found that aides, teachers, and head teachers/directors all engaged in the same duties despite differences in job title. The distinctions in responsibility based on job title were related more to the quantity of time spent performing tasks than than to the nature of the tasks themselves. A person with a Master's degree in child development did maintenance work, and aides were involved in curriculum planning and parent conferences. Much tension in centers revolved around conflicts over distinctions in title and pay without equal distinction in the actual work performed. This suggests that centers need to reexamine their structure. Are the divisions in job title based on skill and experience differences, or do the distinctions reflect the lack of mobility in a field which values on-the-job training but which is unable to offer upward mobility in terms of pay? Open examination of these questions will not generate more funds, but may spark ideas about how to equalize the limited resources that exist. At the very least, there will be an opportunity for a shared recognition of inequities.

---

[9] Other studies not included in the burnout discussion which suggest related center improvements are Hatch (1977) and Monroe (1979).

3) *Improving Break and Substitute Policies:* The provision of breaks and sick days is related to the adequacy of funds. Attitudes of staff and administration, however, can greatly affect break and substitute policy at any budget level. Frequently, people feel, or are made to feel by others, that the need for a break or staying home "with only a cold" are signs of weakness and lack of commitment. Acknowledgement of the value of breaks and staying home when ill can lead to greater staff and administrative cooperation. Slight adjustments in scheduling can enable people to have their 15 minute breaks. A substitute policy that does not leave arrangements to the sick staff member or the person on the floor is another useful step (Child Care Staff Education Project, 1981).

Changes Requiring Expanded Resources

The major cost of child care is staffing (Gurin, 1966). Estimates indicate that 70 to 90% of a center's budget goes to salaries (MAC, 1976). Even when salaries are low, parents using services often have difficulty paying for them (Friedman, 1981). Currently, many women spend almost half their yearly income on child care.[10] Thus, to meet the needs of child care staff for a decent income, and of parents for affordable services, additional sources of funds are required.

Federal and local governments are an obvious source for assisting parents with child care costs, and steps have been taken in this direction. Subsidies at the federal level are provided through several different vehicles. The child care tax credit allowance currently permits parents to claim a maximum $400 per child on their federal tax return. Because the child care tax credit is not refundable, it mainly benefits higher income families who owe taxes at the end of the year. Efforts are now under way to revise the tax credit by making it refundable, and by instituting a sliding scale allowing a greater savings for lower income families.

Title XX of the Social Security Act provides funds for child care services to families earning below 84% of their state median income. However, there are many more income eligible families than there are spaces for them. Approved 1981-82 cuts will further reduce availability (see Footnote 2). Support for welfare recipients' child care expenses is included in their payments, through the

---

[10] Someone earning $7,000 to $8,000 a year, which is common among women wage earners at the minimum wage level, might spend as much as $3,000 per child a year if there are not subsidies available. Of course, parents in higher income brackets often pay no more than 10% of their income for child care. Yet they still complain of high fees (Davis & Solomon, 1980). Some centers suggest that costs for care should be based on a percentage of income, thus raising wealthier families' costs as a way to increase available funds for programs (Nurtury, 1981). The viability of such a strategy depends on the income level of the community and parental acceptance of such a proposal.

Income Disregard Program; however, a proposed cut is currently intended for this program.

The Child Care Food Program is another direct federal subsidy. It offers, at reduced cost, foodstuffs as well as reimbursement for food expenses to family day care and center based programs. This program is currently facing at least a 30% cut in the 1981-82 fiscal year.

Head Start, the federal poverty program initiated in the mid-1960s, provides no cost child care for part of the day to many low income families. Head Start and the tax credit are the only federal child care support programs likely to survive current budget slashing. While state and local governments vary in their degree of commitment to child care, they, like the federal government, are in most instances tightening their budgets. Thus, efforts to maintain and expand child care subsidies from the government face a long, steep battle.

Other possibilities for shifting some of the burden of child care expenses from parents and child care workers, who subsidize child care through their low wages, must be examined. Private foundations are a possibility. Traditionally, support for child care from this source has gone toward non-renewable grants to provide start-up monies or to launch an innovative program. Increased demands from the many human services for foundation funds in this era of shrinking support further reduces the possibility of foundation grants for child care operating budgets.

The greatest untapped resource for child care support is industry. Awareness of this option in the child care community is reflected by the recent plethora of articles and conferences on the topic (GAC, 1980; WRI, 1980; U.S. Dept. of Labor, 1981). In addition, there has been a slight increase in programs sponsored by business, particularly in hospitals where the need for nurses is pressing. Other industries are also examining the feasibility of providing some forms of assistance to their employees with child care needs. Still, most of the activity in this arena is at the discussion level.[11]

Given this checkered, at best, situation of decreasing public monies with only a few possibilities at the workplace level for providing additional funds, some have argued that proprietary care can address the needs of families without subsidy (the so-called "tax-paying" child care). This view overlooks the poor working conditions of child care staff in many of these centers, and the effects of stress and high turnover on the quality of care received by children. In our

---

[11] Many businesses facing increasing costs for other employee benefits (such as health insurance) appear reluctant to become involved in a new, expensive service. And, of course, industry involvement does not guarantee either higher salaries for staff or reduced parent fees for services (Whitebook, 1981).

Some unions have become involved in employment related child care, as reflected in the contract language relating to child care (Creque, 1976; Women's Labor Project, 1980). Union circles have been unusually sensitive to providing decent wages for child care staff (CLUW, 1981).

sample, proprietary center staff earned significantly less and had fewer benefits than workers in other private or public centers. In addition, they experienced less satisfaction and had a higher turnover rate. In other surveys (e.g., CAEYC, 1981), proprietary staff have also fared poorly. These centers typically allot between 50% and 60% of their budget to salaries. If parent fees are to be maintained at reasonable levels, a smaller allotment of the budget for salaries is demanded in order to ensure a profit for investors. One center in our sample allotted 25% of its $100,000 budget to salaries. The owners' share of the profit was 36% of the budget. There are, of course, proprietary centers which do not turn a profit, some of which pay staff slightly higher wages.

Obtaining more financial support for child care involves changing the prevailing view that child care is unskilled work. Until recently, the *Dictionary of Occupational Titles* (published by the U.S. Department of Labor), the most comprehensive source for establishing job qualifications and payscales, rated nursery school teaching and parking lot attending as comparably complex types of work. In the latest edition (1977), nursery school teaching was upgraded to the level of elementary school teacher. Providing family day care or assisting in a nursery school, however, was equated with funeral attending.[12]

As long as child care work is considered unskilled, this will be reflected in its low pay and status. But why is it considered unskilled? Certainly, those performing these tasks do not consider it so. Eighty-two percent (82%) of staff interviewed thought they were continually growing and changing on their jobs, even though 60% of the total group were already "overqualified" by hiring criteria. It may be that, as one staff member said, "It's women's work and so nobody sees it as important." Child care staff must work to change public attitudes about women and the work they have traditionally performed. They must reaffirm the value of our human resources and thus raise the status of those who care for the next generation. Thus, already overworked staff must join together and let people know about the value and skill level of their labor. This involves informing legislators and policy-makers of work conditions, and defin-

---

[12] The mass media perpetuates the image of child care as unskilled work. Two recent examples will suffice. The *Los Angeles Times,* April 26, 1981, carried a picture on the inside of the front page of a woman child care worker who was taking a walk with six toddlers under her supervision. She accomplished this task by having them on a leash. No further comment was made by the paper staff. An episode of "Trapper John" (CBS) which aired spring of 1981 focused on a child care center in a hospital. The teacher was not trained in child care specifically, but of course she could do the job of taking care of 25 children by herself. She was late to the center opening because she was busy putting on her clown suit to entertain the children. She also left a six-foot ladder in the classroom for some unexplained reason and one child fell off it and suffered a serious head injury. Later on in the show, it was revealed that she was only doing child care as a way to work through her feelings about her son, who had been killed in an accident. She had spent some time in a mental institution.

ing minimum employment standards which need to be included in future legislation and recommended by public agencies assisting employers. It requires pressuring organizations which represent child care staff, like the National Association for the Education of Young Children (NAEYC), to maintain and expand their recent recognition of the low status and poor working conditions affecting the field of early childhood education.

The national leadership of NAEYC, as well as local affiliates, have increased their involvement in these issues. In California, a statewide salary study was conducted (CAEYC, 1981) and the predictable and deplorable results have been widely publicized. A Southern California affiliate has recently arranged a major medical health plan benefit for employed members, most of whom are not covered by their employers. At the national level, raising salaries and upgrading the profession has been identified as one priority issue for the coming period. Steps to address this issue have included a day-long session on working conditions at NAEYC'S 1981 conference, as well as a grant to selected NAEYC members to develop handouts on such issues as improving benefits, legal information, occupational health and safety, and parent-staff relations. Future goals might include regular articles in *Young Children,* the organization's periodical, on problems related to working conditions, and developing an outreach project with television and radio spots to inform those people not involved in education about child care work. Beyond these specific tasks, the principal object must be to raise public consciousness and make child care a national concern and priority.

Creating new organizations for staff to offer support and share ideas about common problems such as contracts, grievances, and health coverage is possible and appropriate in many communities. Family day care providers throughout the country have created associations which have been instrumental in raising their professional status and morale and in offering services to members. The Madison Area Day Care Workers United (MADWU), for example, is a coalition of child care employees who publish a newsletter and hold periodic conferences to focus on issues affecting them. The Boston Area Day Care Workers United (BADWU) is a similar organization, which began in the early seventies. (Recently, BADWU has become an affiliate of District 65 of the United Auto Workers.) More short-lived groups and coalitions are also useful. In Santa Cruz in June, 1981, members of the child care community (including the Information and Referral Agency, the local community college's early childhood department, center staff, and family day care providers) joined together for a one day "Very Important Provider" Conference. General information about the status of child care was followed by small group meetings with fellow workers in programs for children of different ages. Although the long term potentialities of such groups are difficult to foresee, in the short term they appear to galvanize child care workers into addressing the problems they face.

Salary surveys also seem to be popular as a way of addressing the concerns of child care staff. In several communities around the country informal groups of child care staff have collected information about center wages as vehicle to raise consciousness and to set new standards. One California group used a survey as a base from which to determine what they considered a minimally decent salary. Many of the centers they surveyed did not meet this minimum (Church Related Nursery Schools, 1981).

Unionizing is another strategy which offers child care staff support and protection, as well as the opportunity to bargain collectively. Currently, most child care staff work without contracts, and those with formal agreements still may not have sufficiently detailed contracts, such as specification of when changes in cost of living increases will be made. As collective bargaining extends to more workers, it will establish a precedent for staff contracts. These agreements may also serve to expand commonly accepted standards for this work force. For example, as unionized workers establish minimal requirements around overtime and pay for meetings, if will become easier for others to follow suit. There is also the potential for unionization to raise consciousness of day care workers themselves about their basic rights and needs. When child care is sponsored in industrial settings, the possibility for unionization can be increased, because many businesses routinely accept collective bargaining. There are, of course, industries who see the offering of child care benefits as a vehicle for impeding unionization among their employees.

In many cases, workers do not identify themselves as ''workers'' but as ''professionals.'' Although many social service and teaching professions have unionized in the last two decades, attitudinal barriers toward organizing remain widespread. And, of course, anti-union setiment amongst employers, parents and the general public complicates this strategy.

Certain aspects of the child care delivery system also pose obstacles to unionization. Specifically, child care workers are located in many different types of programs, with diverse funding structures. For example, while some work within a school district which constitutes a large bargaining unit, others are isolated in privately owned centers with only one or two other employees. Still others find themselves in one of many centers owned by large corporations. Thus, it may not be possible for all child care workers in a community to be represented by the same local union. Public child care staff may choose to join with other public employees, whose union cannot represent private center workers. Currently, this diversity seems to be reflected in the variety of unions with which child care staff are affiliating. These unions include the American Federation of Teachers, the Service Employees International Union, and District 65 of the United Auto Workers. A further problem for child care staff will be their inability to influence union priorities around their concerns (see Footnote 7).

To ameliorate the conditions that lead to burnout, parents, staff, and child advocates require a strategy to distinguish those factors which can be changed within existing institutions. A distinction must be made between factors which can be changed using a center's current resources, and those which involve outside efforts and funds from a source other than the center. Working within the existing structure of the center can be an important first step in confronting the broader problem of burnout. Although tackling burnout by reassessing a center's structure (including resources, staffing, scheduling, and programing) can be time consuming and initially awkward, it often has the effect of energizing the staff and improving work relations by helping people to see the origins of the burnout problem as lying outside their personal inadequacies. Once external factors can be considered as at least partially responsible for burnout, it is easier for the staff to address the larger tasks of legitimatizing child care work and publicizing the needs of child care workers. Such efforts may result in child care acquiring the social support and financial resources it needs to avoid the working conditions which ultimately result in burnout.

REFERENCES

Abt Associates. *Children at the center: Final report of the national day care study.* (Vol. I). Cambridge, MA: March 1979. (ED 168 733, 328pp.)

AIRBS, American Institutes for Research in the Behavioral Sciences. *Project connections: A study of child care information and referral services.* Cambridge, MA: 1980.

CAEYC, California Association for the Education of Young Children. *Early childhood education teacher and staff survey.* Unpublished manuscript, 1981.

Child Care Staff Education Project. Improving substitute policies. *Child Care Information Exchange, July/August 1981,* 23–25.

Church Related Nursery Schools Fellowship Board of Southern California. Staff survey. Unpublished document, 1981.

CLUW, Coalition of Labor Union Women. *Union involvement in child care: Some policy considerations.* Paper presented to California Governor's Advisory Committee on Child Development, Sacramento, May 1981.

Creque, B. *Labor and child care.* Toledo, OH: University of Toledo, 1976.

Davis, J., & Solomon, P. Day care needs among the upper middle classes. *Child Welfare,* September-October 1980, *59*(8).

Freudenberger, H. J. Burn-out: Occupational hazard of the child care worker. *Child Care Quarterly,* Summer 1977, *6*(2), 90–9.[9]

Friedman, D. *Designing a feasibility study: A starting point for considering new management initiatives for working parents.* Paper presented to the conference "New Management Initiatives for Working Parents," Boston, April 1981.

GAC. Governor's Advisory Committee on Child Development. *Employer sponsored child care,* Sacramento, CA: November, 1980.

Gaines, E. *Salaries in early childhood education: Their effect on standards.* Paper presented at the Annual Conference of the Ohio Association for the Education of Young Children, March 1979. (ED 174 329, 13pp.)

Grotberg, E., Chapman, J., & Lazar, J. *A review of the present status and future needs in day care research.* Washington, DC: Office of Child Development, 1971.

Gurin, A. *Cost analysis in day care centers for children: Final Report to U.S. Children's Bureau.* Waltham, MA: Brandeis University, 1966. (ED 042 501, 8pp.)

Hatch, N. A revised work week for caregivers. *Day Care And Early Education,* January-February 1977, *4*(3), 15–16.

Howes, C. *Caregiver behavior and conditions of caregiving.* Unpublished manuscript, Harvard University School of Medicine, Cambridge, MA: 1980.

Hubner, J. *Sources of stress for family day care providers.* Paper presented at Research Needs of Nineties Conference, Anaheim, CA: June 1981.

Katz, L. G. Mothering and teaching: Some important distinctions. In L. G. Katz (Ed.), *Current Topics in Early Childhood Education* (Vol. 3). Norwood, NJ: Ablex, 1980.

MAC, Mayor's Advisory Committee. *Child care: Step by step.* Los Angeles CA: 1976.

Maslach, C., & Pines, A. The burn-out syndrome in the day care setting. *Child Care Quarterly,* Summer 1977, *6*(2), 100–113.

Mattingly, M. Introduction to symposium: Stress and burn-out in child care. *Child Care Quarterly,* Summer 1977, *6*(2), 127–37.

Monroe, M. *Management of child care's most expensive resource—staff time.* Paper presented at the Annual Conference of the National Association for the Education of Young Children, Atlanta, November 1979.

Morgan, G. *Guaranteeing quality in child care.* April 1975. (ED 116 817, 14pp.) not available from EDRS.

Nida, P. *Super-teacher, super burn-out.* Paper presented at the Annual Conference of the National Association for the Education of Young Children, Atlanta, November 1979.

Neugebauer, R. *Organizational analysis of day care.* 1975. (ED 157 616, 88pp.)

Nurtury Preschool. *Sliding scale tuition.* Unpublished document, 1981. Available through Nurtury, 14401 Dickens St., Sherman Oaks, CA 91423.

Oyemade, U., & Chargois, M. *The relationship of staffing characteristics to child outcomes in day care.* 1977. (ED 156 350, 72pp.)

Panetta, S. J. *A study identifying the components of a quality child care center.* Greeley, CO: University of Northern Colorado, 1975. (ED 119 863, 164pp.)

Pettygrove, W. The Child Development Associate credential as a child care staff standard: Accuracy, career development and policy implications *Child Care Quarterly,* Spring 1981, *10*(1), 43–58.

Prescott, E. *Group and family day care: A comparative assessment.* Paper presented at "Family Day Care West—A Working Conference," Pasadena, CA: February 1972. (ED 060 945, 22pp.)

Reed, M. J. Stress in live-in child care. *Child Care Quarterly,* Summer 1977, *6*(2), 114–20.

Rubin, S. Home visiting with family day care providers. *Child Welfare,* 1975, *54,* (9), 645–657.

SDE. *Child care and development services—report of the commission to formulate a state plan for child care and development services in California.* Sacramento, CA: California State Department of Education, 1978.

Seiderman, S. Combatting staff burn-out. *Day Care and Early Education,* Summer 1978, *5*(4), 6–9.

Sutton, B. Consideration of career time in child care work: Observations on child care work experiences. *Child Care Quarterly,* Summer 1977, *6*(2), 121–26.

U.S. Dept. of Labor. *Preschools under the fair labor standards act.* Washington, DC: Employment Standards Administration, Wage and Hour Division, March 1976. (ED 172 941, 10pp.)

U.S. Dept. of Labor. *Dictionary of occupational titles.* Washington, DC: 1977.

U.S. Dept. of Labor. *Employers and child care: Establishing services through the workplace.* Washington, DC: Women's Bureau, Pamphlet 23. January 1981.

West, K. National day care home study. *Child Care Resources,* November 1980, *4*(11).

Women's Labor Project. *Bargaining for equality: A guide to legal and collective bargaining solutions for workplace problems that particularly affect women.* Oakland, CA: Inkworks, 1980.

Woolsey, S. Pied pier politics and the child care debate. In A. S. Rossi, J. Kagan, & T. K. Hauven, (Eds.), *The Family.* New York: Norton, 1978.

WRI, Welfare Research, Incorporated. *On-site day care: The state of the art and models development.* Albany, NY: Empire State Day Care Services Inc., February 1980.

How To Obtain ERIC Documents

Complete copies of most ERIC documents cited here are available in ERIC microfiche collections at approximately 700 libraries in the United States and other countries. For a list of ERIC collections near you, write ERIC/EECE, College of Education, University of Illinois, 805 W. Pennsylvania Ave., Urbana, IL 61801-4897.

ERIC Documents may be ordered in either paper copy (PC), a photocopy of the original, or microfiche (MF), a transparent film card containing up to 98 pages of text. Please include ED number and specify PC or MF. Document prices given in *Resources in Education* (*RIE*) are subject to change. The current price schedule is provided below.

Paper Copy (per ED number): 1–25 pp., $2.00; 26–50 pp., $3.65; 51–75 pp., $5.30; 76–100 pp., $6.95. Add $1.65 for every additional 25 pp. or fraction thereof.

Microfiche (per ED number): 1–480 pp., $.91.

Prices shown do not include mailing, which must be added to all orders. First class postage (for all MF orders up to 32 MF): $.20 for 1–3 MF; $.37 for 4–8 MF; $.54 for 9–14 MF; $.71 for 15–18 MF; $.88 for 19–21 MF; $1.05 for 22–27 MF; $1.22 for 28–32MF. UPS charges (for 33 or more MF and all PC orders): $1.49 for 1 lb; $1.86 for 2 lbs; $2.23 for 3 lbs; $2.59 for 4 lbs. (Each pound equals 75 PC pages or 75 MF.)

Send order and check to ERIC Document Reproduction Service, Computer Microfilm International, P.O. Box 190, Arlington, VA 22210.

The ERIC System and ERIC/EECE

The Educational Resources Information Center/Elementary and Early Childhood Education Clearinghouse (ERIC/EECE) is part of a system of 16 clearinghouses sponsored by the National Institute of Education to provide information about current research and developments in the field of education. The clearinghouses, each focusing on a specific area of education (such as junior colleges, teacher education, languages and linguistics), are located at universities and other institutions throughout the United States.

Each clearinghouse staff searches systematically to acquire current, significant documents relevant to education. These research studies, conference proceedings, curriculum guides, program descriptions and evaluations, and other publications are abstracted and indexed in *Resources in Education* (*RIE*), a monthly journal. *RIE* is available at libraries, or it may be ordered from the Superintendent of Documents, United States Government Printing Office, Washington, DC 20402. The documents themselves are reproduced on microfiche by the ERIC Document Reproduction Service for distribution to libraries and individuals.

Another ERIC publication is *Current Index to Journals in Education* (*CIJE*), a monthly guide to periodical literature which cites articles in more than 700 journals and magazines in the field of education. Most citations include annotations. Articles are indexed in *CIJE* by subject, author, and journal contents. *CIJE* is available at libraries or by subscription from Oryx Press, 2214 North Central at Encanto, Phoenix, AZ 85004.

The Clearinghouse on Elementary and Early Childhood Education (ERIC/ EECE) publishes topical papers, bibliographies, resource lists, and a newsletter for persons interested in child development, child care, and childhood education (for children from birth to age 12). The clearinghouse staff also answers individual information requests and provides computer searches of *RIE* and *CIJE* and other data bases. For more information, write ERIC/EECE, College of Education, University of Illinois, 805 W. Pennsylvania Ave., Urbana, IL 61801-4897.

The ERIC Clearinghouses

ADULT, CAREER, AND
VOCATIONAL EDUCATION
Ohio State University
1960 Kenny Road
Columbus, OH 43210
(614) 486-3655

COUNSELING AND PERSONNEL
SERVICES
The University of Michigan
School of Education Building
Room 2108, East Univ. & South
Univ.
Ann Arbor, MI 48109
(313) 764-9492

*ELEMENTARY AND EARLY
CHILDHOOD EDUCATION
College of Education
University of Illinois
805 W. Pennsylvania Ave
Urbana, IL 61801-4897
(217) 333-1386

EDUCATIONAL MANAGEMENT
University of Oregon
Eugene, OR 97403
(503) 686-5043

HANDICAPPED AND GIFTED
CHLDREN
The Council for Exceptional Children
1920 Association Drive
Reston, VA 22091
(703) 620-3660

HIGHER EDUCATION
George Washington University
1 Dupont Circle N.W., Suite 630
Washington, DC 20036
(202) 296-2597

INFORMATION RESOURCES
School of Education
Syracuse University
130 Huntington Hall
Syracuse, NY 13210
(315) 423-3640

JUNIOR COLLEGES
University of California
96 Powell Library Building
Los Angeles, CA 90024
(213) 825-3931

LANGUAGES AND LINGUISTICS
Center for Applied Linguistics
3520 Prospect Street, N.W.
Washington, DC 20007
(202) 298-9292

READING AND
COMMUNICATION SKILLS
1111 Kenyon Road
Urbana, IL 61801
(217) 328-3870

RURAL EDUCATION AND
SMALL SCHOOLS
New Mexico State University,
Box 3AP
Las Cruces, NM 88003
(505) 646-2623

SCIENCE, MATHEMATICS, AND
ENVIRONMENTAL
EDUCATION
Ohio State University
1200 Chambers Road, Third Floor
Columbus, OH 43212
(614) 422-6717

SOCIAL STUDIES/SOCIAL
SCIENCE EDUCATION
855 Broadway
Boulder, CO 80302
(303) 492-8434

TEACHER EDUATION
1 Dupont Circle N.W., Suite 610
Washington, DC 20036
(202) 393-2450

TESTS, MEASUREMENT AND
EVALUATION
Educational Testing Service
Princeton, NJ 08541
(609) 921-9000, Ext. 2176

URBAN EDUCATION
Teachers College, Box 40
Columbia University
New York, NY 10027
(212) 678-3437

---

* ERIC/EECE is responsible for acquiring research documents on the social, psychological, physical, educational, and cultural development of children from the prenatal period through pre-adolescence (age 12). Theoretical and practical issues related to staff development, administration, curriculum, and parent/community factors affecting programs for children of this age group are also within the scope of the clearinghouse.